The Power of Fantasy

The Power of Fantasy

Where Our Daydreams Come From
And How They Can Help or Harm Us

Lucy Freeman
and
Kerstin Kupfermann

CONTINUUM · NEW YORK

1988

The Continuum Publishing Company
370 Lexington Avenue
New York, NY 10017

Printed in the United States of America

Library of Congress Cataloging-in-Publication Data

Freeman, Lucy.
The power of fantasy: where our daydreams come from and how they
can help or harm us / Lucy Freeman and Kerstin Kupfermann.
p. cm.
Bibliography: p.
ISBN 0-8264-0410-3
1. Fantasy. 2. Subconsciousness. I. Kupfermann, Kerstin.
II. Title.
BF411.F68 1988 88-10055
154.3—dc19 CIP

Contents

Acknowledgments   vii

1   Our Wonderful World of Fantasy   1

2   Where Fantasy Starts   15

3   The Fantasy of Self   42

4   The "Prince Charming" Fantasy   58

5   Fantasies about Sex   78

6   The "Don Juan" and Other Fantasies   90

7   How Dreams Reveal our Fantasies   112

8   The "Revenge" Fantasy   129

9   The "Cruel Mother" Fantasy   145

10   The "Lottery" Fantasy   163

11   The "Body Speaks" of Fantasy   173

12   The "Great Artist" Fantasy   183

13   The Rewards of Knowing Your Fantasies   199

Bibliography   209

Acknowledgments

The authors wish to thank Werner Mark Linz, publisher of Crossroad/Continuum, and Michael Leach, associate publisher, for accepting the idea of a book on understanding the power of fantasy and how it may help or hurt us.

They also want to thank Evander Lomke and Bruce Cassiday, for their sensitive, helpful guidance as editors.

They are indebted to Jacob A. Arlow, M.D., past president of the American Psychoanalytic Association, former editor-in-chief of *The Psychoanalytic Quarterly* and authority on the role of fantasy in our lives, for his views. They also wish to thank William I. Grossman, M.D., a member of the faculty of the New York Psychoanalytic Institute, who has written on topics related to fantasy.

Dr. Irving Kupfermann, Ph. D., Professor of Physiology and Psychiatry, Columbia University and the New York State Psychiatric Institute, made valuable suggestions. David Ross, chief librarian of the Library of the New York Psychoanalytic Institute, was helpful with the research.

Lucy Freeman
Kerstin Kupfermann, D.E.S.

The Power of Fantasy

1

Our Wonderful World of Fantasy

We all enjoy the many pleasures of fantasy to enhance our lives. We daydream of wishes that we believe will bring happiness as we spin into a world where no one can say us nay.

A young woman imagines falling in love with a handsome, eligible young man in the advertising agency where she works. She stares at him dreamily, visualizes herself married to him, making breakfast for him every morning.

A young man sits in a subway, stares at the slim body of the attractive girl in the miniskirt who sits across from him, daydreams of being locked in a hotel room with her for a joyous weekend.

A married woman of fifty-two, her children now on their own, thinks of taking an ocean voyage around the world, visiting exotic foreign ports. She muses, "This is my escape from routine. I know my husband and I will never take such a trip but I can enjoy the thought of it and hope 'maybe someday.' "

A man of forty who gambles regularly at racetrack and lottery stores, dreaming of winning enough money to retire from his routine job as law clerk, assures himself, "One of these days I'll hit it big and be able to spend all the money I want on everything I've always wanted to own."

An actress in a minor part in a Broadway play sees herself soon leaving for Hollywood, becoming as famous as Marilyn Monroe. A writer of rock music visualizes himself as a second James Taylor. A successful architect, married twenty years, no longer in love with his wife, wishes he could meet a desirable woman who will set his flesh aflame with passion.

From the moment we are able to think, we daydream. Our daydreams reflect our desires, hopes, deepest wishes. Some men and women spend as much as half their time daydreaming. Some may even spend most of their waking moments lost in a fantasy world.

What do we mean when we speak of "fantasy"? Acording to Webster's *New World Dictionary* fantasy is an "unreal mental image," an "illusion" or "a mental image as in a daydream, usually pleasant." In the strictest sense of the word, fantasy can be described as a picture in the mind. The word "fantasy" comes from the Greek *phantasies*, the look or appearance of a thing. The literal translation of "fantasy" means "a making visible."

The well-known fairy tale by H. C. Andersen, "The Emperor's New Clothes," expresses the idea of truth versus fantasy. The little child who sees reality with a clear and open mind exclaims, "But the Emperor is naked!" The child's words ring out over the crowd, consisting of sub-missive, well-trained citizens busy flattering the Emperor in the atmosphere of make-believe.

Here we are confronted with an example of how "seeing" is crucial to the original meaning of a fantasy. Fantasies appear as images in the mind that provoke thoughts and wishes. Whoever wrote *Cinderella* indulged in fantasies appealing to every little girl ever born, and often to many young women as they remain in the grip of this fantasy of love and the glass slipper.

How have the poets and the philosophers over the ages viewed fantasy? They seem to mirror artistically both fantasies that inspire us and those that hurl us into depression and terror. For instance, Shakespeare writes in *Twelfth Night:*

> so full of shapes is fancy
> That it alone is high fantastical.

And in *Romeo and Juliet:*

> True, I talk of dreams,
> Which are the children of an idle brain,
> Begot of nothing but vain fantasy.

Milton wrote in *Comus:*

> A thousand fantasies
> Begin to throng into my memory,

Of calling shapes, and beck'ning shadows dire,
And airy tongues that syllable men's names
On sands and shores and desert wildernesses.

Then there are the lines from Edgar Allan Poe in "The Raven":

And the silken sad uncertain rustling of each
　　　purple curtain
Thrilled me—filled me with fantastic terrors
　　　never felt before.
....
Deep into that darkness peering, long I stood
　　　there, wondering, fearing,
Doubting, dreaming dreams no mortal ever dared
　　　to dream before.

And Walter De La Mare in his poem "Memory":

Memory—that strange deceiver!
Who can trust her? How believe her—
While she hoards with equal care
The poor and trivial, rich and rare;
Yet flings away, as wantonly,
Grave fact and loveliest fantasy?

Shelly in *Adonais* writes "Of hopes and fears, and twilight Fantasies." Somehow at twilight, as night approaches, we are induced to daydream of the past, the sun disappearing on the horizon reminds us another day has vanished in the span of our life.

Fantasies in large part run the psychic machine we call our mind. Body and mind are intimately connected. If we have a bodily feeling our mind automatically responds with a fantasy that may either be conscious or unconscious as we perceive something that either pleases us, alarms us or leaves us neutral.

We see a car racing down the street out of control, heading for us. We recognize our life is in danger, possessed by the emotion of fear and the fantasy that the car might kill us. We jump out of the way. Emotion is our bodily feeling, fantasy is how the mind operates at the moment the emotion strikes.

A wife may fantasy her husband is having an affair with his young, pretty secretary. She may either act and accuse him of infidelity or bury her feeling, not wanting to upset him and risk the end of her marriage.

We feel hungry, a physical emotion, and have the fantasy of eating—the fantasy holds the wish to eat. Without the fantasy, at times we might not be so prone to satisfy our hunger.

Fantasies form with a purpose. Sometimes they appease our conscience, sometimes we indulge in them for sheer pleasure, sometimes for imagined vengeance on those who have hurt us, sometimes to regain strength to protect ourselves.

One woman said, "When I feel really threatened it helps if I can fantasy I am like a redwood tree: high, strong, beautiful. This helps me to be strong. When, for the sake of my family, I need to stay very calm, with a strong core at my disposal, I think of myself as the redwood tree that so impressed me when I saw it as a little child in the town where I grew up."

Our fantasies may drive us to success or to failure. To strong religious belief or atheism. To the conviction that earning money will solve all our problems or the belief that others should support us financially. To destroy another human being or to work for the salvation of the world. To a degree, we all have fantasies of both persecution and of rescue. Many of us engage in work that fulfills our fantasy of rescuing others, one that also reveals our hidden wish to be rescued.

A woman of twenty-six who, as a child felt emotionally abandoned by her mother, signed up for the Peace Corps. She set out to rescue impoverished children who had been abandoned by their mothers literally in a country torn by warring factions. Unfortunately this woman was raped by rebel troops and murdered. She had sought a dangerous place in which to try to help others. Many of the homeless who fill our city streets ask to be rescued. Often they walk the sidewalks conducting angry fantasy conversations with "the ghost voices" within, the parents of childhood who rejected them.

Fantasy may have a powerful influence in our life. Freud discovered this power as he connected the fantasies of childhood to the fantasies of our adult years. "Every separate fantasy contains the fulfillment of a wish," he said. He added that our two most powerful wishes were connected to our strong sexual desires and our fury when we felt hurt by someone we loved.

He spoke of fantasy as the way of fighting frustration and rage in a dreamlike fashion. He called fantasy the only kind of thinking of which we are capable as children, when our ability to use reason is not yet developed. As adults, we use fantasy to make our life more tolerable.

Most of us think of fantasy as at least two different things, as Dr. William I. Grossman, a leading psychoanalyst, points out. The most general "is the organizer of meaning in the mental life, the stuff of human interaction and reflection, whether represented in action, imagery, thought or narrative," he explains. The second is the "most easily recognizable exemplar: the daydream."

In the first concept, "when we speak about a mental life, the elements are not sensations, raw imagery, words, phonemes, but something with an organization of representations of experiences—however primitive and undifferentiated," he says. The second, the daydreams, such as those that we enjoy privately or tell friends and are recounted in psychoanalytic treatment have some reference, even if hidden, to a picture of the self.

Many people consciously and unconsciously use the fantasy-daydreams as a source of satisfaction and comfort, excitement, amusement, relief of rage, though there are those who cannot knowingly use fantasy for relief, Grossman states. Some must commit acts they feel an urge to commit. The unconscious fantasy, as referred to in the first definition given above, becomes a "goad to action."

Others evade fantasy by means of concrete and practical activities that allow them no opportunity for any other exercise of imagination for playful purposes, creativity and art. They appear anchored to immediate activities, anticipated activities or to the observation of other people's activities, such as television or sports.

He concludes that "various forms of fantasy activities *have* been important in the lives of many people and are the basis of both consolation and aesthetic experiences. Fantasy is always present, it organizes and directs our behavior—it makes the mental life mental."

We may think of ourselves as living in three worlds. The world of reality, to which we are expected to conform, and the two worlds of fantasy, our private, secret worlds. Fantasy includes both the daydream during which we are aware of our thoughts and wishes and other fantasies related to the daydream that lie in the deepest part of our mind—fantasies of which we are not aware.

We may share the world of reality with others but our two inner worlds of fantasy, the daydream and the desires that underlie it, spark it, so to speak, belong only to us. The daydream is like the chocolate ice cream that floats on the surface of the soda. The buried fantasies are the fizz that seethes underneath, with a strong power of its own.

Beneath our daydreams, which satisfy us in various ways, depending on our personal conflicts, wishes and feelings, lies an undercurrent of unconscious fantasies dating from the earlier days of our life. We keep them from awareness because we have learned they are dangerous to our self-esteem, dealing with sexual desires and murderous wishes, for the most part. The unconscious fantasies retain their original theme over the years, but may be disguised in their choice of object.

A four-year-old girl daydreams about the man she will marry and he is her father. In grammar school the theme is the same, that of love and marriage but she changes the object to a boy her own age. In adolescence, it is usually a boy several years older.

We are taught early in life that many of our most pressing wishes have to be controlled by our conscious mind so we may act in civilized fashion. Our unconscious—the primitive, uncivilized, childlike part of us within—does not know of control. It would willingly carry out wishes mankind has long deemed taboo—incestuous desires, the urge to kill someone who opposes us in any way or inflicts pain, psychic or physical, upon us.

Our vast reservoir of fantasies may become either a cesspool or wishing well, depending on how powerful they are in our lives. By becoming aware of fantasies that underlie daydreams, fantasies that may be threatening, we can lessen the anxiety in our life.

For instance, there are times we all feel as Saint Paul did when he said: "I do not understand my own actions. For I do not what I want, but I do the very thing I hate."

Why do we act this way—"do the very thing" we hate? Commit a deed that may demean us, hurt us or harm those we love. What stirs within that leads us to act against our better judgment? We disregard what we "want" to do, know what we *should* do. Why? Because our conscious wish, the one of which we are aware, is not as powerful as the buried, seething wish that momentarily vanquishes it.

We are all Dr. Jekyll and Mr. Hyde. The Jekyll part shows us as civilized and caring, loving and protecting. But the Hyde part, carefully concealed from our awareness, reveals our fury, our wish to kill, to take revenge on those who hurt us—allows us also to act out unrestrained sexual desire, perverse impulses. The voice of reason which tells us what is "right" becomes momentarily silenced.

This was obvious in a recent incident reported in New York City newspapers. A man deliberately brushed up against a young woman in a subway car, in an open sexual manner. She became incensed, called a policeman and demanded the man be arrested. All too often newspapers describe how a man has kidnapped a child or young woman, attacked and raped her, perhaps even killed her if she resists as he commits a crime— does "the very thing" he "hates," breaking one of our strongest taboos as he loses control of reason.

The difference between a daydream and an unconscious fantasy is that we are in control of our daydreams. We *know* we are daydreaming. And what we consciously know is less apt to hurt us than our unconscious emotions and wishes.

The unconscious fantasies may reflect wishes not acceptable to the conscious mind, as well as wishes that benefit us. Fantasy often works for our protection, as well as our self-destruction or destruction of others. Fantasies of power, such as Adolf Hitler possessed, ended in the death of millions of innocent people, and his own.

But unconscious fantasies may help create our character, influence how we think and govern the way we act. They are often the motivating force behind both our loving and hateful desires. We use fantasy for numerous reasons. To obtain secret enjoyment in a life that is often harsh. To defend against pain. To feel in control when circumstances impose on us a sense of helplessness. To prepare ourselves to accomplish a dreaded or difficult task.

Fantasy can be responsible for whether we are happy or unhappy. When we feel endangered by some threatening situation, in fantasy we can concoct whatever script we please, direct all the actors, produce the action, select the audience, write the reviews. No one can control us, say us nay.

Fantasy includes what we believe to be random thoughts, which often, however, upon closer examination, prove not quite so random after all, but quite purposeful. We may choose, sometimes unconsciously, to mirror our fantasies in reality, as architects, composers, artists and writers do.

We may also use fantasies as a way of thinking that is free from the perils of reality, according to Freud. We do so because we get more pleasure out of the fantasies than reality, which may sometimes be grim or painful. Psychoanalysts often treat men, women and children who have been physically or psychically abused, many of whom use fantasy as a way of enduring otherwise unbearable memories of cruelty.

One male patient told how he and his siblings were locked in the basement while their mother, a prostitute, went out to find customers.

The basement had no water, no toilet facilities and was sparsely lit. This man, as a boy, and his siblings often felt completely abandoned when every so often they had to wait a full day for the return of their mother. To mentally survive, he used to crawl into one of the storage closets, pretend it was an elevator that took him up to a floor where a kind family lived, welcomed him into their circle, gave him all he ever wanted.

Some fantasies are stimulated from within, others by external stimulation such as a sunset, reading of a murder in the headlines or seeing on the street a man and woman kiss ardently. Almost anything that exists can be the starting point of a fantasy.

A cue from the outside that matches a present concern preoccupying our mind is likely to trigger fantasy in the shape of a daydream. People's goals, life-styles and emotions are powerful in setting off daydreams used to cope and to achieve, living as we do in a shifting, stressful, challenging and sometimes dangerous world.

Many of us indulge during sex in a wide variety of intense fantasies that range from substitution of another person to reminiscenses of former sexual acts. These fantasies do not replace the real experience but serve as a way of heightening its pleasure.

There is vital difference between "fantasy," "illusion" and "delusion." What are these all-important differences?

Fantasy refers to a mental image that may be conscious or unconscious, usually associated with a wish. Perceptual "illusions" result from the intrusion of fantasy onto perception. This may apply to our judgment as well. For example, when we are competitively envious of a fine pianist we may entertain a fantasy that he is performing poorly and, as a result, come away with the illusion that he is a poor pianist, explains Dr. Jacob A. Arlow, famous for his contributions to the theories of psychoanalysis.

A person with a "delusion" treats his fantasy as if it were reality, Arlow adds. A man may have the fantasy his wife is betraying him, then kills her, even though she is innocent, as Othello did Desdemona, perceiving his fantasy as real. Those who are mentally ill, who believe they are Napoleon or Jack the Ripper, act on their fantasies as though they were real.

Thus there is vast difference between a fantasy we accept as such and "illusion" and "delusion." The latter two show more intense emotions interfering with our sense of reality. "Illusion" is more destructive to us than fantasy, and "delusion" is even more destructive than "illusion," creating greater distance between fantasy and reality. Delusions may doom us to a psychic darkness out of which there may be no exit. For instance, a psychotic girl four years of age said her last comprehensible sentence, "I have lost my way," just as she felt so overwhelmed emotionally her entire self fragmented.

Fantasy sometimes harms us in other ways. A woman cannot give up sweets though her doctor has insisted she lose twenty pounds for health reasons. But her wish to keep eating ice cream and other rich desserts is stronger than her wish to diet. Her unconscious fantasies overwhelm her conscious use of reason.

She remembers hearing her plump mother tell her, "Be a good girl and finish everything on your plate. If you do, you'll get a special reward—a second helping of dessert." In her unconscious she still hears her mother's voice—love and eating are firmly tied together.

"Be a good little girl and eat what mother has cooked and mother will love you," is the ghost voice that rings louder in her mind than the rational knowledge she must lose weight to preserve her health. She believes herself a "bad" girl if she does not continue to overstuff. Only as she comes to terms with this fantasy will she realize the strong role it plays in threatening her life in the long run as it defeats her desire to lose twenty pounds and remain healthy.

Her inability to diet also rises from other fantasies—every act destructive to us stems from what psychoanalysts call "overdetermination," several or many causes. To this woman, eating, as it is for all of us, may be both a sensual and a violent act. Food entering our mouth is our first sensuous feeling as a baby and our entire psychosexual development flows from that first feeling. A baby craves food not only to stay alive but to have his hunger appeased. If he is not fed, as any mother knows, he will protest with cries and screams.

Eating is also associated with fantasies of violence, a cannibalistic way of destroying someone who has frustrated or angered us, as well as, in fantasy, taking within us the power he possesses. When our primitive ancestors were hungry and no animals or fish were at hand, they may have eaten their enemies, perhaps even hated relatives. As man's mind developed and he could empathize with another human being, he realized cannibalism was not humane.

When fantasies become too harmful, result in aberrant, destructive acts against the self or others, some may end up in mental hospitals or prisons. But even fantasy of a less destructive nature may harm us, such as when someone walks away from job after job, feeling he does not get sufficient praise. Or a woman or man is propelled from one sexual affair to the next, obliterating all hope for a lasting, intimate relationship. Or a person is plunged into the void of depression, not knowing how to understand his unconscious fantasies.

The study of fantasy is ongoing in the world of psychoanalysis where unconscious fantasy is thought a "major conceptual instrument," as Arlow describes it in his article, "Unconscious Fantasy." He says that unconscious fantasy "articulates the form and nature of the dynamic unconscious conflicts that mold the individual's life. It is a mental process that represents a variation in the function of daydreaming."

Unconscious fantasy is a thought process free of the testing of reality. It remains subordinate to the "pleasure principle" alone. It abandons dependence on other people, customs, laws.

Arlow calls the power of unconscious fantasy "ubiquitous." Through its influence on people, as individuals and in the mass "it is an ever-present force in shaping not only individual destiny but human destiny," he concludes, referring to nations and the world.

What is the relationship between fantasy and emotion? Arlow says, "They are inseparable." Every "perceptual experience," especially in the early years of life, is accompanied by some "emotional tone." All of our experiences are processed in our mind as pleasurable or unpleasurable, familiar or unfamiliar as we react to whatever happens to us. Arlow explains that every experience is "metaphorically assimilated, since no two experiences are identical and sequences of associations are grouped together based on certain familiar combining elements."

Thus all emotion holds within it our thoughts. Thoughts and feeling tone are inseparable: together they constitute what we call emotion. An unpleasant feeling tone, accompanied by a thought that something terrible has happened, is what we experience as sadness or depression, Arlow states.

He concludes: "One could conjecture that human beings could not really bear the strictures that civilized life impose upon the drives if it were not for their ability to abrogate these prohibitions in various ways—in dreams by night, in daydreams during waking hours, and through communal participation in art, literature, religion and similar activities."

Fantasy represents one aspect of the process of resolving a conflict by what psychoanalysts call a "compromise formation," that is, we do not act out the wish, which we know may be harmful to us and others, but instead bury it in the unconscious. Some of our attempts to bring about a compromise are unsuccessful. Or other "fantasy formations" may unite the conflicting elements into an experience that gives us pleasure.

Incidentally the term "reaction formation" occurs when we show in our behavior toward others a wish of the opposite nature to the one we originally held, which we realize is taboo. Our defense is to behave in a directly opposite fashion, denying the forbidden fantasy. We appear friendly when we really feel hostile. We seem to love when we actually hate. We show pleasure when we feel disgust.

Arlow also pointed out that at certain times in life when we are about five or six, conflicts that center on our growing sexual and aggressive wishes become modified. They are integrated into a basic fantasy that becomes the "vehicle for some conflicted wish." Later in our life, versions of the fantasies grow and change but the basic wish remains the same: "like the character and settings of a novel may change but the plot line remains the same."

Freud compared our universe of fantasies and daydreams to a national park preserve where the original state of nature is kept in pristine form. He called daydreaming a universal activity and fantasies the "vehicle" for our instinctual drives. At the start of his work Freud recognized that symptoms, dreams, moods and character traits represented what he called "derivative expressions of unconscious fantasies." The wishes involved in unconscious fantasies tended to be more primitive, more bizarre and in opposition to morality and reality. Then he recognized this was not true of all unconscious fantasies. They included elements of defense, adaptation and considerations of moral judgment, as well as fear of punishment.

Fantasy may be inspired by any emotion that needs an outlet but cannot be expressed in reality because we fear it may alienate us from those we love. Fantasy serves as partial expression, a substitute expression, of that emotion. If someone hurts us but we dare not tell him of the hurt for fear we will lose his love, we may dream up all sorts of revenge: picture him dying of a slow, painful death, run over by an auto, knifed by a mugger. If we do not dare such wicked thoughts consciously, we may dream at night that someone who looks like our tormentor is slain by a burglar or fading away from cancer.

We can all recall moments from childhood when we had fantasies about what life would be like when we grew up. A twenty-nine-year-old woman, a jazz singer, told her husband, "I couldn't wait from the age of nine to get out of the house. Every day as a child I raged against being bossed by my controlling mother and father. I yearned desperately to be on my own." In this age of greater opportunity for women, many more young girls dream of careers and new freedoms.

As we grow up we have to hide from the world the deeper wishes embodied in our fantasies, chiefly sexual desires, hatred, envy, jealousy, greed. We feel ashamed of such fantasies, believe the thoughts contained in them are forbidden. We are not ashamed of daydreams when they are within the limits of society's approval—to fall in love, achieve fame, earn great wealth. Sometimes fantasizing prevents us from acting on destructive thoughts. It is healthy to daydream, if not excessively.

A fifteen-year-old girl's daydream was to become a doctor like her beloved father. She earned her medical degree, thus achieving the daydream. But strong fantasies lurked beneath that daydream, fantasies of which she was not aware: to be a man, like her father; to achieve fame so he and her mother would love her more; to rescue sick men and women from pain as she had wished to be rescued from the emotional pain of a childhood where she often had been left for weeks in the care of a nurse as her parents took long trips to distant places.

A fantasy represents mixtures of both external and internal reality, according to Joan Riviere, a British psychoanalyst, who studied with Freud. She described fantasy as a "weapon which cuts both ways; it can be used to create goodness, and to destroy and expel badness."

If we live too deeply in fantasy we are unable to fulfill our potential in love, work, creativity. A blurring may occur and there will be no distinction between reality and fantasy. One severely disturbed woman talked in her analysis about how, as a child, fantasy became her only way out of a destructive reality that threw her almost daily into panic. Both her mother and father often struck her, gave her little love or protection so she felt an outcast.

Fantasy became her way of emotionally and socially trying to stay in touch with people, not to tune them out, resort to hallucination. As she grew up, at times she found it difficult to recognize the difference between her previous reality and her fantasies. She would ask herself over and over, "Did I really experience this or was it just my imagination?"

Fantasies can either free us or bind us more tightly to the unreal past, in the words of Elizabeth Thorne, psychoanalyst, current president of the

National Psychological Association for Psychoanalysis as well as president from 1977 to 1980. "Fantasies that free us are those which help us visualize future goals and inspire us to achieve them," she says. "On the other hand, our explanations about the past may be so filled with wishful fantasies that they mislead us."

She asks, "When is our picture of the past sheer fantasy or true memory, or perhaps both?" She answers, "Who's to say? We are always trying to make sense of the world so we build neat assemblies of apparent cause and effect, but life doesn't proceed in a simple cause-and-effect way. Also, we want to ignore aspects of ourselves that we don't like. So we may end up with a myth, a fantasy, instead of a useful history."

She concludes, "Some people dare not face reality and have to live too much in fantasy, as Eugene O'Neill so masterfully portrayed in his plays *The Iceman Cometh* and *Long Day's Journey Into Night*. It takes time and effort to give up the anesthesia of such fantasies masquerading as facts. When we do, then fantasies can proliferate in their true role, as the delights and inspirations of the spirit."

For our emotional survival as an adult we need to know the difference between fantasy and reality—those fantasies that enhance our life and those that are harmful. If we are aware of our angry fantasies and face past hurts, they lose their power to harm us.

We may choose to act on fantasies of love, hate, sex and power or live them out vicariously, watching others enact them. We may enjoy murder on the television screen, movie theater or stage, thrill to the chase in which the killer is caught. Or we may exult in the screen images of the illicit affair.

No longer, like our earlier ancestors, do we attack our enemy with a spear, kill on sight. But we may devastate him with words, "cut him down" with icy sarcasm that wounds in a different but still a hurtful way. The "thick-skinned" survive the verbal wounds but the "thin-skinned," like the vulnerable child, may suffer emotional wounds that never heal.

We may also use fantasies for constructive, profitable deeds. Some build successful businesses based on the fantasies of buyers, fantasies related to cosmetics, perfumes, cigarettes, alcohol. Pornography is profitable because it arouses forbidden sexual fantasies related to childhood. Gambling hotels cater to the "get rich quick and you will be happy" fantasy.

All of us need a certain amount of fantasy to get through grim times. Frustrations and disappointments are part of living and we use fantasy to cope with them, dream of better times ahead. If we detest our work, we may fantasy ourself in a more stimulating job. If we dislike living alone, we may fantasy finding someone to marry.

We may also have fantasies of power. In childhood we wish not only to defeat our frustrating parents but siblings or the teacher or the neighborhood bully. Later in life we want power over our fellow men in the form of money and success, as well as sexual power.

As we mature, we learn reality is quite a different world from that of fantasy. Reality means, for most of us, that we work hard to live in comfort, that we think rationally in order to survive emotionally with those we love. We learn to accept that we may have fantasies about anything we wish, no matter how forbidden, as long as we do not act on the destructive fantasies.

In a sense, we are what we fantasize. Fantasy can either destroy us if it leads to suicide or murder, or it can enhance our feelings about ourselves and others. Fantasy is part of our spontaneous reaction to an experience, both good and bad. It is how our mind responds to an emotion, such as the feeling of anger and wish for revenge after a slap in the face or, its opposite, a loving feeling and wish to be closer after a kiss. Fantasy may lie at the root of either happiness or anguish.

This book will discuss the various fantasies we all hold. They include: the fantasy of the self; the fantasies of childhood; the fantasy of love and marriage (the Prince Charming fantasy); fantasies about sex; fantasies that lead to perversion (the Don Juan fantasy). Also: the fantasies in our dreams at night; the fantasies that cause murder (the revenge fantasy); the "mother" fantasy related to depression; the fantasies in addiction, such as gambling and taking drugs; the fantasies in creativity; the fantasies in psychosomatic illness.

Following the description of all these fantasies, the concluding chapter will tell how we can feel more at ease with both our daydreams and our hidden fantasies.

2
Where Fantasy Starts

We cannot escape fantasy any more than we can escape breathing. A fantasy accompanies every emotion we feel. Dr. Martin Grotjahn, psychoanalyst, has written eloquently of the nature of fantasy in childhood:

"The greatest mental dread of a child: that he may some day lose control of his bad thoughts, and they may suddenly get loose like a swarm of bats from a cave after sunset. We live in constant dread that our unconscious may find its way to consciousness and may overwhelm our controls."

A child has limited ability to judge reality, having neither the experience nor the emotional maturity. He equates fantasy with reality—as he believes, so is it. The child fears the power of his fantasy. He believes his wishes always come true, he lives in the grip of magical omnipotence—the wish, the fantasy, is the same as the deed: "I feel like killing my mother and therefore I have killed her."

When do our fantasies first appear? When do we try to make sense of the strange world that surrounds us? The mind of the infant is ready at birth to receive and respond to impressions, research has shown.

Even the fetus responds to sound. Judith Geizhals, Ph.D., in a personal communication to one of the authors of this book, described how during her pregnancy, like many mothers, she would talk to her fetus. Knowing she expected a girl, she named her Emily.

When Dr. Geizhals felt Emily kicking she would say, while gently patting her pregnant belly, "Hi, Emily." After the delivery Emily was allowed to remain on her mother's belly for a short while, then whisked away for tests. Hearing Emily cry from across the room her mother called

15

out, "Hi, Emily," and to her amazement Emily stopped crying. When this occurred a second time, the nurse said, "You know your mommy's voice," and smiled. When mothers name the fetus, talk to it as though it were a person, they are less likely to fear something will happen to the fetus before it is born, that they will bear a deformed child.

Our first fantasies center on our mother, the first face we see. Freud wrote of the start of love that "the sucking of the child at the mother's breast is the model for every love relation." In the beginning with all of us is not the Word but, closely allied, where the words are emitted, the Mouth. During our first months on earth we learn to know the world by the sensations of sucking, swallowing, spitting. To the baby it is an oral world.

As our mother's arms enfold us we learn the feeling of tenderness and caring, the touch of intimacy. She is the source of our original fantasies, ones we never forget though they are deeply buried in memory. Our ancient fantasies and the emotions they aroused center on the feminine figure who first fed us, kept us warm, bathed us, comforted us when we cried. We became accustomed to her face and whatever she bestowed on us we welcomed, from milk to a soft furry animal.

Then a male figure strode into the picture and he occasionally held us, cooed at us, perhaps even fed us and diapered us. His voice was deeper than our mother's. We grew accustomed to his face too, though he did not spend as much time with us as our mother did.

Dr. D. W. Winnicott, the famous British psychoanalyst, called holding a baby a form of loving, adding it is perhaps "the only way in which a mother can show the infant her love. There are those who can hold an infant and those who cannot; the latter quickly produce in the infant a sense of insecurity, and distressed crying."

The mother's love, he maintains, is expressed at the breast as the infant gradually becomes aware of the satisfaction given by someone familiar who extends tender, loving care. In this dawning awareness, there starts for the infant a relationship on which he will base impressions of his surroundings. On these impressions will be built inner thought processes that influence his fantasy life.

A four-month-old infant reacts differently to each face when shown pictures expressing various emotions such as happiness or anger. At six months of age his mother can gradually introduce him to a situation of delayed gratification and introduce new and strange objects, like a cup to sip from, instead of sucking at the breast or bottle. By eight months most babies have learned what behavior brings an approving smile or kiss as opposed to an angry, disapproving frown or slap. During the first year of life a baby becomes increasingly skillful in interpreting facial expressions of those who surround him.

Our most poignant fantasies go back to the years when our mother healed our hurts, kept us warm, taught us to talk, walk, bathe and dress. When we become depressed and lonely, we long for her, wish she were near to comfort us. Many a grown man or woman, in moments of fear or anguish, will call out to an empty room, "Mother, where are you? I need you." A physician reported one of the most heartbreaking cries he ever heard came from an eighty-year-old man about to undergo an operation. As he was wheeled into the operating room he called out tremulously, "I want my mother. Where is she?"

The happier our childhood, the less we will be driven as adults by unconscious fantasy. Sufficient emotional nurturing will set us free of terrorizing unconscious conflicts. We will always have conflicts but they strike fear in us only if we are unaware of them. Awareness means we can make peace with them, realize they are part of existence, know we cannot express our every impulse of hate and sexual desire.

Love, as shown by a mother toward a child, helps the child, and later the adult, keep destructive fantasies at bay as the child learns his first feelings of love. Childish love knows no bounds, it demands exclusive possession, is satisfied with nothing less than all. The demand made by so many adults that they fully possess the one they love comes from this child-concept of love. When directed toward another adult, it is bound to emotionally suffocate him.

Our first love may also be our first hate when our fantasies of being cherished turn to ones of revenge at times we feel ignored or abandoned. A child will scream as though he is dying when he needs food and when he is in pain. Our two greatest fears are death by starvation and physical injury.

Sometimes children hate their mother for not understanding what they need or for opposing a wish but this occurs only because she means so much to them that even a sharp look may strike rage in their hearts. They hate because the mother has the power to hurt. We usually do not hate those who have no power to hurt us.

Winnicott says further fantasies of infants are concerned not only with the external environment but with the "interrelationship of the people and bits of people that are being fantastically taken into him—at first along with his ingestion of food and subsequently as an independent procedure—and that build up the inner reality."

He adds, "A child feels that things inside are good or bad, just as things outside are good or bad. . . . The child's ability to keep alive what he loves and to retain his belief in his own love has an important bearing on how good or bad the things inside him and outside him feel to him to be; and this is to some extent true even of the infant of only a few months."

Winnicott concludes: "It can only be inferred, then, that the psychology of the small child and of the infant is not so simple as it would at first seem to be, and that a quite complex mental structure may be allowed even to the newborn infant." He adds, "At the present time [1956] there is a general acceptance among psychoanalysts of the view that there is a psychology of the newborn infant."

The baby tends to identify fantasy with the things going on inside his body, an inner world alive with movement and feelings, Winnicott states. First comes his recognition of the oral instinct, his feeling, "I want to suck, eat, bite. I feel satisfied after sucking, eating, biting." This is followed by his oral fantasy, "When hungry I think of food, when I eat I think of taking food in. I think of what I like to keep inside, and I think of what I want to be rid of and I think of getting rid of it." Through analysis of older children and adults, clear insight has been gained into the many ways in which fantasies of the appetite become involved as a defense against anxiety and depression in our life.

Following the oral fantasy, Winnicott says, "there comes a more sophisticated linking up of this theme of oral fantasy with the 'inner world.' " No case of vomiting or diarrhea, or anorexia or constipation in the child, he maintained, can be fully explained without reference to the child's conscious and unconscious fantasies about the inside of his body.

"Most doctors prefer to keep to the simple idea of pain without fantasy . . . but the fact remains that children will often give an account of their inner world when asked about their inner discomforts," he concludes. One child described a war being waged in his stomach between Spaniards and English fighting with swords. Another recounted a fantasy of little people sitting around a table in his stomach waiting for the food to be passed down his throat.

Winnicott refers to studies by Melanie Klein, a British psychoanalyst, that show the infant is engaged in "a constant interchange and testing between inner and outer reality; the inner reality is always being built up and enriched by instinctual experiences in relation to external objects [his mother and father] . . . and the outer world is constantly being perceived and the infant's relationship to it enriched because of the existence in him of a lively inner world."

An infant's one weapon is the scream. His temper tantrums bring his mother to his side so she will feed him or lessen his pain if he is cold or his stomach hurts, or relieve his wetness. A baby needs his mother to survive and his scream tells her his survival is endangered.

Hunger pangs to an adult are gnawing enough but to a baby, who is all sensation and cannot reason, to be hungry feels like the end of the world, comparable to a giant brandishing a knife above him. He may have the fantasy that a delay in feeding is an attempt at murder. The wails of a hungry baby are a plea to spare his life by feeding him.

This fantasy still operates unconsciously in those adults who become unreasonably furious if kept waiting in a restaurant. This is the original fury they felt as a baby endangered by the slow arrival of food, as the fantasy still persists that lack of food may mean their death. One wealthy stockbroker would hurl curses at the waiter if he were slow in bringing the food.

We are all barbarians at birth. No person can understand himself well unless he realizes that at the times of childhood when he felt starved, an angry voice raged within. Dr. Edward Glover, a psychoanalyst, remarked that we ask a child to learn in four or five years what it took mankind hundreds of thousands of years to learn—to become civilized. If a child is asked to suppress too many feelings too quickly, his fantasies will be intense and he will suffer. Just as he will also suffer if asked to suppress too few feelings but is uncritically indulged.

It is necessary we all learn to steer a course between what Freud called the "Scylla of giving the instincts free play and the Charybdis of frustrating them." Indulgence is not love though some parents believe it to be.

Often a child is indulged by a mother who has lost her husband through divorce and bestows all her feelings of love on the child so that he has the fantasy that he can do no wrong, that he is the one in control. Some parents indulge a child one moment, then turn on him angrily the next. This confuses the child; he has the fantasy that he can never please them.

Parents may compete with each other in a show of affection and bribes to win the child's allegiance and he will fantasize that bribes can produce love. A child may be overwhelmed by parents who demand he give more than he is able. His fantasies about such expectations may cause him to try to become mature at once and lose all sense of childhood play and joyousness.

The overprotective mother harms her child by worrying about him incessantly. She communicates the fantasy that something dreadful will happen to him and only she can save him. She robs the child of true initiative and independence, makes him afraid to strike out on his own. He will be furious at her for making him feel so dependent but usually dares not express his anger for fear he will lose her love. As destructive as a mother may be, the child has the enduring fantasy that she is his only protection against the dangers of the world. This holds true for his father, too.

Every child finds it difficult to tolerate frustration. As primitive tribes openly show, the child and the adult believe in magic. The child's world of magic includes the fantasy that he will get everything he wants and at once. This is one of the psychological distinctions between child and adult. The child cannot tolerate much of a delay, give up pleasure, knowing that a richer, deeper pleasure awaits if he can postpone the immediate gratification. The latter is the sign of a mature person, one in control of his feelings.

A deep hatred spewed in adulthood on mate or children is hatred originally felt in childhood against uncaring, cruel parents. Many children wait impatiently for the day they are old enough to leave home, torn between wanting revenge on parents they believe tortured them psychologically or physically, and the anguish of knowing how much they depended on such parents who, they feel, in spite of their brutality, really loved them.

No matter how wise and temperate his parents, each child is bound at times to feel angry because of what Freud called "the human condition." Humans differ from animals whose young grow quickly without much concern on the part of their parents. Humans, on the other hand, come into the world weak and helpless, cannot survive without years of intense care for their most elementary needs. The fact that we must depend on our mother to fulfill our needs for such a long time means we become very dependent on her and feel we have to repress many feelings of anger at frustrations.

To a child his parents seem at times bent on forbidding pleasure. Giving up pleasure is difficult for all of us but especially for a child. So he indulges in the fantasy of pleasures denied. He relinquishes pleasure in the world of reality but it continues within, free of anyone's demands. Denied a chocolate ice cream cone, a child may dream of eating his way through fields of chocolate ice cream cones. Denied the pleasurable physical touch of a mother, who grimaces when her child tries to embrace her, he can freely fantasize embraces that last for hours.

We cannot give way, as a child, to our fantasies of destroying at will when we feel frustrated. Our parents, being human, are bound to be imperfect. Even the most sensitive, understanding parents cannot meet all the demands of a baby.

It seems ironic that as children we spend years defiantly wishing to be big while as grownups we seethe in anger at having to give up the pleasures of dependency in childhood and face the harsh realities of life. Every adult, in part of his heart, fantasizes remaining a child, cries out in a far part of him, "Mother, take care of me!"

The early years are the time most of our basic, primitive fantasies originate, fantasies that may haunt us all our life. The fantasies are our attempt to explain whatever puzzles, frightens, confuses, angers us. They are constructed in our mind mainly around erotic desires and fear of death—being killed by our parents or killing them. While an infant does not know the meaning of murder he does know a parent may vanish and then he will be left alone, helpless and doomed to die—annihilated.

Life's greatest tragedy for a child is to be apart from his mother when he needs her. It is no wonder so many murders occur as one person threatens to leave another, or after he has left. There is no greater torment than to be abandoned by someone you need for survival.

The terror of abandonment is one of the child's greatest fears. He cannot live without his mother. This was shown by the studies of Dr. René Spitz who reported that babies deprived of their mothers and taken care of in hospitals often became very depressed. Some faded away, regressed, died because there was no one to give them the touch of love.

Fantasies that follow any threat his mother will desert him and the subsequent persistence of these fantasies may play a critical role in the maturing of a wide variety of a child's mental functions, according to Dr. Gregory Rochlin, a well-known psychoanalyst. Children ask in essence, "Who will love me, take care of me, when I am left alone? No one will want me and I will perish." Their greatest fear is reflected in the frightening fantasy of complete annihilation, extinction.

A four-year-old psychotic girl, poorly anchored in reality but unusually skilled in depicting her fears with the help of pencil and paper, drew a picture of herself as coming apart—all the body parts split from the torso. She showed it to her mother, shrieked, told of her fear of going to the dentist to have a tooth pulled. After she returned from the dentist, minus the tooth, she rushed to the mirror to make sure visually she was still in one piece.

It is a child's view that there is little danger "except if one is worthless," Rochlin explains. "What is no good is given up. To be angry and hateful is to be no good." The burdens of a child's life are often lightened through fantasies, wishes and beliefs in the reverse of what is oppressive, he adds.

During what is called the oral and anal phases of our psychosexual development, we devise many fantasies as recompense for inevitable frustrations. These include learning to give up the breast or bottle and becoming toilet-trained, giving up our right to urinate or defecate at will. Further fantasies follow on the heels of the frustration we suffer from all the "no's" we hear as we grow up.

Our aggressive or hostile fantasies become more numerous and stronger in the anal stage. Feces in fantasy may become weapons that maim or kill. Urine may be fantasied as a weapon by which we drown the enemy or humiliate and shame him. Or we may have the fantasy that urine and feces are gifts we bestow on our mother.

The power struggles that go on in many a marriage stem in large part from fantasies in the anal period—who is in control of whom. Many a husband or wife experiences the giving of love or pleasing the partner as "doing one's duty," but then feels humiliated and, like the child who resents submission to a tyrannical mother, becomes angry and resentful. Such fantasies result in power struggles between husbands and wives, may cause extramarital affairs or divorce.

If a child has been toilet-trained prematurely or too harshly, or allowed to indulge himself too long without being toilet-trained, we may assume his parents handled other learning situations in similar fashion. When treatment is harsh, the child feels he must perform regardless of whether he is able to or not and has fantasies of someday getting even. As an adult he feels obligated to please his mate as he once did his parents, but unconsciously will resent it. The resentment is strong because he is not pleasing spontaneously out of love but because he is angrily "doing his duty" for fear of reprisals if he does not comply.

The child who has not been expected to master the tensions of toilet training until he is three years old or even later may bring to adulthood the fantasy he can "shit all over the place" and may have difficulty loving anyone. He will expect his partner to submit to his narcissistic wishes. He may do little or nothing to give his sexual partner pleasure, believing sex is conducted only for him; in his mind the partner, like the mother of infancy, has no needs of her own and is there only to minister to his wishes.

Many sexual problems of adults are related to fantasies at the time of toilet training. Not only are the organs of excretion the same as, or close to, the sexual organs but a childhood fantasy may persist that sex is a form of evacuation. An adult may be unable to separate the fantasy of shame and guilt connected with the toilet from the act of sex if the toilet training has left him with a sense of failure that he has not been able to produce in a satisfactory way. He may feel he is no good, just like "a piece of shit." Self-doubt is connected with the fantasies of having nothing good to offer.

Because bowel and urine training constitute the first strong demand for control that a mother places on the child, conflicts are bound to arise. The result will determine whether the child, as an adult, is cooperative with those he loves or obstinate, defiant and rebellious. If this anal period has not been too permeated by an atmosphere of battles of wills, anger and hatred, the adult will not be troubled by lasting fantasies of self-doubt, rage and guilt.

As the child gradually resolves the conflict between the urge to express his wish to control the universe and the desire to keep the love of his mother and father by conforming to what he sees as their unreasonable demands, his fantasies become less narcissistic. By the age of three, he should be able to express love as well as receive it. While at first he may love both parents indiscriminately, about four he will turn with greater intensity to the parent of the opposite sex, in preparation for the later love of his life, a mate.

We are not born with a conscience; we have to learn some fantasies can never be gratified because they go against the taboos of civilization. A little girl of four feels her first passion for her father, wants him all to herself. This is the start of love for someone of the opposite sex as she is primed at an appropriate age to seek a father for her own children. But she does not know this as yet. Her fantasy is that she wants to marry her father and take her mother's place. The boy feels the same way about his mother. Both sexes must learn to accept the frustration of these natural sexual fantasies.

One reason psychoanalysis is successful in relieving emotional pain is that, with the help of the analyst, we trace fantasies to memories of earlier times in life when we felt frightened or vengeful or sexually aroused. We reveal the specifics in our lives that led to a particular fantasy still causing deep conflict. We find out what we have been unable to endure and have defended against through the use of fantasy.

One man could not understand why the sight of flames sent him into a panic. When he saw a building on fire he swiftly ran away. He did not smoke because he could not light a match, averted his eyes when anyone else did. During analysis he recalled that when he was a little boy his mother, whenever he misbehaved, would threaten him, as she lit a cigarette, "I am going to burn a hole in you if you ever disobey me again." She had never carried out her threat but he lived with the fantasy she might. There are other reasons children set fires: loneliness, anger at parents, need to make an impression, to be paid attention to, using the sight of the flames as a way of counteracting a feeling of deadness or to symbolize their inner feelings of being afire with either erotic or vengeful desires.

Fantasy and reality constantly wage war within us as children when sexual desires and aggressive wishes arise and are either carried out or repressed. Part of us accepts reality, knowing we must, to win the love of parents and the respect of society. But part of us fights reality, not wanting to give up the comfortable feeling of omnipotence and the luxury of dependence on our mother and father. The feeling of fusion with the mother is never completely given up. But it lessens in degree as we become aware of the dependence and gain more confidence in ourself to make our own decisions.

We are supposed to achieve a mature capacity to love when we reach the final or genital stage of sexual development. By then we should be capable of the feeling of tenderness in addition to sexual desire, for tenderness is essential to mature love.

Our goal should then be not to dominate, to possess, to subjugate but to give and share love. This is quite different from the first years of life when we fantasy the object of our love, our mother, as someone who exists only for our pleasure, as someone we own, merged with her.

If we have successfully reached the genital stage, we do not treat the one we love as a possession but a human being in his own right. But if we are still deeply involved in fantasies of the oral and anal phases we will treat those we supposedly love as our slaves.

The adult who as a child grew up in excessive fear of parents and in anger at them may be driven by the fantasy he must control the one he sexually desires, and if he cannot, he wishes to destroy his sexual partner.

One woman of twenty-five married a man of thirty-seven who tried to dominate all aspects of her life. "I can't breathe without his directing me," she told the lawyer she sought to arrange for a divorce. "He wants to know everything I do every minute of the day and night. It's like living in prison." She added, "And when I start to object, he hits me. Hard. I won't take it any longer."

By the same token, when an adult wishes to get rid of someone he hates, he may in fantasy vomit the person out of his life with angry words, as he did food as a baby. Or expel the enemy in fantasy as he once did in anger, and may still do, with feces. The expression "shit on you" is not uncommon in angry adults and adolescents.

If we have successfully reached and developed in a mature way during the genital stage, with the fantasies whirling in all stages successfully suppressed (a conscious act), no longer needing to haunt us through repression (an unconscious act), we will be capable of loving someone of the opposite sex. We will be able to spend the rest of our life enjoying a fair amount of pleasure, accepting the frustrations that are part of reality.

The normal development of psychosexual growth ends in becoming a man or woman in the fullest sense—capable of pleasurable sexual activity, capable of restraining anger except when justified. There is however a long and fairly difficult path to traverse emotionally from the complete self-centeredness of our first months on earth to the point where we can freely bestow what was originally self-love on someone else.

Two things are involved. We have to give up fantasies of narcissism and then accept our feelings of ambivalence—the great swing between love and hate. To quote Dr. Karl Abraham, one of the early psychoanalysts, "Every attraction to another person is, as it were, sicklied o'er with the pale cast of auto-erotism," erotic feelings for the self.

To achieve mature love means not only the use of the genitals as primary in sexual intimacy but the ability to enjoy the other person as companion and friend as well as lover. It means we see him as human not as an object of our fantasy.

Every stage of sexual development holds its own particular threats that arouse anxiety. During the oral stage we feel psychically helpless for we have little or no judgment or reason, cannot care for ourselves. We feel endangered, fear we might lose our sense of self, resulting in complete annihilation. During the anal stage we fear loss of our mother's love if we do not learn control of our excretory functions. In the phallic stage, which comes between the anal and genital stage, both boys and girls fantasy castration as punishment. The last source of fear is the loss of the love object. A boy gives up his fantasy of killing his father so he can have his mother all to himself for the sake of keeping the father, who is not just hated but also loved.

Children at various ages, depending on their psychosexual development, interpret differently the meaning of a parental act that may shape their individual fantasy life. For instance, a rather aggressive, impulsive mother, prone to cruel tricks, decided to play a practical joke on her three daughters who were one, three and four years old. She placed beneath the blankets of the bed of each one a wooden Chinese toy snake (the kind that wiggles). That night her three girls stretched their feet under the blankets as they climbed into their beds and each quickly withdrew her toes in fear. All later revealed their individual fantasies about the toy snake.

The youngest saw it as a devouring monster who would swallow her. The middle child was afraid someone had made a bowel movement in her bed and was terrified about what her "neat" mother would say if she discovered the forbidden feces. She feared her mother's reaction if she knew of her daughter's rebellious wish to defecate at times on the floor, not in the toilet.

The oldest girl, who was four, after overcoming her first shocked belief that this was an animal who could hurt her, became amused. She told her mother she had fantasies of putting the snake in front of her genital area in the bathroom at the day-care center she attended, competing with the boys. She also fantasized her mother might like her even more than she did her father if she realized her daughter possessed the same treasured "thing" as her husband.

As we grow up, the old fantasies of fear should lose their threat since the dangers of each infantile stage have, in reality, lost their emotional power as we learn to use reason. The disappearance of anxiety stirred by our fantasies depends however on how loving and wise our parents, how threatened we felt in infancy, and how deep and strong the fantasies called into use as defense against the pain of fear and anger.

There are adults who live as though the old dangers still swing overhead, the Sword of Damocles of daily life. They are not aware of the ancient threats but remain oppressed by the feeling something vague and unknown threatens them, something from which there is no escape and against which they are powerless.

They cannot overcome the fear of loss of love enough to be able to give love. They never become free enough of feelings of dependency to feel independent enough to give strength to others. They remain childlike in their reaction to danger, in fear of unreal villains. But unreal villains are nonetheless terrifying, for psychic reality may be even more painful than actual reality, otherwise no one would go mad. The woman who cannot sleep at night fearing a burglar will break in, rape and murder her is more terrified by her fantasy than by any threat of an atom bomb.

Many men and women consciously feel they want to love and be loved but find themselves unable to do so. They fail when they try to be happy with one person. Something within strongly opposes their conscious wish. The opposition comes from the infantile wishes and fantasies blocking fulfillment of mature love.

Such men and women possess high overestimation of the value of food, the value of feces and the value of the penis. They unconsciously fear being eaten or eating, beaten or beating, castrated or castrating. These fears mask their overwhelming wish to devour (from the oral stage), to beat (from the anal stage) and to castrate (from the phallic stage). They have never been able, because of fear and anger, to cope successfully with the fantasies at each stage.

No love is pure, as Freud said. There will always be some hate in any intimate relationship, for we are not saints. But when adult sexual feelings are freed in large part from the hunger and anger of the earlier psychosexual stages, and are accompanied by tenderness and affection, this is probably as near adult love as we can achieve.

If we remain too caught in the fantasies of the earlier stages, feel too emotionally hungry, too angry, adult love is impossible, for we bring too much fear and rage to the relationship. The capacity to love depends thus on our early experiences and memories. With loving, understanding parents we are guaranteed the easiest time possible. With parents who treat us neither as puppet nor toy, nor as an appendage, nor as a little savage, but as a small human being who needs compassion and protection, a child grows into an adult able to love. Parents who understand their own fantasies and needs are the ones most apt to give a child the chance to know love.

The fantasies in every stage of our psychosexual development contribute either to our eventual success or failure in choosing a mate wisely and to remain married. Whether or not we have been able to give up dependency on the mother and give up also the erotic attachment to the parent of the opposite sex are crucial factors for our future ability to love fully and freely.

Layers and layers of fantasies exist in our mind, hundreds of them by the time we reach adolescence, many clustered around our feelings of love and hate. The form of an unconscious fantasy develops and grows with time, expressing "the forces at play at the particular time in the person's life, and the level of functioning and maturity of the ego, as it attempts at different stages to integrate the demands of wishes in keeping with the ego's growing adaptive and defensive responsibilities," according to Arlow.

Thus in one form or another fantasies persist our whole life. The organization of some very important fantasies takes shape in connection with the beginning of the Oedipus complex. But fantasies begin far before that phase. A mother emotionally distraught at a child's birth, not wanting the child, is unlikely at any time in the child's life to help him achieve a state of mind that leads to effective emotional growth and his fantasies will be influenced.

When Catherine, thirty years old, was a little girl, she had been given at birth two golden hearts to wear around her neck on a chain. In her fantasy these hearts every so often frightened her as they turned into two granite blocks growing in size until she felt they choked her, she was on the verge of being killed. Her mother had died when Catherine was thirteen after a six-year illness. Catherine stopped wearing the golden hearts, hid them in an attempt to get away from her fearful fantasy.

During her analysis Catherine realized the depth of her mother's resentment at having three daughters and no son to take over a large business that her husband had started. Catherine's mother had been a social butterfly for whom appearance meant a great deal. Catherine recalled as a girl her mother discussing the possibility of "swapping one of her girls" for one of the sons of her sister-in-law—the joking quality had completely escaped the terrified Catherine. She had remembered instead her mother hysterically crying when she learned her third and last child was also a girl. Catherine realized her fantasy of the golden hearts killing her might have reflected her mother's death wish against her unwanted daughters.

Catherine had hidden her rage against her mother over the years by being placid, the "good girl," neat and obedient—defensive maneuvers against her fury. When her mother died, she dressed up in her mother's clothes, acted out her oedipal attachment to her father in literal fashion—stepping into her mother's shoes. She became furious when her widowed father started seeing other women.

In her analysis, Catherine realized the various conflicts from the oral, anal and oedipal phases that had fueled her fears, pertained to her relationship to her mother at the various developmental stages. She was able at last to take out hesitantly the two golden hearts on the chain, place them around her neck, at first fearing the old fantasy of death would return. But it did not, she had faced it, made it conscious and rid herself of the ghosts of the past that had unrealistically haunted her.

The early breakup of parents with small children does not bode well for the easy solution of life's natural emotional conflicts of the child. His fantasies are apt to be fraught with fear and confusion. Since a small child's perception of himself is colored by omnipotent fantasies he feels the cause of divorce cannot only be related to the parents' conflicts but he is somehow responsible. Such fantasies can take on overwhelming proportions. A four-year-old girl, Eliza, injured herself severely, in part to punish herself for her fantasized crime of wishing to separate her parents so she could possess her father, yet also hoping her parents would become so preoccupied with her injury they would stop fighting and reunite in their care and love for her. She hoped she had given them an interest in common so they would not seek the divorce, which, of course, she was not able to stop.

The ability of our instinctual wishes to evoke what are called "derivatives" of the original unconscious fantasy varies in intensity, depending on a number of factors that act in unison, Arlow states. Foremost among these forces is "the intensity of the conflict over the instinctual drives," the sexual and the aggressive.

He cites as an extreme example those severe cases of obsessive-compulsive neurosis that border on psychosis—cases in which the person is so overwhelmed by his wishes to kill with gas and feces that he can perceive nothing but dangerous poisons in the air around him, inside and outside his home.

Arlow mentions the experience of a man who became almost violent with his employer. While deep in thought about his most recent quarrel with the employer, the man passed a sign he had seen regularly on visits to his psychoanalyst. Familiar with the sign, the man knew it referred to the owner of the shop, "Maeder." But now, as he passed the sign, he mistakenly perceived it as "Murder"—fulfilling his wish to get rid of his hated employer.

A second set of factors that governs the evoking of an unconscious fantasy concerns the nature of the current experience, particularly "the data of perception," in Arlow's words. Current experiences and "perceptions" often stir up a persistent unconscious fantasy.

A twenty-two-year-old woman could never wear a black dress, any other color she admired and bought. One day she was speaking to a friend about her mother, recalled, "She always wore black, she thought it was chic." The color black sparked her fantasy of the oedipal battle for her father. Never having resolved it, she dared not, in any way, resemble her hated mother, black awakened her forbidden yearning for her father.

Commenting on the fantasies of childhood, Freud wrote: "the loss of love, or failure, leave behind them a permanent injury to self-regard in the form of a narcissistic scar which . . . contributes more than anything to the sense of inferiority. The lessening of affection he [the child] receives, the increasing demands of education, hard work and occasional punishment . . . these show him at last the full extent to which he has been scorned."

If we want to see infantile fantasy lived out at perhaps its fullest, there is the description given by psychiatrist Wulf Sachs in *Black Hamlet*. Born in Russia but later a citizen of the Union of South Africa, Sachs lived in Johannesburg where he became a practicing psychoanalyst, a member of the British and International Psychoanalytical Societies. He wrote of his treatment of John Chavafambira, a native African medicine man, showing John's fantasies and conflicts placed against the background of two worlds—white and black—worlds in collision. Sachs spent many years studying John's personality as both patient and friend.

Sachs commented: "To the primitive African, the belief in witchcraft is real and logical. There is no such thing as imaginary feeling. There is no such phenomenon as imaginary pain or imaginary vision. . . . The African fears malicious spirits which he actually sees and hears. He lives in constant fear and turns to the witch doctors, in whom he places unconditional belief and trust."

There is belief in evil spirits that continuously act against everyone. It is like a child's world: you can poison a person from twenty miles away or stick a pin in a doll fashioned like the one you want to kill, believing he will die. Or a certain medicine will save your life if you are fatally ill.

In *Black Hamlet* Sachs describes the psychoanalytic treatment of John, medicine man of this tribe in darkest Africa. He unveils the same passion for his mother as the stockbroker living in a penthouse in Manhattan feels for his mother. Hence the title of the book.

Sachs portrays in depth the fantasies that exist in "the child that slumbers within the adult," as Freud put it. The child is driven by his strong desires and impulses that lead him to create imaginary satisfactions in a rich fantasy life. If extreme, this may result in a state in which the adult cannot distinguish between fantasy and reality.

Many of the child's fantasies reflect the parent's fantasies. One woman, as a girl, saw her mother terrified of the rain and cold weather because she, as a little girl, had seen two brothers, caught out in winter storms, die of pneumonia (no penicillin in those days). The mother conveyed to her daughter the peril of rain and cold weather, as though these conditions meant death, perpetuating a fantasy unto another generation.

Many fantasies are conveyed by parents about certain foods as "bad" or "good," fantasies not based on reality. These are conscious fantasies; no attempt is made to disguise or hide them. But there are also the unconscious fantasies, the unspoken ones, that may be handed down by parents. Through facial expressions, a mother may signal she disapproves of an adolescent daughter kissing her date goodnight—any sexual contact is "bad." A father may cut off a daughter each time she starts to speak, as though she has no mind of her own, and she may fantasy herself as worthless, meaningless to a man.

The child is constantly engaged in what analysts call "internalizing" aspects and attitudes of parents. A woman complained to her therapist, "I resent being so much like my mother. I seem to have copied all her traits."

The analyst said, "Who did you expect to be like as you grew up? Mahatma Gandhi?" He was pointing out that she would naturally copy the two persons to whom she was closest, her mother and father. Freud noted that there exists a period of "childhood amnesia" during the first six years of life when few experiences, fantasies and wishes are recalled by the adult. In the famous case of the "Wolf Man," who often dreamt of five wolves perched in trees outside his window at night, waiting to attack him, Freud interpreted this as a memory of seeing the primal scene (parental intercourse) when he was eighteen months old and slept in his parents' bedroom. Freud said he debated whether the Wolf Man dealt with fantasy or reality, but concluded this made no difference since his terror was based on feelings real to him.

All discussion about fantasy, Freud wrote in *A General Introduction to Psychoanalysis,* "seems to lead to but one impression, that childhood experiences of this kind are in some way necessarily required by the neurosis, that they belong to its unvarying inventory. If they can be found in real events, well and good; but if reality has not supplied them, they will be evolved out of hints and elaborated by phantasy. The effect is the same, and even today we have not succeeded in tracing any variations in the results according as phantasy or reality plays the greater part in these experiences."

Freud not only produced the theory of how the unconscious operated, he also provided a method to reach what he called "the primary process," concealed by our rational everyday thoughts. It is only when this rational mask is either removed or reduced to a minimum that the unconscious becomes known to us, as Reuben Fine points out in *The Development of Freud's Thoughts.*

The primary process refers to our unorganized mental activities characterized by our unconscious mental life. The process includes free discharge of our psychic energy without regard to the demands of environment, reality or logic. Freud provided a way to make conscious the primary process by asking patients to freely associate, to tell what came to mind. He also asked them to describe their dreams, which he then interpreted.

As the child gradually resolves the conflict between the urge to express his instinctual wishes and the desire to maintain the security of his relationship with his parents by conforming to their demands, he becomes less involved with his own needs. In the struggle to resolve the oedipal conflict he represses hostile wishes, displaces them onto other objects such as animals or persons outside the home.

Incidentally, the history of the treatment of children by parents and society has been a cruel one, causing terrifying fantasies in the child. The hatred of parents for children in ancient Carthage, for instance, resulted in the ritual slaying of children. This was dramatically shown in relics of that age which included urns holding the remains of sacrificed children. These urns arrived in New York, along with art treasures uncrated at the American Museum of Natural History, as revealed in a story in *The New York Times* on September 1, 1987. In the midst of magnificent bronze figures, opulent jewelry and ornaments, sat cremation urns and religious paraphernalia used in the sacrifice of 20,000 children from about 800 B.C. until Carthage's destruction by Roman invaders in 146 B.C. The urns, unearthed near Tunis on the north African coast, are regarded by scholars as the largest cemetery of sacrificed humans ever discovered.

The fantasies of parents who favored such ritual slaying of children were that their death helped control the growth of the population and helped the families keep fortunes intact, archaeologists stated. The children's death ensured that an estate would descend intact to a single heir (the basis of many a modern murder mystery). The children ranged in age from stillborn fetuses to four years. Primitive civilization was cruel to children. It has taken time for parents to acknowledge fantasies that are still hostile and murderous toward their children.

The child's earliest reality is "wholly fantasy"; the child does not differentiate between objects, organs, animate or inanimate, inside and outside, Grotjahn points out. All reality is at first symbolic reality. Only after his ego develops and his body is differentiated as "I" does the child develop a true relation to reality.

Fairy tales, by showing both the fantasy world and the world of reality, help children mature. Grotjahn in *The Voice of the Symbol* describes fairy tales as "collective dreams, closely related to daydreams and similar to the highly individualized night dreams." Children do not separate the unconscious from the conscious, they understand the meanings of the circus and the clown and of the fairy tale without the aid of the adult and his intelligence, he says.

Grotjahn concludes: "The natural brilliance of the unspoiled child stands in shocking contrast to the stupidity of the average adult, who has invented the term 'common sense' as an excuse for his limitations. The child uses his fantasy and imagination in order to understand, while the adult tries to think rationally. . . . The fantasy and imagination of the child may turn a chair or a table into a living being. . . . A parent should take lessons from his children and start again to listen unashamedly with 'the third ear' as the child does." He adds that the adjusted person recognizes the world in both its realistic and symbolic aspects.

The fantasy world of the child is dramatically portrayed in *The Adventures of Alice in Wonderland*. The relation between author and child is unusual in that Lewis Carroll takes the side of a girl as he reduces the world of the adult to absurdity. The author is a male writing about a female heroine with whom he is deeply identified. Carroll's real name was Charles Dodgson and it is possible he took the female name "Carol," adding an "r", as part of a bisexual identity.

Grotjahn points out that in this highly complex, unusually rich symbolic representation of the fantasies of a child's mind the author succeeds in being amusing and confusing simultaneously. Grotjahn says, "a wilful, vicious hostility runs wild and heightens the hopeless confusion," with much of the anxiety connected with changes in Alice's body image. There is portrayed a "hostile, destructive, frightful method of growing. . . . Alice grows so fast that she threatens to burst the whole house she is in" and as a last resort "puts one arm out of the window and one foot up the chimney."

Grotjahn calls this a hostile birth fantasy, says its destructiveness for mother and child "could hardly be better expressed." It is the kind of associations analysts hear from patients trying to work through their feelings toward mothers who seem always to have been pregnant, as Lewis Carroll's mother was with one or the other of ten babies, Grotjahn notes.

Alice may also represent Carroll's confusion and wonderment about different parts of the body. She changes size, like the boy who experiences his penis sometimes erect (strong and large), sometimes flaccid (insignificant and small), looking as though it is about to disappear in the mind of the frightened boy. The changes in length and volume displaced onto the person of Alice are reassuring, become a special way of envisioning and accepting a confusing fact of life to both boys and girls.

According to Grotjahn, the destructive fight against all logic and rational thinking extends to the language and the "inexhaustible play on words," in this classic by Carroll. In some places words are "cut to pieces and live as such; they unite with other parts of words and take on new meanings until sometimes no meaning at all is left." The printed word makes no sense but children probably accept "this hostile and playful defiance," Grotjahn says, better than adults.

Alice's adventures lack integration and show little love, concern or tenderness, he states, feelings children "develop much later, if at all." He calls Alice's wanderings a "gigantic, teasing hoax" in that they show the child that repressions are secure enough to withstand teasing in fantasy that may sometimes create more anxiety than the child can handle. He adds that some children react to the circus with fear or nightmares and some may react to Alice's journey with intense dislike.

Possibly one of the most remembered fantasies in adults is the Red Queen's easy disposal of anyone she immediately dislikes, without even knowing them—"Off with his head!" This appeals to every child, who has often had this thought when his parents deprive him of a pleasure or in any way interfere with his wishes and fantasies.

Finally Alice meets the Queen "who is as dreadful as the Duchess and quite like her." The King is "only vaguely outlined and not very impressive," as Carroll probably fantasied his father, Grotjahn observes. They have ten children, as in Carroll's family, not counting himself and Grotjahn notes, "Life is created easily and taken away with similar ease, nullifying the act of creation by one sweeping destruction, which ends in a catastrophic tumbling down of a pack of cards." The queen-mother is included in the final act of destruction—death to the mother who did little but add siblings to Carroll's precarious childhood.

In his fantasy tale, Carroll reached classical heights as he portrayed fantasy with humor and artistry so that it has appealed to children and adults alike and will no doubt remain popular as long as man can read. The book ends with a trial in which Alice is mysteriously involved, almost like the hero of Kafka's *The Trial,* Grotjahn points out. Alice solves the situation by retreating to reality, awakening and putting to rest, at least temporarily, her fantasy life—the fantasy life of the author and his millions of readers attempting to get in touch with their unconscious fantasies as they feel on some level understood and accepted.

Grotjahn also points out that children view television for its fantasy and passive pleasure, a chance to escape real-life worries and real-life boredom. He classifies viewers as "fantasy seekers" and "reality seekers." Television fantasy productions offer escape from threats and anxiety, provide wish fulfillment and pleasure, unlike shows based on reality that invite alertness, activity, effort, such as the 1987 midsummer Congressional hearings on the Iran-Contra involvements.

The valuable purpose fairy tales serve in the life of a child is also described by Bruno Bettelheim in *The Uses of Enchantment: The Meaning and Importance of Fairy Tales.* He points out that today, as in times past, the most important and also the most difficult task in raising a child is to help him find "meaning in life," and fairy tales help him master the psychological problems of growing up.

These problems include overcoming the feeling the world is his, oedipal conflicts, sibling rivalry, relinquishing childhood dependencies, gaining a feeling of identity and self-worth and moral obligation. A child achieves this understanding by identifying with the story and figures in fairy tales. He also gains the ability to cope "not through rational comprehension of the nature and content of his unconscious but by becoming familiar with it through spinning out daydreams—ruminating, rearranging, and fantasizing about suitable story elements in response to unconscious pressures."

Bettelheim says that by doing the above, the child "fits unconscious content into conscious fantasies, which then enable him to deal with that content." Fairy tales also have unequaled value because they offer new dimensions to the child's imagination otherwise impossible for him to discover on his own. The form and structure of fairy tales suggest images to the child by which he can structure his daydreams and use them to give a better direction to his life.

In opposition to the belief a child must be diverted from what troubles him most—his formless, nameless anxieties and his chaotic, angry and even violent fantasies—Bettelheim believes a child should not be exposed only to "the sunny side of things . . . only conscious reality or pleasant and wish-fulfilling images," because "such one-sided fare nourishes the mind only in a one-sided way, and real life is not all sunny."

He decries the "widespread refusal" to let children know that the source of much unhappiness in life is due to human nature, the propensity of all men to act aggressively, asocially and selfishly, out of their anxiety and anger. Parents want children to believe inherently all men are good but children know *they* are not always good and even when they are, would often prefer not to be. This contradicts what they are told by parents and therefore makes the child a monster in his own eyes.

As the German poet Schiller wrote, "Deeper meaning resides in the fairy tales told to me in my childhood than in the truth that is taught by life." Parents, encouraged by the culture in which they live, pretend, particularly where children are concerned, "that the dark side of man does not exist," according to Bettelheim. Whereas Freud's philosophy holds "that only by struggling courageously against what seem like overwhelming odds can man succeed in wringing meaning out of existence."

This is exactly the message fairy tales get across to the child: a struggle against severe difficulties in life is unavoidable—an intrinsic part of human existence—and if you do not shy away from but steadfastly meet unexpected and often unjust hardships, you can master all obstacles and emerge triumphant and victorious.

Fairy tales, proceeding as the child's mind does, helps the child by showing how reality may emerge from fantasy. The fairy tale offers "fantasy materials which suggest to the child in symbolic form what the battle to achieve self-realization is all about, and it guarantees a happy ending," Bettelheim says.

Referring to the "inescapable cauldron of emotions which every child, in his own way, has to manage at a certain age," he says that fairy tales, unlike any other form of literature, direct the child to discover his identity and calling, and suggest what experiences are needed to develop his character further. Fairy tales "intimate that a rewarding, good life is within one's reach despite adversity—but only if one does not shy away from the hazardous struggles without which one can never achieve true identity." The stories promise that if a child dares to engage in "this fearsome and taxing search, benevolent powers will come to his aid, and he will succeed." The stories also warn that those who are too timorous and narrow-minded to risk themselves in finding themselves must face a humdrum existence—if an even worse fate does not befall them.

The typical fairy tale splitting of the mother into a good (usually dead) mother and an evil stepmother "serves the child well," Bettelheim holds. It is not only a means of preserving an internal all-good mother when the real mother is not all-good, but it also permits anger at this bad "stepmother" without endangering the goodwill of the true mother, viewed as a different person.

All the fairy stories that show the mother or stepmother as "wicked" or other members of the family as "evil" contain fantasies the youngster recognizes as such but also partly believes. They center on what Freud called the child's "family romance," the fantasy one's parents are not really one's own but that one is the child of some exalted personages.

Children's dreams show wishes fulfilled and anxieties given tangible form—an animal attacks or devours an unknown person. A child's ego is still weak and in the process of building. Animals are often used to represent the conquering of terror.

Maurice Sendak, writer and illustrator, is among the few who understand the child's mind. In *Where the Wild Things Are,* the boy Max represents a rebellious, angry three-year-old child struggling with his rage and temper tantrums, his "monsters", and the book describes how he learns to tame them by looking straight into their eyes, facing his own fury. The story ends in a reassuring way as Max finds symbolic evidence of his mother's unconditional love waiting for him in the meal that is still hot. In this final drawing Max is relieved at not having his fearful fantasy of being rejected come true.

It has been twenty-four years since the publication of this book but children still delight in the story and Sendak's macabre illustrations, as he became the first artist to deal openly with the buried feelings of children. In an interview on December 16, 1987, on the Arts and Entertainment Channel in New York, talking about his creative process, Sendak said in answer to the question who the monsters in the drawings represented, "Well, they were all my uncles and aunts."

He also revealed when he was two years old, the Lindbergh baby was kidnapped and Sendak's father was so frightened by this that he slept in the same room as his young son to protect him. Sendak said he never shook that fear of being separated from his parents, inheriting it from his father.

Selma H. Fraiberg in *The Magic Years* tells of her niece Jannie who, when she was two years and eight months old, in front of her aunt pulled on white cotton gloves, clasped her patent leather purse in imitation of a lady leaving for an afternoon engagement, turned and frowned at the air behind her. Then she said firmly, "No, Laughing Tiger, You *cannot* come with us for an ice cream cone. You stay right there. But Jannie can come with us. Come along Jannie!" She stepped out the door with her uncle, swinging her purse grandly.

Ms. Fraiberg, after she composed herself, asked the child's grand-mother, "*Who* is Laughing Tiger?" The grandmother replied, "He is the latest one." The two women understood each other. There had been a steady arrival of imaginary companions, chairs reserved at the table for rabbits, dogs and bears. The real child, Jannie, who directed this menag-erie, often did not answer to her own name.

The grandmother looked distraught and Ms. Fraiberg asked, "Why *Laughing Tiger?*"

"He doesn't roar. He never scares children. He doesn't bite. He just laughs."

"Why couldn't he go for an ice-cream cone?"

"He has to learn to mind. He can't have everything his own way. Anyway that's the way it was explained to me."

At dinner that night, Ms. Fraiberg's niece did not even notice her until she was about to sit down. Whereupon Jannie cried out, "Watch out! You were sitting on Laughing Tiger!"

Laughing Tiger remained with Jannie for several months, he never showed the ferocity of his species, gave no cause for alarm. He endured all the civilized teachings of his young mistress without rebelling or a nervous breakdown. A few months after Jannie's third birthday he disappeared and nobody missed him, Ms. Fraiberg reported.

She explained that Laughing Tiger was "the direct descendant of the savage and ferocious beasts who disturb the sleep of small children." He came into being at a time Jannie was very afraid of dogs in the neighborhood who could bite and might eat up a little girl. She felt small and helpless before the imagined danger.

To help her ward off this danger, she created a "bashful and cowardly beast" who, at one word from his mistress, would shrink into his corner. Ms. Fraiberg called this transformation of a tiger into an obedient beast "probably a caricature of the civilizing process which the little girl is undergoing." The rewards, the deprivations, the absurd demands she made upon Laughing Tiger were a caricature of the whims and wishes of the grown-ups as she perceived them.

The reformed tiger, in fantasy, was also a caricature of a little girl, and the natural attributes of a tiger—its uncontrolled impulsive and ferocious qualities—represented those tendencies within her undergoing a transformation. She acted more severe and demanding than the mother and father who civilized her. This confirmed the psychological truth that the most zealous crusaders against vice are the reformed criminals, as the strength of their original impulses to commit a crime is given over to the opposing wish, Ms. Fraiberg pointed out.

In the ordinary home such experiences with invisible tigers or a reasonable facsimile thereof have a good effect on the mental health of children, Ms. Fraiberg states. Laughing Tiger was an important factor in the eventual dissolution of Jannie's fear of dogs and other animals as she learned to conquer her fear. But if a child feels his mother or father "dangerous," if he has reason to fear a parent because that parent beats him or consistently ignores him as though he were not in the room or criticizes him constantly, he will have difficulty dealing with his fear through imaginative play because his fears are real.

"Whenever reality reinforces a child's fantasied dangers, the child will have more difficulty in overcoming them," Ms. Fraiberg points out. "This is why, on principle, we avoid any methods of handling a child which could reinforce his fantasies of danger."

While a parent may not regard a spanking as a physical attack or assault on a child's body, the child may regard it as such, feel hurt physically and emotionally. Ms. Fraiberg urges parents to "try not to behave in such a way that a child feels a real danger."

She points out there is a difference in the child who tries to overcome his fear of tigers by becoming a tiger in his *play* and the child who has a fantasy in which he believes he is in danger of attack as a tiger and attacks first in self-defense. She reports that when such a child, who attacks other children because of his fantasied fear of attack, talks about himself in clinical treatment, "we find the most fantastic fears as the motive force behind their behavior." The tigers have invaded his real world and the therapist has to help the child understand his fear, whereupon his aggressive behavior subsides.

She warns that if a child of any age abandons the real world and cannot form human relationships, prefers to *be* his imaginary animal, there is cause for concern. "But we must not confuse the neurotic uses of imagination with the healthy," she says. "It can be demonstrated that the child's contact with the real world is *strengthened* by his periodic excursions into fantasy."

Destructive fantasies become entrenched in the unconscious if a child has suffered too much psychological pain too early. If his self-esteem is crippled from the start he is apt to retreat to this world of fantasy because the reality of his life is too painful.

If a child is cruelly beaten by a mother or father, he cannot fight back for he believes he will lose what little love they are able to give (though some young sons and daughters have been known to kill their mothers or fathers). But the child can fantasy he is David slaying Goliath, at least feel imaginary vengeance. If he does not allow himself to acknowledge his anger in some way, the result may be the autistic or schizophrenic child, or, later in life, the emotionally disturbed adult.

Love is a complicated emotion built on many fantasies as it develops. If a child grows up in an understanding, empathic, protective atmosphere, he will believe "bad" or dangerous impulses can be controlled without living in fear of them. If he does not feel loved, he is constantly guarding against his fantasies of hate and terror breaking loose and harming himself or someone to whom he is close or a stranger on whom he projects them.

If childhood is fairly peaceful, if parents give us love, respect and trust, our fantasies will be for the most part loving, creative, realistic. But if parents are cruel, did not want us born, fail to protect us, our fantasies will be filled with hatred and wishes for revenge.

The play of a child is determined by his wishes, Freud maintained, chiefly the wish to be grown-up and in command of his life. A child in play "imitates what is known to him of the lives of adults." Children take on the roles of various family members—Mom, Dad, Grandma, Grandpa, imitating grown-up behavior.

Since no parent is perfect (perhaps the greatest fantasy of all) the child, later the adult, faces the fact that life will hold many frustrations and disappointments—alas, far from paradise. The acceptance of this reality reduces the angry fantasies that consume us all to some degree.

It is natural to have fantasies of omnipotence and greed as a child, to want to be the only one, to expect every wish to come true and at once. What determines whether these fantasies rule our life, creating deep unhappiness, is our capacity to move slowly into the realm of reality, attain a sense of self.

What does "self," a word loosely thrown around today, mean? Many books are written about the "true" self as opposed to the "false" self. Is the self something we can define? Examine? Change?

3

The Fantasy of Self

There is a hunger in all of us to know "Who am I?" Socrates advised, quoting the sentence inscribed upon the Delphic Oracle of Apollo, "Know thyself." This knowledge entails becoming aware of fantasies that may threaten what we call the sense of self.

Without knowledge of the deeper fantasies that stir us we may lack strong belief in our inner self. We may feel as though we were on a ship tossed about at sea without a compass.

We start to develop a sense of self early in life as we go through many experiences with our parents. One mother, who lived in New York, was trying to decide whether to send her eight-year-old son, Adam, for a six-week stay with her sister who owned a farm outside of London. The mother had reservations about her son's ability to manage away from home for the first time, though she knew he was very self-reliant.

When he begged to be allowed to fly to London, she said, "I'll think about it." He went to his room, returned three hours later with a collage, handed it to her, saying, "This is me." He had fashioned on a foot-long sheet of paper an animated rocket with four strong engines and a boyish creature at the wheel, ready to take off on a flight into the universe.

She laughed, said, "If that's the way you feel, ready to leave Mother Earth, I'm reassured. I'll allow you to fly to London." She thought, I will give him a chance to prove he is mature enough to be responsible for himself since he believes he is ready to be launched into the world.

He telephoned from London he was having a fine time. While with his aunt, he made a mischievous mistake when he let out her sheep from their enclosure and they ate her entire vegetable garden. He offered to pay for this by painting her barn as recompense. He returned home feeling more self-confident than ever.

In contrast, a nine-year-old girl, Karin, had a poor self-image, shown when she and her two younger sisters had their portraits painted at their mother's request. Karin was a depressed, emotionally starved child, who had never received much attention from her mother and father after the birth of her two sisters. The artist at once picked up on the difference between Karin and her siblings, reflected in the way he painted them.

One evening her mother found Karin crying bitterly in her room, asked, "What's the matter?" Karin said forlornly, "I look so sad and ugly in the painting." The mother talked to the artist about the way he had portrayed her oldest daughter. He said, "I can't paint Karin any other way than she appears. But I will do one thing to brighten up her portrait. I will change the dark green background drapery to a green forest with rays of sun streaming through the leaves and I will add a bright red scarf around Karin's neck." Even so, Karin could never stand the painting, her lack of self-esteem unmasked.

Winnicott, who possessed extensive knowledge of mothers and young children, concluded that what he called "good enough mothering" was crucial for a child when it came to developing a strong sense of self. An early conflict occurred in children who did not receive this care and it possessed profound significance for their future sense of self. The conflict was caused by a "failed relationship" between mother and infant.

He believed the innate growth potential of the infant expresses itself in various spontaneous signs. When the "good enough mother" responds naturally to her baby's signals with "primary maternal preoccupation," the "fit" between her response and her baby's experiences give the baby a sense of wholeness and of trust about the importance of reality. He will possess a belief in the world as, for the most part, a rewarding place in which to exist.

This core of feeling gives rise to what Winnicott named the "true self" as the "full maturational potential" emerged and was experienced "not with pain but joy." The child's confidence in the mother permits him to give up his sense of omnipotence gradually, along with the disillusionment this involves.

The "true self" potential recedes more and more from the child's inherent capacity for relatedness to those he loves if the child is frustrated beyond his tolerance—especially, in Winnicott's words, when the mother is felt "as forcing herself on the infant, of impinging on it with her responses that are not in tune with the spontaneous needs of the child." For instance, when she responds to the child's call for food with angry words. Or allows him to lie for hours in a wet diaper and shows facial expressions of disgust. Or does not protect him from the cold.

These negative experiences gradually become organized into what Winnicott calls the "false self." This self complies with the mother's demands and tries to accept her obvious dislike at times, an acceptance that hides the rage in the child. As the mismatch between the mother's and the child's responses increases, so do the fantasies of revenge in the child, as well as the stunting of his emotional development.

It is not unusual to walk along the streets of large cities and occasionally see a mother striking a little child in fury because the child is crying or will not obey, at which the child only screams louder. His rage increases with each slap and though eventually he will cease crying and obey his mother, he will not forget his anger at her for not understanding he is in pain.

Winnicott concludes that the experiences structured into the true and false selves are not those of gratification of our instincts but a result of our early emotional experiences. Good experiences pertaining to the gratification of instincts reinforce the true self but its slow structuring is founded on the quality of the relationship between infant and mother.

One important fact in the developing of this relationship, according to Winnicott, is the degree to which the mother has wanted the child. If she considers him a nuisance, a burden, this builds up his false self. If she has for the most part desired him, enjoys his presence, his true self expands.

The capacity for a child to enjoy play is dependent on the mother's love, Winnicott holds: at first on her active input and later on her reliable availability when he needs her. The way in which the child senses the "self" has to be mirrored by the trusted parent. Winnicott is convinced that the emergence of play and creativity is dependent on the quality of the mother's love from the very start.

Thus our sense of self—whether we feel shattered or whole, not driven by repressed anger at what psychoanalyst Dr. Joseph Sandler calls the "ghost voices of the past"—starts in the crib as we first eagerly reach out to touch what lies in sight, seeking to learn what exists around us. A baby's tiny fingers grasp whatever is at hand. He usually tries to stuff it into his mouth for, at this stage, he knows only of being fed as a way of relating to anyone or anything.

Before long he starts to coo as he sees the face of the caretaker, his mother, approach to feed him, to warm him or to comfort him if he is in pain. He takes in with his eyes, his ears and his as yet unformed mind, her features, expressions, touch, the warmth of her body, her manner of feeding and the rhythm of her movements, whether slow or fast, nervous or composed.

As the baby slowly develops he absorbs a growing number of visual images that include the persons who walk in and out of his room. He hears the spoken word, which he identifies by sound. He imitates laughter and smiles. He soon learns of a second caretaker, his father, and perhaps brothers and sisters who kiss him, tickle him, laugh at his awkward movements as he learns to use his limbs.

As Winnicott theorized, the self starts to form in the first days of life. If a mother is loving, protective and caring, our world is loving, protective and caring. If a mother is harsh, destructive and neglectful, our world will feel harsh, destructive and neglectful.

Every baby needs a mother who understands his signals of distress. When he cries out he feels some threat to survival; he does not cry to annoy his parents but because of pain. If his mother is impervious to his hunger or discomfort or hurt, he feels abandoned. We read of headlines where a mother or father has murdered a child who will not stop screaming, not realizing he is asking for help rather than trying to annoy them. Usually the screams remind them of their own when they were babies, or the screams of siblings.

We also come into psychic being by the process analysts call "internalization." We "take in" or "internalize" the acts, spoken words, facial expressions and emotional reactions of our mother and father. The self is created in large part through this process of internalization, which occurs as naturally as breathing. We cannot stop it, it is an unconscious process, as impervious to our conscious will as the beat of our hearts.

After we start to understand words, we internalize the commands of our parents. We hear them instruct us not to touch fire because it will burn our fingers. Or they command us to eat carrots and spinach because they are good for us. But more important than the orders of parents are the feelings of parents that convey to us their hidden thoughts and emotions, tell us when they love or hate us. We also internalize what our parents *are*. Loving at times, perhaps cruel other times. Wise at times, perhaps foolhardy other times. Protective in some ways, harmful in others.

Within a family no two children internalize exactly the same things. This explains why we cannot say a brother and sister have the same mother or father. Each child sees his mother and father in different images, has different fantasies about them, according to his particular experiences with the parent. What each chooses consciously or unconsciously to take in from a parent varies with his needs at the moment and his feelings about that parent, how his memories have affected him. A little girl sees shadows on the wall as monstrous and menacing. Her brother sees the same shadows as beautiful and entrancing.

In our choices of what we take in we are also shaped by our parent's unconscious and conscious fantasies about and wishes for us. This differs markedly from child to child. One child may be wanted and loved, another unwanted and hated, born at a time a mother and father were in conflict, when the mother wished an abortion. Or a mother may encourage creativity in one child, show contempt for another who wants to achieve in an area where the mother feels competitive. Or a mother may be jealous of one child, not of another. Or a father may have wanted a boy but finds himself with three daughters, wishing at least one were a son, and the daughters will sense his wish, feel unwanted.

Each of us is unique in that, while we have two hands and ten fingers, our fingerprints differ and set us apart from everyone else. So too each psyche is unique, with its special fantasies and experiences that form memories. If we could compare the memory tapes of the mind we would find no two persons matched.

For centuries it was thought a child inherited his emotional and psychological characteristics from his parents. We know now "inherited" is the wrong word—"imitated," perhaps, or, more accurately, "internalized" whatever was available to him in the aura in which he grew up.

We have no trouble recognizing the power of the physical hunger that impels us to eat in order to keep alive. But we are less aware of the equally powerful emotional hunger that drives us to devour knowledge of how to cope with the world, ourselves and those we love. We start to fulfill this emotional hunger from the day we are born, perhaps even in the womb. A mother's reactions to us as an infant, and our reactions to her, form the staff of emotional life.

At first an infant is unable to decide if an experience is "good" or "bad." But as the child's capacity to evaluate experience grows, he learns the difference betwen "good" and "bad," according to the parents' definitions. He then becomes aware of "reality," the outside world. He also learns that psychological reactions accompany each bodily sensation. If his psychic world holds excessive pain, he will use fantasy excessively to combat what he feels as danger.

Internalizing the good parent makes it possible for us to give up demanding that our mother and father take care of us and enables us to take care of ourselves if the internalizations are primarily healthy ones. At first when our mother leaves the room we, as a baby, become frantic, fear we will be deserted, no one will care for us. Slowly, along with our biological development, our brain develops memory and our emotional capacity grows. We are soon able to retain in our minds the image of our mother to comfort us when she disappears. We rely on her to return, as she has in the past. We are learning the feeling of trust. This internal image, the representation of her in our mind, makes us less dependent on her and ready to try coping by ourself.

If a baby is left hungry and shivering in the cold, he will internalize the hunger and feeling of "cold" as part of his experiences. But if his mother feeds him regularly, keeps him warm, he will internalize feelings of comfort and consistency. He does not need to put his psychic energy into fantasies that defend against fear, anger and the wish for revenge but may use the energy to develop what some therapists call a "harmonious self."

With an uncaring parent, too much of the psychic energy of the child goes into repressing anger and desiring vengeance, rather than using it to learn, to be creative, to be empathic. An impending sense of death is paramount when there is fear in the air. Babies see everything as exaggerated; they have not yet learned to evaluate experiences.

When the child can stand up and walk, start to depend on himself, he explores everything around him. This is the start of what psychoanalyst Dr. Phyllis Greenacre calls "the love affair with the world." The child moves from centering all interest in his own body to the development of relationships with others. This adds up to a complex group of enduring images in his mind associated with feelings that range from joy to anger, despair to happiness, pain to pleasure. Perceptions of his mother and father, and scene after scene within the home are internalized, writ forever on the screen of memory.

As yet the child's perceptions are literal and concrete. He cannot give meaning to them nor connect the act he perceives to a coherent pattern. He sees acts as still pictures that cause a variety of emotions. The internalization of these feelings and images experienced in a positive way are integrated as such and become part of the self. They do not create conflicts.

But when feelings and images are threatening, like monsters in the dark, when the child senses danger in the air, he is caught in fantasies of conflict and confusion. Dangerous images will interfere with his future psychological development.

Thus the self emerges in large part from our fantasies as we take in the environment which at first consists of the goddess and god of the nursery, our mother and father. What they evoke in us, how these evocations are registered within our mind and become part of our mental structure, how we separate them out gradually so we may create our own individuality, is constantly being studied by learning theorists, child development specialists and psychoanalysts.

As the child's mind develops he starts to perceive how he is viewed by his parents—good and/or bad. He internalizes his parents' opinion of him as part of his self-image. He is aware there is a difference between himself and all others. He also, to some extent, realizes what can be expected of him by others. His images of people and the world around him have become quite stabilized.

His perception of reality has increased, he can distinguish between his inner world and the outer world. No longer does he imagine he and his mother are merged. He realizes two people are involved in the relationship, though he still feels close to her. He identifies with parts of her or attitudes or physical mannerisms, unconsciously copying his mother's smile or her walk. He may identify with her mood, follow her into a depression. We are only starting to realize the extreme sensitivity and vulnerability of the very young child.

Alice Miller, a Swiss psychoanalyst, author of *Prisoners of Childhood* and *The Search for the True Self*, writes poignantly on the development of the "true" and the "false" selves as rooted in childhood. She holds that genuine feelings, the real source of vitality in life, reflect themselves in independent thinking and creativity as we see it expressed in various kinds of productivity, such as fantasy.

Miller describes a man in analysis who recalled how hard he tried during childhood not to give vent to any sign of sadness by crying, aware this would make his beloved mother upset and unsure of herself—to remain "cheerful" had saved her life in childhood, he had somehow understood.

As an adult he learned what had prompted this "demand" on him by his mother. She had grown up in a concentration camp where, together with eighty other children, she had watched their parents led to the gas chambers. Not a single child had cried. But her child had paid a high price for maintaining a state of denial of his feelings in order to help his mother keep her emotional equilibrium. His false self was expressed in cheerfulness, his true self allowed to emerge only in what he thought the obsessive perversion of masturbation, for which he felt shame until he went into analysis. Then he understood how his mother's tragedy had been perpetuated on her child.

Most parents aim to bring up a child to be self-reliant. But the child at risk in reaching this goal is the one whose parents are not available to him and are unable to become attuned to what seems their child's specific endowment. Instead, the parents make their child fit their needs, fulfill their narcissistic fantasies about what they would like the child to be. Or they use the child as a showpiece to gain attention and admiration in situations where the child's accomplishments are regarded as the parents' own. Usually the expectation exists that the child will personify their fantasies about what a "perfect" human being should be—compensation for not having achieved their fantasized goals. As children they had to fulfill the dreams of their parents—part of a vicious circle of generations who felt a lack of self-esteem.

The result of becoming a "nice," kind, easygoing, submissive, nonassertive child and adult may mean losing touch with our inner desires, depriving ourselves of becoming a person in our own right, entitled to feel sexual desire or rage when we are hurt. At the age of twenty many a young person finds himself in a state of severe depression. He is estranged from the true self, with one overriding question on his mind: "Who am I?" And the answer: "I don't know."

Karen Horney in *Neurosis and Human Growth* and *The Struggle Toward Self-Realization* wrote of the "true" and the "false" selves even before Miller and Winnicott. She describes how people with self-hate, self-contempt and self-doubts focus their energies on building up a false, idealized self. She speaks of the "tyranny of inner dictates" under which the person lives, governed by the code of "shoulds." She explains:

"He should be the utmost of honesty, generosity, considerateness, justice, dignity, courage, unselfishness. He should be the perfect lover, husband and teacher. . . . He should never feel hurt, and he should always be serene and unruffled. . . . He should always control his feelings. He should be able to solve every problem of his own, or of others, in no time. . . . He should never be tired or fall ill. . . . He should do things in one hour which can only be done in two or three hours."

This list of rigid inner dictates makes life difficult and impossible for living in a humane way because inherent in them is complete disregard for the person's own emotional state and his human limits. There are rare individuals who come close to the goal of "always" being understanding, sympathetic and helpful to others. Victor Hugo, for instance, created such a person in the bishop of Digne in *Les Miserables*—the priest who felt fulfilled in reaching out to criminals. He was the symbol for those who feel they should be helpful and compassionate to everyone. But there is something still amiss, for such a person is driven by the "should," the voice of his demanding, authoritative parents whose opinions he dared not oppose as a child.

All of us hear the voices of the past to some degree, for it is through those voices we have learned how to act, how to think, how to cope (or not to cope) with frustration and disappointment. And, most important, how to love and to hate. The positive voices help us mold our lives happily, build up more of the "real" self—the self we feel is truly ours, untainted by intrusive, destructive wishes and thoughts. It is a self no longer based on the "should's" and "should not's" of childhood but on our own convictions.

As we become aware of the hostile forces within, we gain control of them. Freedom from domination by phantoms of earlier days brings a changed feeling toward ourselves and others. We possess far greater confidence and esteem for the self, no longer haunted by the false self. We realize it is natural for us to be somewhat like the mother and father who were our nearest and dearest, who were with us hour after hour, day after day, throughout childhood and adolescence—our models for better or for worse.

We recognize the patterns of negative attitudes that we internalized. We face head-on the childish feelings and thoughts that formerly controlled us. With the facing, rather than the denial and then the projection of them onto others, we become free of them. We accept the voices within that caused us at times to suffer, know the greater pain is not to acknowledge the voices.

We no longer feel the child who is powerless and must give in to the parent, even when he is thoughtless and cruel. The reality is that the scene has changed and we are now the ones in command of the self—a self we respect and love, feel tender toward, just as we do the ones we love. The voices within, ones that have been hurtful, are muted, the self is no longer split into a good or bad part but becomes whole. You cannot change your past but by understanding it you change your present and future. By understanding both the good and the destructive internalizations, you change your life.

To know the self is to overcome the illusions we have about ourselves, maintains Grotjahn. It is to fully face the painful infantile experiences of the past and expectations for the future which do not fit into present reality. In the case of marriage, he adds, it means to overcome unreal expectations and still remain in love. He cites Rembrandt who, after painting a portrait of his wife, remarked to a critical connoisseur, "No, she is not beautiful, but she is my wife and I love her."

"To be master of oneself and to a modest extent to be the master of one's outer reality is the basis of happiness," Grotjahn says. "The happy man knows who he is—he has found his identity, what he was looking for."

Both illusion and delusion deal with what we might call a shattered self. Over the centuries men have written of voices within that at times seem to be giving commands and taking over what we think of as the self. No real people stand behind these inner voices but originally there were real people. The voices are those of persons once desperately loved and hated, now speaking from within, voices that exert an internal force stronger than the person's own voice. He reacts to the voices as though they were real, obeys what they suggest, be it to finish every morsel of food on the plate or murder someone he loves who, he believes, has betrayed him, or a stranger who has never harmed him but serves as a substitute target.

We all walk around with voices inside to a greater or lesser degree, for in growing up we have internalized the words, the acts and directions of our parents and think of these as parts of our self. Sometimes the voices are alien and we feel a sense of uneasiness at their presence, even though we are only dimly aware of them, or perhaps not at all but feel somehow distressed. The voices make us feel that we act falsely: our true self is being exploited, negated, crippled. Something inside cries out for an integrated, whole self.

In his book *The Analysis of the Self* Dr. Heinz Kohut wrote, "The more secure a person is regarding his own acceptability, the more certain his sense of who he is, and the more safely internalized his system of values—the more self-confidently and effectively will he be able to offer his love without undue fear of rejection and humiliation."

Many fantasies lead to either a fear of failure or of success. Dr. Leon Tec, in *The Fear of Success,* says the wish to succeed may create so much tension and consume so much energy that unconsciously we fear success, though consciously the fear may be experienced as the fear of failure.

"Every person consciously wants to succeed in the area or areas that he considers important, whether it is money, family, friendship or career; at the same time, every person consciously wants to avoid failure in those areas," he says. The wish to succeed is a positive force, a force of initiative, the power of positive thinking. The fantasy of failure is a negative force which, when pronounced, may be paralyzing and interfere with the attempt to take necessary risks, go against the odds.

The fear of success can be defined as an unconscious fear of what one consciously considers important and desirable. It may be seen as the person's unconscious fear that his success is not justified, that he is a fraud. Dr. Tec cites as example the suicide of Marilyn Monroe as the "extreme manifestation" of the fear of success. He writes:

"Marilyn Monroe's life was a narrative of self-destruction, and whether she meant to die when she took barbiturates while she was drinking is immaterial. If her performance ability had been supported by self esteem and a trust in herself and others, she could have thrived on her status rather than have been destroyed by it." She never felt she deserved success because of her childhood (no father, and a mother who deserted her when she was eighteen months old, spending most of the rest of her life in mental hospitals). Marilyn, feeling unworthy of success and guilty at her achievements, literally threw away her life at the age of thirty-six.

Success in the unconscious part of our mind may also be seen as the murder of rivals in the family, a parent or sibling. Some sons and daughters dare not be "better than" a mother or father or sibling because they think of this as murder of the parent or sibling. There is also guilt over the oedipal conflict and the childhood wish for success in eliminating the parent of the same sex.

"Narratives of the Self" was the title of a paper delivered by psychoanalyst Roy Schafer at a symposium celebrating the fortieth anniversary of the Columbia University Center for Psychoanalytic Training and Research, held April 24 to 26, 1985, at the Waldorf Astoria in New York. The symposium was entitled, "Psychoanalysis, the Second Century: Recent Advances in New Directions."

Schafer explained that the concept of the self can be approached in two ways: as posing a significant feature of the self psychology of everyday life and as posing a significant problem for the construction of theory about the self in psychoanalysis. He added, "These two approaches need not be as different as one might expect," and said that "both approaches may be characterized as the construction of narratives."

In his paper, which will appear as part of a book of essays to be published shortly by Columbia University Psychoanalytic Center, he concludes by saying, "To make a long story short, the self appears in so many guises and places in the self psychology of everyday life and its corresponding presentation by analysands in the course of analysis—it is, one might say, so mercurial—that one should be warned to use the utmost caution when introducing the concept of self into psychoanalytic theory."

In an article, "The Pursuit of Failure and the Idealization of Unhappiness," Schafer reveals that in work with patients he found that the theme of pursuing failure was relatively more conspicuous in analytic work with men while the idealization of unhappiness was relatively more conspicuous in women.

He cited the example of a young man whose "ideal" self focused on being an underachiever. In his psychic reality, to be an underachiever was to conform to the role his family appeared to have assigned to him early in his life. "This role warded off envy and disparagement by his siblings; it also earned parental love in the form of his father's compassionate help when, but only when, the boy was in trouble," Schafer explained. "Typically, feelings of being a 'good kid' were associated with lack of achievement and steady self-disparagement." In another case, a young man's pursuit of failure served unconsciously to protect the self-esteem of his apparently weak, unsuccessful father.

In discussing woman's idealization of unhappiness, Schafer described a woman who made a slip of the tongue. Intending to say, upon being confronted with a threatening situation, that she had experienced cold chills going down her spine, she said, "Cold thrills went down my spine."

This woman had a lifelong history of attempting to relieve others of their unhappiness by absorbing their unhappiness into herself. "Unconsciously, as many women in our culture seem to do, she incorporated their unhappiness and she suffered for others," Schafer explained. "In doing so, she felt she was being a good girl, that is, kind, compassionate, supportive, undemanding, even self-sacrificing. From a young age she had done this to an extreme degree with all members of her family." She received approval and love for this "Christlike" role. In her fantasy, she gained love and importance by being unhappy but added a false sense of worth to her "self" through suffering. Schafer added that such idealization of unhappiness is an important feature of the psychology of women in our society, as is the pursuit of failure undertaken by men.

He said the pursuit of failure and the idealization of unhappiness "are not mutually exclusive," that for the most part, the examples he presented under one gender could have been presented under the other—both themes were developed in all the cases mentioned, though to different degrees.

In recent years there have been many books, both popular and in the psychoanalytic literature, focusing on the self. Kohut describes a man who used fantasy as a way of getting in touch with himself when fearful that his sense of self would fall apart. His fear was so intense it was difficult for him to go to sleep. Reflecting on this fear, he remembered as a boy being alone in the country and finding it difficult to fall asleep, felt threatened in an environment he experienced as nonsupportive, nonempathic and inimical.

He was afraid if he gave up conscious control—fell asleep—his body-mind self would break apart. So he created a fantasy game to counteract this fear: he lay in bed for hours imagining himself making long excursions on "the landscape," his body. He traveled from one part to another, in his mind, from nose to toes, over his navel, shoulder, ear and back, reassuring himself he was still there, all in one piece, held together by a self that inspected all the body parts. He was in a creative way effectively helping himself regain control of the totality of his body-self by focusing his attention on all the body parts that momentarily felt endangered. His mother was unable to provide emotional support to her young child that set up the nucleus of self-acceptance and security, qualities she lacked.

Self-esteem, unlike certain other aspects of the self, seems perishable. It is easily lost and difficult to recapture. It is indispensable but unstable, readily affected by a variety of influences, and care must be taken to insure its preservation, Rochlin says. Its loss must be redeemed; a forfeited, damaged or decreased self-esteem is not acceptable. Whatever lowers self-esteem needs to be faced. The condition of self-esteem is not permanently achieved, it requires constant attention for its maintenance, he believes.

The effect of early losses of loved ones on the concept of the self may be devastating. To lose a mother, father, sibling or other relative is likely to be the hardest blow life can deal. Grief at such a loss, both real and fantasized, affects our image of ourself, sometimes to a severe degree. So much of our energy is wrapped up in mourning the loss that we may have little to invest in love or work.

The fantasy of our own death is not easy to face. As Dr. Robert Langs, author of *The Bipersonal Field,* once commented, "What a burden man bears, it's a wonder most of us are sane, knowing we inevitably face death."

Regardless of the extreme isolation that may develop in the child possessed by fantasies related to his loss, the relationship with the loved one still exists in the child's mind. Rochlin cites the "bizarre hallucinations" of chronically psychotic adults that reveal the hallucinated voices are those of parents or parental figures.

Children who are orphaned, or young children who, after their parents divorce, in some instances never see the absent parent again, or young children who suffer the death of a parent, may fantasy the parent will never return. For years, they find themselves searching strange faces, hoping to find a sign of recognition that will restore the loved one. The search for a lost parent and fantasies about the eventual reunion are common, the restitution of someone loved and believed lost is "a timeless theme," Rochlin says.

Man has many traditional ways of not relinquishing his fantasy that the lost one will return, even though dead. Naming a child after someone valued who has died perpetuates the fantasy that there is part of the lost person in the living child. Each time the parent thinks of the child or looks at him, unconsciously he maintains his tie to the dead person.

A young mother of twenty-one named her daughter after her own mother, Cecilia, who had died when this mother was only two years old. The young mother, as a result of therapy, realized she had unconsciously expected her daughter to nurture her, to make up for the loss of her mother. Need for restitution at our losses never ceases; it is a continuing process as studies in grief, mourning and depression show.

Our feelings about the self start with the fantasies our mother has about us when she first feeds us, takes care of us, changes our diapers. The way she does this, whether with calm and caring or haste and distaste will later affect our feelings about food, feeding and the nursing process. How we feel about our whole self—whether valuable or a nuisance—will be influenced by our mother's fantasies and feelings during our early life.

Dr. Abraham pointed out that the adult who is optimistic has been well-fed and nourished and loved as an infant whereas the pessimistic adult, as a child, was allowed to cry when hungry or remain uncomfortable for hours in wet diapers. In other words, if a child has an emotionally responsive mother he will be responsive emotionally to others as an adult and choose those emotionally responsive to him to love and as friends.

An intriguing article, "The Self as Fantasy: Fantasy as Theory," by Dr. Grossman, mentioned earlier, was originally delivered as a paper before the December 1980 annual winter meeting in New York of the American Psychoanalytic Association. He posed the question: "Is the self but a fantasy?" He was suggesting each of us possesses many fantasies about what we are or would like to be or do not wish to be, which add up to what we think of as the "self."

In calling the "self-concept" a theory or a fantasy, he explains he does not wish in any way to diminish its importance in regulating behavior, for fantasy plays an important role in organizing and directing behavior. He says, "Fantasy plays a much greater role in our mental lives than most people are likely to know about if they think 'fantasy-daydream.' " Fantasies are "complex structures" in the mind that have an effect on our mental organization and are also a part of it.

He makes the point in this paper that "the self depends on a person's idea of himself, which, from a psychoanalytic point of view, makes the self a fantasy. Our fantasies are related to our capacity for reflection, fantasy is a complex structure, there are many-faceted views of the self in ordinary discourse."

For Freud, myths were theories and theories, myths—he spoke of the theory of drives, both sexual and aggressive as "our mythology," Grossman states. He cites Freud as saying our memories are selected and formed with a purpose, memories are not "*from* our childhood" but "*relating* to our childhood."

Grossman concludes that when the child in us speaks in our dreams or when we are awake, we often do not understand what that child says. Psychoanalysts try to understand the child in the patient "but it is no longer the same child." Grossman explains, "The childhood we reconstruct is virtual, in the sense of a virtual image. It is the part of childhood that is significant now."

In the process of being psychoanalyzed, the person learns to reflect about his behavior both past and present. Particularly the behavior that has brought pain and a lowering of self-esteem. One woman of thirty-two went into analysis because she was disgusted with herself for her promiscuity, her inability to settle down with one man.

"I desperately want to marry and have children but I seem attracted to the wrong kind of man," she told the analyst. "Either he doesn't want to marry me or I don't want to marry him."

As she became better acquainted with her fantasies and feelings about her mother and father as she grew up, she realized she had identified in large part with her handsome, professionally successful father, an actor who made no secret of his affairs with other women, though he remained at home with wife and daughter.

The analyst helped her understand she had unconsciously copied her father's sexual behavior, she had never resolved her oedipal conflict, she was still in love with the father who had adored her, never in her heart wishing to marry another man and bear his children. After several years of analysis, during which she faced childhood fantasies, she felt free enough of conflicting feelings to marry a man she loved and bear a son.

Most women marry without feeling as much in conflict as this woman. But over half of all marriages end in divorce. Why does the first intense feeling of "love" often disappear so quickly in a puff of anger? Why has the "Prince Charming" fantasy failed to come true for so many women?

4

The "Prince Charming" Fantasy

From childhood on we are brought up on the fantasy that there is such a thing as perfect love. The Sleeping Beauty awakened by the Prince lives happily ever after, enfolded in his arms. Cinderella steps into the glass slipper and love enduring is hers.

Through the ages poets and philsophers have painted poignant images of the glory of love and also the tragedy, of highest joy and deepest despair. More has been written of the riddle of love than any other human emotion.

"Who ever loved that loved not at first sight?" asked Christopher Marlowe in the sixteenth century, proclaiming love as a magical spell fusing two strangers at first glance. Love is described as a desperate, hungry craving appeased only by the vision of the beloved. Love and death are placed side by side as though death were the only answer should lovers be torn from each other's arms. Romeo and Juliet live in all of us.

The conviction that the wild, wondrous feeling of love can be captured for a lifetime propels enamored souls into marriage which, they believe, will bring joy everlasting. Sometimes love lasts for years, sometimes only for months, perhaps only days before the rapture ebbs and turns to fear, rage, indifference, hate.

Former lovers become tortured by the thought that ecstasy has vanished. Possibly the question most often asked over the centuries, asked in anguish and sorrow, is "What destroyed our love?"

What shatters romance? Why does fiery, all-consuming passion so easily smolder into ashes of disillusionment? Whose fault is it? Can it be we are looking for the impossible in our search for love?

58

Are we forced to agree with Shakespeare?

> For to be wise, and love,
> Exceeds man's might; that dwells with gods above.

Sir Walter Scott in *The Lay of the Last Minstrel* put the definition of love in poetic form, relating love to fantasy:

> True love's the gift which God has given
> To man alone beneath the heaven:
> It is not fantasy's hot fire,
> Whose wishes, soon as granted, fly.

Though we may have fantasies about anything under the sun, our strongest fantasies focus on love and hate. Fantasies about sex and rage may be equally divided but today we have society's permission to become aware of, talk freely about, even act out, our sexual fantasies. Whereas we still must hide our feelings of fury until they are at explosive power.

The new women's liberation entitles them to sexual fulfillment. In centuries past only man possessed that right; women were supposed to be sexual slaves, as they still are in many areas of the world. Unfortunately women are finding that "fantasy's hot fire," as Scott described it, soon dies down, peters out.

We might ask, as Cole Porter's popular song of the past was titled, "What Is This Thing Called Love?" Is it nature's way of making sure the human race propagates? Is lasting love possible, given the human condition?

A cavalcade of fantasies whirl in the name of love. Love is a feeling that develops in complexity from the day we are born and nestle in our mother's arms, as Winnicott pointed out. At that stage love is selfish, we want our mother all to ourself, fiercely resent any rival. As we develop physically and emotionally, our fantasy of love goes through many phases, hopefully ending in mature love that, in addition to sexual desire, holds tenderness, caring and respect for our sexual partner.

Freud was the first to bring sex out of the closet, so to speak, as he examined in excruciating carefulness the formation and essence of love. Describing the sensation of passionate love, he said, "Against all the evidence of his senses the man in love declares that he and his beloved are one, and is prepared to behave as if it were a fact."

The fantasy of "oneness" in love does many of us in. It is the fantasy of our earliest days when we felt fused with our mother—the original "blissful" state we still seek to recreate in the name of "love." But this fantasy reflects infant love, not the love of one adult for another.

For centuries in America men and women have thought of love as the emotion that leads to marriage and children. Loveless marriages were arranged by parents in foreign nations where sex was not a part of love but a need apart from love for the man, with women expected to endure sex when demanded by the man.

But in our culture the past few decades have seen vast changes in accepted sexual practices. Premarital sexual intercourse with men and women living together out of wedlock is accepted today, as is the bringing up of a child by a single parent, usually the mother, married or unmarried. "Swinging" and "switching partners" as well as group sex were popular before the AIDS epidemic.

Are people perhaps not monogamous creatures? Is it in our spirit to be attracted to a number of members of the opposite sex as we try to attain that elusive state of mind we call happiness? Why is it so difficult for so many of us to achieve a happy marriage?

Strong fantasies interfere with our struggle to maintain monogamy: the false illusions with which we enter marriage based on the romantic notion of love; the belief a happy marriage occurs magically, instantaneously; the conviction it is not our own conflicts that cause disillusionment with the other person, but something wrong in him.

And no matter how miserable a man or woman's life has been up to the hour they become joined "as one," they cling to the fantasy the other person will be the perfect match, enrich their life as it has never been enriched. By his side, the man believes, stands a tender, compassionate woman, ready to comfort him always. The trouble is that this tender, compassionate woman in the flowing white satin wedding gown, is fantasying the very same thing. She thinks, "He will give me everything I want, have always wanted."

Each makes a preposterous demand, one no adult should ever make of another. Each believes he is marrying because he has fallen desperately in love. But he is, unconsciously, marrying to be loved in a way his mother was supposed to have loved him—completely, all-out—but never did. He has the fantasy of a love that no mother, no human, could ever provide, for it is an impossible love, given the sad but true fact that we are all ambivalent, some more than others, toward those we love.

So many marriages fail because they are based on the childish fantasy of wanting to be loved wholeheartedly, unconditionally. Neither partner is willing to compromise or accept the necessary sacrifices and frustrations inherent in marrying and adjusting to round-the-clock life with another person, but continues to insist on his impossible demands.

One wife, married fifteen years, could not bear to let her husband out of her sight. It was all she could do to accept the fact he had to leave the house to go to work in the morning as a lawyer for a large Manhattan firm. If, on a weekend, he went to visit his mother or sister without her, she felt abandoned. If he dared look at another woman, she would accuse him of wanting to have sex with the woman. The husband became torn between a fondness and sexual attraction for his wife and the feeling his life was not his own. They started to fight over her possessiveness and jealousy. The more he gave in to her, the more she seemed to demand.

He started to assert himself. He realized he had been as selfish as she, playing the role of a compliant little boy, weak in the face of a tyrannical mother, expecting the wife-mother to take care of his every need. They learned to trust each other more, each one slowly gaining more self-confidence, aware of the infantile fantasies that had ruled them.

The idea of "romantic love" that we fantasize is absolutely antithetical to the love that endures. Those experts who have studied the conflicts of contemporary married life note the chasm that exists between what young lovers expect and what can be realistically expected in marriage.

Romantic love holds in it the conscious overidealization of the beloved who is, at the same time, unconsciously stripped of his sexuality. The overidealization stems from the fantasy that the new marital partner will be the wished-for good mother of childhood. But because of this fantasy, the partner then becomes, like the mother of earlier days, taboo as far as sex is concerned. This is one of the unconscious fantasies we all bring to marriage from the days we were a five-year old and fantasied we were passionately in love with the parent of the opposite sex. We remain trapped somewhat in the oedipal conflict unless we are aware of it and come to peaceful resolution.

The chivalrous, romantic lover throughout history rarely demonstrated his passion physically, except perhaps by a fleeting kiss. This courtly ideal derives in part from medieval cults that worshipped the Virgin—the wished-for virginal mother who, like Mary, gave birth without a sexual partner.

In literature of the past the fantasy of romantic love was not always requited and often not even acknowledged. Our hearts are still touched by the love of Cyrano de Bergerac for Roxanne. Not daring to confess his love, Cyrano wooed her for another man. Sometimes, as in *Romeo and Juliet,* the declaration of love was followed by the death of the lovers. In *Tristan and Isolde,* after consummation, the guilty lovers died.

Since the fantasy of romantic love is based on the idealization of the loved one, it cannot possibly withstand the confrontations with reality day-to-day married life brings. Seeing a wife of several weeks in hair curlers or brushing her teeth may fill a husband with disgust. Watching her husband clip his toenails or hearing him pass gas in the bathroom may bring feelings of revulsion to a bride. To some, the first show of anger on the face of the marital partner means the marriage is over.

Romantic love, which centers on the self, is the product of what psycho-analysts call "a constellation" of fantasies. Lovers project onto each other their fantasy of the "perfect person." As Juliet said to Romeo, "The more I give to thee, / The more I have, for both are infinite." Alas, this feeling seldom lasts beyond the honeymoon when the demand to give is now made of the marital partner as reality sets in.

Unfortunately the qualities ascribed in courtship to the romanticized one have little to do with the qualities he possesses but are mainly fantasies about him—fantasies that do not take in his limitations and needs. There is vast difference between feeling "in love," which makes fantastic and obsessional demands on the other person, and love based on the ability to look at the self and the other person as possessing human frailties.

Freud compared the feelings within the romantic lover to the state of madness. The essence of the "romantic ideal" is exclusive possession, the demand the loved one show no interest in anyone else. The intense overidealization that is part of romantic love is shown in some of Freud's early letters to his fiancée, Martha Bernays. They were written before he discovered the theories of psychoanalysis and the dramatic and often traumatic influence of the oedipal conflict, as well as the preoedipal feelings of love for the parent.

At one point Freud wrote Martha during their long courtship: "What I meant to convey was how much the magic of your being expresses itself in your countenance and your body. How much there is visible in your appearance that reveals how sweet, generous, and reasonable you are . . .

In your face it is the pure noble beauty of your brow and your eyes that shows in almost every picture."

As Freud was later to say about any feeling, act or fantasy that was excessive, romantic love also carries with it "the seeds of its own destruction." When the shadow of reality falls on romantic love, the man and woman start to give less to each other, to focus more on their own needs, expect more of the mate. It is the juxtaposition of giving less and the fantasy of expecting more that sets fire to the romantic ideal, sparks the often deadly conflicts that arise.

It is now that sex, as has been said, "rears its ugly head," where before it was thought hallowed. Because romantic love is so idealized, the sexual yearnings for the partner become accompanied by guilt and anxiety. Total withdrawal may set in, even feelings of revulsion for the formerly adored one.

One woman, after six months of marriage, found her husband turning angry each time they faced the act of sex. He would revile her, accusing, "You're no good. I don't love you any more." She did not know what he meant by "no good," but dared not ask. He started to drink heavily, and to beat her. She went to a psychoanalyst to find out what had gone wrong with the marriage.

She told the analyst, "I can't understand what has happened to Jim. He was so loving before we married six months ago. Now all he does is scream at me, 'Change! Change, you bitch! I don't like you the way you are.'" She asked the analyst, "What does he mean? I'm just the same as I was six months ago."

The analyst helped her realize her husband was asking her to be the good mother he never had when he screamed "Change! Change!"—his own infantile demand of a mother who had been emotionally disturbed. The analyst told this wife, "No woman could possibly meet your husband's demands." then he suggested, "But we have to look at the reasons why you married such a man."

She slowly faced her fantasies of what marriage meant, realized she too had wanted "the good mother" to take care of her. She had not seen her husband as he really was, nor had he seen her as she was. Both were caught in fantasies that clustered around the conflicts of earlier days.

This couple, as do many, could not acknowledge that a perpetual honeymoon is an impossible dream. They believed their feelings would remain the same as in the early days of courtship. The childish wish was still too strong: "If you really loved me you would know what I need and devote all your efforts to meeting my needs." It was a wish based on the child's fantasy that his mother is all-powerful and can give continuously with no needs of her own. When a spouse is unable to satisfy this unrealistic demand, the mate becomes furious, unable to cope with his strong feelings of disillusionment. There will always be a certain disillusionment in marriage but it is the excessive one that causes the breakups.

Rare is the married person involved in an illicit affair who does not rave about the "romantic" feeling, compared to the "deadened" feeling for his marital partner. Because the fantasy of romantic love has long been crushed in the marriage, he feels he must seek it elsewhere. The fantasy does not die, only the marriage.

Is it natural to wander from one love to the next? Not according to experts in human behavior. They say it is a sign of emotional health to be faithful sexually to one person. This has nothing to do with "morality," though it happens to coincide with convention. Rather, it has to do with emotional maturity.

What do we mean by emotional maturity? When Freud was asked the definition of maturity, he said, "To be able to love and to work." We should be able to form a mutually loving relationship with one member of the opposite sex and also pursue work we enjoy.

Monogamy, according to the experts, provides many emotional rewards if there is an underlying feeling of love, tenderness, respect and friendship. It relieves the feeling of loneliness, which we all experience to some degree. It provides constant, dependable company. There is a sharing not only of sexual pleasure but of the tasks that are a part of life. A man or woman may want a certain amount of privacy and in a mature relationship this is easily given by the mate.

Elaborating on Freud's definition, Erik Erikson, a noted psychoanalyst, described the mature person as one who feels limited hatred and can love a member of the opposite sex "with whom he is able and willing to regulate the cycle of work, procreation and recreation so as to secure to the offspring, too, a satisfactory development." This is an ideal prescription for maturity, for we all hold "limited hatred", and face occasional frustrations and regressions that may destroy love unless we become aware of them. Then we are able to control our feelings, not dump them on others.

Maturity implies that we are capable of loving ourselves and giving up the fantasy of perfection as a prerequisite for love. Of utmost importance is the acceptance of our own imperfections without guilt or shame. Only then are we able to accept the imperfections of someone we love, knowing he is human too. We will also possess a sufficient sense of self-esteem so criticism from others does not make us feel worthless or inferior. We depend on our own judgment and reason, not on fantasies of the past that haunt us or others.

A divorced woman of forty wondered whether to stop seeing a friend of fifteen years because she was too caustic, too critical of everyone, including this woman. When her friend said to her one day, "You can never make up your mind about anything, go fuck yourself," the woman broke off the relationship, saying to her friend, "If you can use that language to me, just forget our friendship."

In therapy, this woman told her analyst what she had done. He helped her understand that her friend, who was not in therapy, was unable to handle her life with self-awareness. She antagonized all her friends out of her own low self-esteem, was more to be pitied than scorned. The woman then called up her friend, said, "Let's have dinner some night this week, maybe go to a movie," and the relationship was restored. The friend apologized for her profanity.

Emotional maturity means recognizing our own fantasies of dependency and those of others. It means not allowing ourselves or others to exploit feelings of dependency. Emotional maturity implies the ability to know fantasy from reality and to be able to become attached to another person without seeking a symbiotic relationship that destroys love, trust and respect.

In the words of psychoanalyst Herbert Strean: "We can admire the loved one without being infatuated and can enjoy intimacy and mutual devotion without engulfing or fearing we will be engulfed." He adds, "Unlike the man or woman who needs an illicit affair to buttress a shaky self-image or to discharge hostility, the mature husband and wife enjoy themselves and each other in a mutually trusting, intimate and devoted relationship."

Strean points out that studies have shown that unhappily married couples have difficulty in "honest social interaction and friendship." Jealous feelings appear that involve fear of loss and "lingering feelings of possessiveness or desire to control the mate." Though the couples demand equality, often they each discover this demand entails different degrees of commitment. A wife might insist her husband be faithful, the husband might see no reason why he should not have an occasional affair if his wife does not know about it but at the same time forbids her to relate sexually to another man.

The millions of married men and women who plunge into affairs each year are examined by Strean in his book *The Extramarital Affair*. He concludes the affair is a reflection of the man or woman's earliest fantasies about sex and their present level of emotional maturity. He shows how failure to resolve childhood conflicts underlies the decision to engage in and continue an affair while trying to preserve an unhappy marriage. He explains the conscious and unconscious factors at work in undertaking and sustaining both the affair and the marriage.

Many men experience marital problems due to fantasies connected to unresolved oedipal conflicts, he notes. Because they fantasize the wife as the incestuous mother, sex becomes forbidden in marriage and impotence results, after which the man embarks on an illicit affair or seeks prostitutes (the "bad" woman with whom sex is permissible, as contrasted to the "good" motherly wife). Or the husband may spend most of his time with "the boys" and join them in "blasting their wives," as Strean puts it. This also applies to wives who marry because they seek a man "just like dear old daddy" and then feel guilty about having sex with him.

In his research Strean discovered that what one marital partner criticizes in the other is what the critical partner unconsciously wants. The wife who claims her husband is "impotent" unconsciously sought such a man because she felt she could not cope with a "sexy" one. The man who criticizes his wife for being "bossy" sought her because this trait reminded him unconsciously of his controlling mother to whom he was still emotionally attached.

Thus marriage proves that part of life to which both men and women bring their deepest fantasies. They imagine another person can undo all the hurts and pain of the past. That with one phrase, "I thee wed," all buried conflicts will miraculously turn into blessings.

The passionate feelings of a honeymoon enhance the fantasy marriage is a cure-all and only rainbows ring the marital horizon. But the demands of unconscious fantasies may wreck the marriage for they are far more powerful than any conscious wish for love.

Today there is not always a clear-cut line between masculine and feminine work or duties in the house. Some men are better cooks or shoppers than their wives, whereas a wife may earn more money at her job or be a better tennis player. But if they love each other and can consider mutual needs, these differences can be accepted without a competitive fantasy becoming aroused.

A sensitive composer of thirty-four resented the fact that his wife, a fashion model, earned more than he did at concerts, helped pay for his treatment with a psychoanalyst.

"Damn it, it doesn't seem right," he said over and over to his analyst.

"But she loves you," the analyst pointed out, "or she wouldn't want to help support you and pay for your treatment."

"I feel guilty about it," he protested.

"Are you sure the guilt isn't because you feel competitive and resent a woman earning more than you?"

"Maybe," he said grudgingly.

He had entered analysis because of severe headaches for which doctors could find no organic cause. After five months on the couch, the headaches disappeared. As he was able to look more deeply at his fantasy of competing with a woman (originally his mother and an older sister) and his reluctance to accept gifts from a woman, he could acknowledge his wife's generosity and wish to help him achieve a happier life.

There is little more emotionally satisfying than living in harmony with a member of the opposite sex, sharing the pleasurable, intimate moments that create the strongest ties between man and woman. There is reward, comparable to no other, in discovering the emotional depths and richnesses in someone else. Depths and richnesses that lead to bringing out the best in us—which is what psychoanalysts do in a sense on one level (though we feel it is the worst in us as we bring it to consciousness). Compatability with a sexual partner in marriage is mature love devoid of the troubling fantasies that may have crippled it in the past.

One of Freud's many words of wisdom was that "from the beginning everything sexual should be treated like everything else worth knowing." Shakespeare might have proved right, that only the gods were wise and could love, had not Freud uncovered the reasons why so many people were incapable of a love that included tenderness and understanding of the other person. He gave no simple answer but then life, of which love is the major theme, does not have one.

Through his study of the mind of man Freud permitted us to know why love, as we think of it, often cannot last. The inner world of our mind, the world we hide from all others and often from ourselves, works against the love of fairy-tale vintage. Hundreds of fantasies and memories merge to form our vision of love. We prepare for love and are prepared for it by our mother and our father from the day we are born.

Before Freud gave us a realistic look at love, man believed the desire to love started to flower during adolescence, then exploded into full passion in adult years. When love sometimes became expressed in chaotic, confused ways—when men seduced children, or raped women—society condemned them, not understanding the many distorted paths love might take when its natural development was crippled or thwarted.

A revolution in our concept of love occurred in 1905. Freud made a stunning discovery, in the literal sense of the word "stunning." It was one that at first shocked and antagonized the world, an antagonism that has not as yet disappeared, though psychoanalysis is far more accepted now than in Freud's early days.

Freud blasted the fantasy that sexual feelings did not appear until adolescence. He traced the existence of erotic feelings from the cradle on. He described the development of what he called the "libido" (the sexual drive or instinct) over the years until it reached the final stage of maturity.

We all want to be loved and, in turn, to love. Perhaps this is the most important of all realities. What good is anything else—fame, fortune—if life lacks love? But if our fantasies are too intense, if they in large part overpower our wish to know reality, it will be difficult to love another person.

It is, as has been said, our fantasies that lead to the idea of romantic love. The "spell" of love is no mystery, it is cast by our own purposeful imagination, aided and abetted by the world of reality which urges us, through powerful advertising campaigns to fall in love, marry and have children. Freud called this "the debt with which all of us are charged." Fantasy thus is also based on the real need in most people to procreate and continue the human race, miserable though many may be. To pay this debt, we swiftly surrender to the popular idea of love, not realizing it conceals dark, often devastating secrets.

Shakespeare may have been wrong in believing only the gods could be wise and love but he was near truth when he wrote, "There are more things in heaven and earth, Horatio, / Than are dreamt of in your philosophy." Shakespeare sensed well the role of fantasy. The "more things" were the fantasies that haunted the soul, some of them known to us, many of them unknown, but all relevant to what we call love.

We think we fall in love blindly but the opposite is true. We may not be aware why we choose someone beyond being fascinated by the color of his hair, the tone of his voice or the way he walks. But our unconscious has selected the partner for specific reasons, not always wise ones.

In one way or another he satisfies our unconscious fantasies but, because they are unreasonable, primitive and narcissistic, no one could possibly fulfill them. So when the one we supposedly "love madly" fails to live up to our unreal expectations, dooms the attainment of our fantasies, we feel in a fury, as though irretrievably betrayed. And love turns to hate.

For those whose lives are not drastically controlled by destructive fantasies, the slight disillusionament that inevitably follows the first passionate period is bearable. They are able to enjoy marriage, mate and children. But for those whose fantasy life is destructive to themselves and others, the disillusionment may be so devastating that love has no chance to survive. This is what happens to the one out of every two married couples who seek divorce.

When we fall in love in frantic fashion, love is doomed from the start. The foundation of such love is sheer fantasy; we do not know the person (or ourselves) and fail to feel tenderness, affection and the desire to give and receive mature love. Such desperate love is infantile love choked by fantasy. It does not stand a chance; the demands it makes are unreal, strictly those of an angry, yearning child.

The urgent, instant passion portrayed so dramatically in most films and books as hero and heroine fall in love within a split second and supposedly live happily ever after is what psychoanalysts call "immature love"—love based on childhood fantasy. Love that may also be shaded by a hatred displaced from the parent of childhood onto a current target. This hatred, concealed at first, may eventually explode from its prison in the mind.

Mature, or adult love, is founded not on fantasy, not on what one *wishes* the other person to be, but on reality, on what the other person *is*. It comes out of knowing him, loving him, respecting him, wanting to share with him not only sexual intimacy but emotional and intellectual life as well.

Mature love is not a demanding, possessive love that swallows up the other person, a love that erupts from emptiness. It is an enriching love that flows from fullness. It enables a man and a woman to exist as an entity, with a certain privacy of their own, yet also with a sense of delight in being a twosome. Each wishes the best of everything for the other. Each sees the other as an individual in his own right, with independent needs, rather than a slave living to fill demands.

Mature love is based on that deep awareness of the self that enables each to understand the other, not to use him but to share with him both life's pleasures and suffering. The more self-understanding you have, the more likely you are capable of mature love.

The ability to love maturely has nothing to do with your intelligence. You may be a celebrated scientist, or noted poet or artist, but unable to love. You may be brilliant intellectually but enmeshed in so many fantasies you cannot achieve a close, lasting relationship with a member of the opposite sex. On the other hand, a man or woman who has never gained distinction in the headlines may be free enough of childhood emotional chains to give freely of love.

Those incapable of mature love still demand that the world of reality carry out their fantasies. The romantic illusion of the secretary who dreams of marrying her boss as she stares into space sitting idly at her desk, even though he has an attractive wife with whom he seems in love, hides fantasies that are far from mere romance. She is still the little girl wishing to take papa from mama, wanting to be the only one in his life. This was a natural feeling when she was five years old but a fantasy that should have been relegated to natural suppression as she grew up and made peace with it. Either her mother or father, or both, have intensified over the years her wish to remain "daddy's little darling."

Marriage reveals hidden fantasies by forcing them into the open whereas previously they could be successfully evaded. Some men who have been homosexual will marry, believing a woman will help them become heterosexual. Others who are heterosexual marry in the hope it will stop their promiscuity, provide the brake for their runaway sexual drive. Such false hopes never work because the many fantasies inherent in them are too powerful.

Sometimes a marriage is undertaken because the man or woman think they *should* marry, despite all secret doubts and fears. They think of themselves as a pariah because all their friends are married. Marriages made for such a reason rarely survive because there is little desire to know the other person, little tenderness for him, little thought besides the selfish one, "I want to get married."

It is pure fantasy to expect another person to change our lives. Each of us has to make our own happiness. If we are happy before we marry, we will be happy in marriage. If we are unhappy before marriage, the marriage will reflect that unhappiness. No "magic" outside self-awareness, which is not magic but hard work, helps us live more happily if we are unhappy to start with.

Unfortunately, the person with deep emotional conflicts is likely to marry someone who also has deep emotional conflicts, though they may not appear on the surface. Unhappiness, like water, seeks its own level.

Thus, unhappy marriages are usually made on the basis of this intense, urgent sense of passion that suspends seeing the other as he really is, an intensity that sweeps away all wisdom. Swift courtship blocks the chance to get acquainted and there is often the rude awakening. Some marriages do work out after a brief courtship but they are rare. It takes time to know another's likes and dislikes, to discover whether interests are mutual, to decide whether life will be more pleasurable or more painful if spent with that particular person as lover and companion.

To romantically love a stranger is easy. Living in closeness is far more difficult. Then you cannot escape yourself, or the one you believe you love, who often turns into someone quite different.

When passion palls, many a husband and wife look at each other in despair and wonder what on earth led them to believe they wanted to live with such an impossible creature. Some men think they are marrying sweet tender women but find instead spoiled little girls demanding to be taken care of, or bossy, dominating women who insist their wishes come first.

Some women think they are marrying strong, wise men, only to find frightened, tantrum-ridden little boys, or aggressive, cruel bullies who think only of their own exaggerated needs.

We can become aware of what someone is really like if we are not so blind we will not see—if we take time to know the other person, to find out if he is thoughtless, heartless or harsh. The saying, "All is fair in love and war," gives deception its due but also tells us we should go slowly and study the ways in which we may be deceived if we do not look closely at someone we believe we love but see him through the clouded eyes of fantasy.

Failure to love is never a matter of blame. It does not help to blame oneself or the other person. Nobody is forced to fall in love or to marry. Each one chooses for himself and shares the responsibility if there is failure. When there is intense unconscious fantasy, it is difficult for two people to look into each other's hearts and to love. The only way to understand fantasy and thus escape its thrall is for each one to look inside himself, discover the carefully guarded secrets that keep him from being able to give or take love.

Some women whose husbands assault them may have selected such men for reasons that arise out of their unconscious fantasies. The men act out a brutality and hatred the woman fantasizes she might express but never has dared. Her hatred of such a husband, which she is unable as a rule to face, runs just as deep as the hatred he openly expresses for her.

Many people take out their hatred on those they profess to love, in subtle ways, not aware they express it. The man who must tell a woman the intimate details of his past love affairs, for whatever reason he may give, is expressing his hostility toward her, toward all women. He degrades other women by talking about them as he degrades her, telling her she is only one of many.

Some married couples boast they always tell each other the truth about everything, including occasional illicit affairs. They think they are being modern and courageous but they too express anger at one another. The impulse to tell everything—except in the office of a therapist—is suspect. Only to the therapist do you tell all, and then for a laudable reason—to understand your fantasies so you may live more at ease with yourself and others.

When a marriage partner is used as a confessional, it may temporarily ease the conscience of the one who spills out his secrets. But far from binding the two together in greater closeness, it often destroys love and trust.

If a marriage or love affair turns out unhappily, it is wise for the person to say, "This is my doing and next time perhaps I can choose more wisely if I understand that I picked this particular person out of my own desperate needs."

As you face what, in you, led to the unhappy marriage, you can then make up your mind as to whether it is worthwhile to remain in it or if you have a better chance of happiness with someone else. Without self-understanding, the tendency will be to marry someone exactly like the first partner. The unconscious reasons for choice remain the same if the underlying fantasies are not understood.

Many choose to remain in a wretched marriage, enduring the agony. Each receives some measure of gratification from the other. It is said of such couples, "They seem to enjoy their misery." The misery fulfills some unconscious needs. They may welcome the punishment inflicted on them and which they are inflicting on the mate. They may be secretly enjoying the pain because it relieves the deep guilt felt because of their fantasies.

When two people marry driven by unconscious fantasies, the discord between them is apt to show in their sexual life. They will not want each other sexually. Or one will want the other out of intense hunger, only to be frustrated as the partner refuses sex. Their sexual life may become half-hearted, then fully halted. The husband may accuse the woman of being unfeminine and she may accuse him of not being a man (the cause of many a murder of a wife by a husband, as she fails to realize the depth of his fear he is impotent).

A couple may accuse each other of infidelity, sometimes warranted, sometimes not. But the unhappy sexual life is only part of the story. Those who are not compatible sexually are usually also unable to bear the psychic rigors of married life.

Some who love and have sex before marriage when there is an atmosphere of secrecy and illicitness find that marriage ends the sexual desire. One man and woman enjoyed a love affair outside their separate marriages for thirteen years. Then they divorced their mates to marry each other. The marriage lasted one month. As long as love was forbidden, they could enjoy it. Without the aura of danger to excite them, love collapsed.

If we know the self and like the self, not demanding perfection of ourselves or anyone else, we will not choose a mate who is threatening or cruel. If we are able to admit our own fears and hatreds, dependencies and needs, realize they are carried from childhhod, we will not need to make unreal demands on anyone else. As we recognize our own rages, we no longer have to hate others for expressing what lies in us. We can like them as human beings, not gods or idols expected to make us happy.

One young man had a reputation among his friends as an eternal suitor, of liking "to court and then to run away." He made love to one woman after another, telling each at the start, "I have never been so in love, we will be happy together forever." His longest "forever" lasted six months. The moment a woman wanted to get close to him, showed she was human and had weaknesses as well as strengths, he fled. He could not tolerate his own weaknesses mirrored in his feminine partners.

A man and woman who live in intimacy cannot criticize each other constantly and expect love to endure. They may make demands on each other that come out of the marriage but not demands on each other that come out of their inner worlds. If they want the marriage to last, before they can give love or accept it they have to free themselves of the parasitic fantasies that bring an end to love. Each can do this only by being honest with the self, each time they feel like criticizing the other person, and admit, "It is really myself I am talking about." Strong feelings against someone else are usually aroused in us because they portray something we dislike inside ourselves.

By facing the fantasies we have guarded against over the years, we prevent ourselves from making the same mistake again and again. When we are bound to the ghosts of the past, we can only repeat the errors. We cannot make a free choice of love. We select not wisely but hungrily, loving not too well. We are apt to seek the same situation again and again, even though painful, then turn away from it when it becomes unbearable.

To be unaware of our hidden wishes and fantasies is to live unfulfilled. If our head whirls with fantasies of the forbidden, we do not possess the energy to tackle life's real challenges. Nor will we be truly lovable as we express the hate in the fantasies—not the love.

When we fall "madly" in love, driven by fantasies, the word "falls" seems particularly appropriate. It connotes we cannot help ourselves, that something beyond our control compels us to infantile love. Sometimes we may be vaguely aware what it is but usually we deny the fantasies that catapult us into such catastrophe. Our precarious façade can withstand the heat of inner hatred only so long. Then our feelings roar out, emotional disaster crashes about us. But if we can face the fiery feelings, they become as ashes, no longer inflame us.

We realize that feelings of envy, rage and guilt, which we have tried to conceal from ourselves over the years, belong to every man and woman. The word "human" implies that each of us is capable of every feeling that exists. It is how we cope with the feeling and the fantasies accompanying it that determines whether we find a love that lasts.

Freud said that "every psychoanalytic treatment is an attempt to free repressed love." The treatment does so by examining the person's fantasies. Whenever there is an abundance of repressed love or repressed hate, fantasy overwhelms us.

If love cannot be felt freely, hate lies somewhere near. In the unconscious, where our repressions are stored, love and hate, though inharmonious and opposed in our conscious thoughts, exist easily alongside each other.

Allied to fantasies of love and marriage are those that emerge in giving birth and rearing a child. Dr. Marianne Kris, a psychoanalyst, taking data from a family research project for many years at Yale University, studied the records of many family members in analysis.

She pointed out that the arrival of the first child solidifies the sexual identity of each parent, deepening the identification with his own parents. She explained: "The first child, so long as it is the only one, frequently is looked upon as the miracle, symbolizing for the parents the magic, the wonder of having achieved in reality what, in their childhood, was relegated to the fantasy and play-acting world." By the time the second child arrives, the parents are usually more solidified in their roles as parents, there is less of a feeling of unreality.

But expectations fraught with unconscious fantasies continue to play an important role in the way the children will be brought up. The order of birth of the children seems important in deciding the parent's expectations and responses to the children, reflecting their past situations as children with their parents. This is why, to a certain degree, the emotional development of each sibling differs. Each parent will unconsciously be steered in certain ways in bringing up each child, depending on what that child represents in terms of the parent's past experiences in his family of origin as well as conflicts and unconscious fantasies.

Each child will react to the parent's unconscious expectations, which play a role in the way the child sees himself and copes with life. The parent projects onto the child the image of his own successful or flawed self and/ or other images of his original family, based on his relations with his mother, father, sibling or grandparent. His fantasies may either promote or hinder genetic predispositions in the development of his child's characteristics.

A young couple, Fred and Lisa, attended well-baby clinic sessions while Lisa was pregnant with her first child. She spoke often of her beautiful older sister Eva, the exalted first-born, who became her father's pet. Lisa described Eva as "spoiled rotten," never asked to take responsibility, "the doll on a pedestal, the parents' show piece." Lisa expressed envy, resentfulness and fury as she talked of her sister, claiming she had never been considered "special" as Eva had been. Eva grew up to be a demanding, unhappy woman who relied heavily on morphine to get through the day and died in her early twenties.

Lisa could not rid herself of the eerie feeling that her first born would be "a good-for-nothing" person too. When Monica was born, the workers in the well-baby clinic marveled at how well she looked, a strong, energetic, engaging child with a high level of alertness. But no observations from outsiders could in any way comfort Lisa. When she nursed Monica she fantasied the fire in the fireplace reflected itself in the eyes of her child, forming crosses, indicating Monica would not live to grow into adulthood.

During the early years, when taking care of her daughter, Lisa sometimes surprised herself by being inattentive, letting Monica get into hazardous situations, one of which almost cost her life when she lost her foothold in the waters of the local beach. As an older child, Monica became prone to accidents, she had not been given enough protection in her life and was therefore severely handicapped in her ability to take care of herself. Her father tried to make her feel less neglected, at which Lisa became jealous of the attention he bestowed on Monica, tried in various ways to interrupt the father-daughter play.

Later, during her psychotherapy, Lisa discovered she had fantasied her daughter as Eva, her older sister, both the first-born in their families. She had been unduly pessimistic about Monica's development and unwittingly promoted certain fantasies to interfere in her care of her daughter. Lisa also discovered how her feelings of jealousy, competition and anger at seeing her husband play with their daughter were rooted in her own childhood experiences.

She remembered her father playing with her envied, hated sister. She also recalled her guilt feelings after her sister's death, since so many times as a child she had wished her older sister would disappear forever. She fantasied she should be punished by some disaster happening to her firstborn child. And Monica did die as a teenager due to the taking in of her mother's negative fantasies.

This illustrates in shorthand fashion the complicated relationship between parent and child dictated by the parent's past fantasies. It shows how unconscious fantasies that have clustered around childhood relationships can directly influence the way the next generation will be brought up.

Thus children in the same family are often raised very differently by a parent because of the latter's fantasies. When Lisa found herself pregnant with her third child, she felt elated because she, like her parents, had wished for a boy. Here was her chance to produce "the son," who would personify the idealized image of the child her parents were never blessed with (they had only two daughters).

Lisa gave birth to a boy who had a slight neurological dysfunction. He was a more passive, less vigorous child than his two sisters. But he became the apple of his parents' eyes, the prime creation. He was provided with the necessary treatments for the neurological condition as his parents worked diligently with him to strengthen his ability to function. They felt great hope and expectations as they minimized the negative odds against their somewhat handicapped son.

The parents made certain he would get the best opportunities to carry out his personal interests. He overcame his handicap, possessed a self-caring, positive attitude about himself (the attitude his parents had shown him), fared far better in school than anyone would have expected when observing him as a newborn infant.

This boy's emotional development had been enhanced by the fact there were no parental conflicts or negative expectations to mar his ability to develop. He had been a wanted child: nothing in his mother's past contaminated her capacity to provide good nurturing, a nurturing lacking in the case of her daugher who at birth had shown a much better predisposition for high levels of development but failed to live up to her innate potentials. He could later express love far more easily than his sisters.

In mankind's slow march toward becoming truly civilized, we are learning how important it is to know the fantasies that drive us to unhappy love affairs and marriages. Among our strongest fantasies are those that stem from sexual desires.

What are the specific fantasies that accompany our sexual wishes? Do men and women differ in these fantasies? What purpose do such sexual fantasies serve?

5

Fantasies about Sex

The hidden power of fantasy, one of Freud's most important early discoveries, he called "the great secret." He came upon it unexpectedly during the analysis of his first patients, all women, suffering from what was, in Vienna in the 1890s, called "hysteria."

As the women trusted him enough to reveal the secrets of their hearts, they insisted that as little girls they had been seduced by their fathers. Though he believed them at first, after treating a number, Freud concluded they had not been incestuously attacked but were only expressing the strong wish natural to every little girl who, at four or five, wanted to marry her father, the first man in her life. The women were not aware of lying, so powerful the childhood fantasy now unconscious.

This was clearly shown in the case of Anna O., who, Freud said, led him to his theories of psychoanalysis. She was not his patient but treated by his close friend and mentor, Dr. Josef Breuer, at the time Freud was finishing medical school in Vienna. Breuer told Freud at the last session of Anna O.'s treatment he became alarmed when she acted out a phantom pregnancy. She imagined he had seduced her and she was now bearing his child. She had fallen in love with him as every woman patient does, transferring to the analyst the love she felt as a child for her father. Anna O.'s real name was Bertha Pappenheim; she was the daughter of wealthy parents and later became a famous social worker in Germany.

Freud reached the conclusion that Anna O. was expressing her sexual fantasies about her father, to whom she had been very close and who had died during her treatment with Breuer. For a woman to admit she yearns for sex with her father seems obscene, dangerous to her sense of self. This

78

may be the wish of the little girl who says frankly, "I want to marry daddy," but for the adult woman to be still enmeshed in her earlier fantasy is unthinkable to her and to society.

But if at its origin the wish was too passionate, or never faced because of fear, the woman may be possessed by it all her life, never able to love a man. This happened with Anna O., who never married, who, from her letters to friends, never even fell in love again. The emotional origins on which her fantasy thrived were never unearthed in her treatment with Breuer, for psychoanalysis had not yet come into being.

At each phase of what Freud named our "psychosexual development," new fantasies arise about sexual desires. In the first, or oral stage, our fantasies center on the mouth as the origin and recipient of sexual feelings. In the second, or anal stage, when we are toilet trained, the anal passage takes on a sexual tinge. In the third, or phallic stage, the phallus comes into our awareness. In the final, or genital stage, the genitals come into their own as the site of sexual expression. Remnants of each phase may be part of the adult sexual act but unless the main emphasis is on genital sex it is considered infantile sex.

If during each psychosexual stage—oral, anal and phallic—both parent and child go through it in a spirit of cooperation and with an attitude of belief in each other and positive expectation even at times of failure, the child as an adult will be self-reliant, have high self-esteem and a positive expectation of his own ability to achieve and be productive. He will be an optimist, not a pessimist.

Dr. Martin Stein, a psychoanalyst, states that unconscious fantasies from childhood determine whether a marriage will last. In his chapter, "The Unconscious Meaning of the Marital Bond" in *Neurotic Interaction in Marriage,* he discusses a single unconscious fantasy he found played a prominent role in the entering into and perpetuation of the marriages of four neurotic men he analyzed.

In its simplest form the fantasy may be expressed, Stein said, as the man imagining "My wife is my phallus" or "My wife is part of my body." In each of these men, who showed the same fantasy operating in somewhat different fashion, the fantasy played a large role in their serious marital conflicts. The unconscious anatomical significance of the fantasy, Stein pointed out, had to be understood and worked through by the patient before progress could be made in solving the problems of his marriage, or, for that matter, "in other aspects of his life."

He described one husband who treated his wife like a "tool," an appendage, a part of his body. Unconsciously, his sexual relations with her were "a kind of masturbation, independent of her needs and feelings."

Stein asked rhetorically, "Why had this fantasy remained so important?" Then he answered that the fantasy of being castrated, which this man carried from boyhood, led to the fantasy that his active, competent, scolding, vivacious wife was his phallus. He felt he was not a man without her. He could not think of her as a human being, even struck her at times when he got angry, causing her to weep (in his unconscious, to urinate or ejaculate). She sensed this and once told him in a fit of anger, "You don't want a wife, you want a penis and balls to play with," sensing his childhood wishes.

One of the most perceptive and entertaining accounts of the "phallus-girl" equation is found in Shaw's *Pygmalion*, Stein pointed out. Professor Higgins, a devoted student of linguistics and a confirmed bachelor of eccentric tastes, has for clearly selfish reasons transformed Eliza, a Cockney flower girl, "a squashed cabbage leaf," into a lovely, charming woman. This miracle has been accomplished chiefly through the correction of her speech.

Eliza then attacks him for his lack of human feelings for her, charges he uses her as a "baby or a puppy" or a slave. As she asserts her independence, Higgins feels panic and anger, pleads, "You and I and Pickering," his masculine friend, "will be three old bachelors together instead of only two men and a silly girl." He has in fantasy bestowed on Eliza a penis. Stein concludes that Shaw had an excellent sense of reality in that he did not allow Eliza to marry Higgins, who was unable to regard her as anything but an appendage to be used and exhibited. (In the musical *My Fair Lady* the implication is he does marry her.) Stein concludes, "As usual, Shaw has struck at the heart of the argument. He ends the epilogue, 'Galatea never does like Pygmalion: his relation to her is too godlike to be altogether agreeable.'"

The fantasies of boys and men about sex differ from those of girls and women for the most part as each gender faces conflicts of its own. From birth, the boy has been primarily dependent on his mother for comfort and security. While the object of his love, his mother, does not change during the crucial oedipal period, unlike the girl who must switch her passion and love from her mother to her father, the nature of the boy's relationship to his mother changes.

He continues to value his mother as a source of security but about the age of four or five starts to have fantasies of a more romantic and sexual nature. He notices his father caressing and kissing his mother and fantasizes himself his mother's lover. But he is afraid to compete with his father, considering him a dangerous rival who can destroy him in a moment. The boy fantasizes his father's disapproval, anger and punitive feelings because of his own competitive fantasies.

Noticing the absence of a penis in girls, the boy fears his father may castrate him because of his wish to supplant his father. Unless he is helped to overcome this fear and the guilt that follows, he may never be at ease sexually with a woman, may even become homosexual, fearing the sight of a woman's genitals which arouse the fantasy of castration with the folds mistaken for the healing of a cut.

The fantasies of girls and women differ quite markedly from those of boys and men. Girls not only have fantasies about the difference in the sexual organs of men and women but about menstruation. Little has been written about the deep, dark fantasies that accompany what psychoanalyst Norman Shelly has called "the bloody rage"—the fear and anger many girls feel when they first learn of the menstrual period and resent it. Probably every girl, when she first has her monthly menstrual period is alarmed by this new function of her body, one that will later enable her to bear a child. Those girls who have seen their mothers accept menstruation as a natural occurence and show little fear and anger at it are likely to be the ones who also accept it as part of a woman's life. They have the proud feeling, "Now I am no longer a child." This end to childhood for other girls, who may be abnormally dependent on their mothers, will not be welcomed, however, and they may resent what they think of as a new burden to femininity.

As one girl said to her mother in angry tone, "It's damned unfair of mother nature to inflict such an outrage on women and not on men. Why should they go scot-free?" A man might respond, "We have to shave each day and that's a nuisance. Why should a woman complain?"

The bleeding of menstruation causes the emergence of many fantasies. Dr. Karen Horney wrote, "Every woman's analysis shows that with the appearance of menstrual blood, cruel impulses and fantasies of both an active and passive nature are awakened in her." These are often preceded in the days before menstruation begins by feelings of self-depreciation, and depression—all of which recede, however, at the onset of the bleeding, when the woman feels relief, she added.

For many women, pregnancy is a time when fantasies of loss, injury and death may be activated. Dr. Helene E. Deutsch says, "The optimistic idea 'I shall have a child' assumes the character of an ecstatic experience that is at once opposed by the pessimistic negation 'I shall have no child, I have no right to have one, I shall lose it, I shall pay for it with my death.' " This need for punishment is connected with her early oedipal wish to have a child by her beloved father which meant she was a sinner and deserved death.

Shaving does not exactly balance the menstrual "curse," as some girls, chiefly the tomboys, call it, or the pain they may endure each month, largely because of their psychological fear of menstruation and ensuing anger. Girls have the fantasies that menstruation represents castration, mutilation, identification with their "damaged" mother, the loss of part of the self, as well as a stigma associated with being a woman.

A woman of twenty-six who went into analysis because of anxiety feelings told her analyst she had suffered intense pain each monthly menstruation period since she first had a period when she was eleven years old. She talked about her fear of menstruation, said all her friends called it "the curse." She confessed, "I hated it when I first got it and I still hate it."

She discovered that after two months of therapy all pain conneced with the period had vanished and never returned. Her ability to speak of her fantasies in connection to the period and to her mother, whom she outwardly despised but inwardly was very dependent upon, had a beneficial effect on her body, her need to inflict pain on herself for a function she had despised. She was able, after analysis, to marry and bore two children, wrote the analyst a letter thanking him for helping her accept her femininity.

According to recent research, parents show different responses to boys as contrasted to girls from birth on. These responses may, to a certain degree, influence the child's later perception of his gender identity, the image of himself as related to the values of being a boy or a girl, his expectations and coping mechanisms—all reflected in his fantasies.

Observations show, for instance, that from birth on boys are generally handled more roughly, particularly by their fathers. Also the interactions between a boy and his parents are more action-oriented because of the parental expectation (fantasy) that boys should be more "aggressive doers" than girls. We might speculate that later in life this attitude would, to a certain degree, promote what seems to be the males' lesser capacity to endure being "good, quiet listeners" to women, possessed as males are by the fantasy of being doers (finders of solutions).

Realistically, in today's world, where a woman is allowed to be competent, she does not need to look to the man to be the omnipotent, magically performing "doer," the problem solver. The most recent Hite report shows women feel disillusioned in finding an empathic understanding listener, women seem to unite in the feeling this quality cannot be found in a man.

According to the latest psychoanalytic research, mothers feel that boys are "more cuddly" than girls while fathers feel just the opposite, consider girls "more cuddly." No doubt this parental image is reflected to some degree in the child's image of himself. Perhaps the parent's readiness to cuddle with the child of the opposite sex will influence that child to have later feelings related to the experience of closeness versus distance.

A teenage girl, set on revenge against her father who, she felt, never showed any interest in her began to understand why she felt so hostile while listening to her father describe how he used to lift her up as a little girl, hold her high in the air, when he returned from work in the evening. He was expressing the feeling she was the "princess on the pedestal" for whose sake it was worth working hard. But she had imagined his lifting her high in the air as a further attempt to put distance between them, for his work took him away from home much of the time.

To survive mentally what she fantasied as her father's neglect, she developed fantasies as to how she could attract his attention, bring him closer. She tried to be like him—a boy, then a man. If she could look like him, she fantasized, he would become part of her, they would be inseparable. As a rageful, frustrated teenager she also indulged in fantasies about how she would compete with him, take away females by becoming far more attractive than he could aspire to be. She lived out this fantasy in reality by emphasizing a male look, courting females in her teenage years. In her revenge, she even went so far as to try to embarrass him by exhibiting homosexual overtures toward females in his presence.

Until recent times the mother, main caretaker of her children, has been seen by them in general as more powerful, stronger than the father, who does not run their daily life by giving them food, clothes, toys and other necessities. In the eyes of her children, the mother is the person who makes things magically come about. Consequently, it is common to see not only girls dress up as mothers in the doll corners of nursery school and day-care centers but also boys who wish to show themselves as equally powerful members of the household. Young preschool boys put on their mothers' makeup and perfume not just as a way of wanting to explore everything that exists but also to feel as powerful as their seemingly all-powerful mothers.

A mother's attitude toward her own body and her feeling about herself as a female is of great importance in the development of a girl and her sense of her own sexual identity. Take one little girl's reaction to her mother and her pregnancy. Four-year-old Elizabeth was told by her mother of a third pregnancy—Elizabeth had an older brother, Adam—and wondered whether the next baby would be a boy or girl.

Elizabeth's mother felt comfortable about being a female and told her little daughter lovingly about the "fun of being a woman," said she enjoyed a third "little one" growing inside her. Elizabeth took this all in, happily announced she too was "expecting" and not just one but many little babies. Her entire belly in her fantasy, turned into a voluminous house of many rooms, fourteen in all, one room for each baby. At four o'clock each afternoon in her fantasy her little babies came out through a door located in the area of her belly button so she could count them all, take a look at them. Then they returned inside her to develop further, later expected to come out "for good," she announced.

Several psychoanalysts have written about the unconscious fantasy of the woman that she is an appendage of the man, that "girl equals phallus," as psychoanalyst Dr. Annie Reich described it. Women who fantasy themselves as appendages of a man often marry men who wish them to be the phallus, as mentioned earlier by Dr. Stein.

Since Freud introduced the concept of "penis envy" in girls many psychoanalytic articles have been written about this. Analysts seem to agree that the wish to be a man, to possess a phallus, is strong in girls during both the oedipal and phallic stages (between four and five years of age) but that if the girl is allowed to feel and express her femininity, she successfully gives up this fantasy. If however her mother and father have strong wishes that she had been a boy, the fantasy may remain deeply imprinted in her unconscious and in later life she will consider the fantasy as an essential part of reality.

Girls are brought up to be compliant, to conceal all signs of inner rage at deprivations. Fantasies of hate remain repressed, causing guilt and low self-esteem. Women are just starting to realize the difference between assertion, which embodies the freedom to work, to stand up for themselves not angrily but justifiably, and aggression, which often holds hostility.

During the oedipal stage girls also experience different fantasies and conflicts than boys. In contrast to the boy, who continues to rely on his mother as a source of love and security even though she is the object of his passion, the girl has to direct her sexual fantasies toward her father and become a rival with the mother—the parent who has been her main emotional support. Inasmuch as she has depended almost solely on her mother for her gratifications, she is faced with the conflict of deciding whether to give up dependence on her mother and possibly her mother's love or risk feeling emotionally stunted at not exploring her feelings of love for her father.

If these unresolved oedipal conflicts still exist in a woman, she may experience sex and intimacy with a man as incestuous and forbidden. If she marries, she may repudiate her husband, not having worked through her oedipal fears. She may have the fantasy that marriage and motherhood are an oedipal victory over her original love, her mother, and feel so guilty she does not enjoy either.

If a mother or father makes it difficult for a little girl to transfer her love to the father, if the mother is jealous of her or the father withdraws from all attempts by a daughter to win his heart and affection, this will seriously impede her natural psychosexual development and she will have difficulty relating to a man, still embedded in childhood fantasies.

Punitive responses by parents to oedipal competition may stimulate in the child the development of a strict conscience and lay the groundwork for sexual inhibitions. The child feels that his sexual fantasies are "bad" and avoids much intimacy with the opposite sex, both in adolescence and later years.

According to Erik Erikson, the dilemma to be resolved in this oedipal period with boys and girls is their taking initiative versus feeling guilt. The child who feels guilty about his sexual fantasies and activities may become passive. But if this phallic-oedipal period has been essentially free of conflicts, the maturing child will enrich his capacity to achieve and to love. He will be able to form a pleasurable, trusting attachment to members of the opposite sex, to admire the loved one without feelings of guilt.

The fantasies of any one stage do not disappear when that stage ends but overlap with new fantasies. A fantasy is never forgotten, it remains in the unconscious, becomes part of what analysts call a "fantasy constellation," grouped around a particular wish and feelings about it. The power of a fantasy to determine our behavior depends on whether we have been able to become aware of it, relegate it to its proper place in repressed memories or whether, because it is still used to defend against a terrifying feeling or wish of which we are unaware, it still influences us in a negative way.

Both boys and girls have fantasies during the oedipal phase, fantasies that can cause much pain in later life. Freud warned, "It is inevitable and perfectly normal that a child should take his parents as the first objects of his love. But his libido should not remain fixated to these first objects."

And a second warning: "It has an ugly sound and paradoxical as well, but nevertheless it must be said that whoever is to be really free and happy in love must have overcome his deference for women and come to terms with the idea of incest with mother or sister." He referred to boys but also meant girls needed to come to the same terms with their father or brother.

It may seem strange Freud coupled "deference" with "the idea of incest" as he wrote we must overcome "deference" and "come to terms with the idea of incest" to be "really free and happy in love." He admitted this had a paradoxical sound.

Yet the deference, the wish to please, to be loved completely and forever by the parent of the opposite sex, is very much part of "the idea of incest." Coming to terms with the "idea of incest" means accepting the impulse to love the parent of the opposite sex as natural. The normal impulse may have been overstimulated by a parent who did not understand what he was doing, such as appearing naked in front of the child on many occasions and deliberately, or keeping the child in a cot in the parents' bedroom until the child is three or four. This type of parental behavior can only over-whelm the child, will stimulate and intensify his sexual fantasies as well as his aggressive ones, as a way of the wrong type of comfort.

When a parent actually seduces a child he inflicts a psychological wound. For a child to have his sexual fantasies come true in reality leaves him with indelible emotional scars for life, expressing themselves in ways such as a poor self-image, unbearable guilt feelings and an intense need for punishment of the self.

As children, we tend to exaggerate feelings, see the world in black and white, know no shades of gray. Thus a warm hug and a kiss from a parent can represent sexual seduction to an eager, responsive child, just as a mild word of indifference can be felt as fatal rejection or a sharp scowl inter-preted as the wrath of Medusa.

A child cannot explain his sexual fantasies to his parents, the giants on whom he depends for survival. And if the child, who eternally seeks closeness and safety, cannot find it in his parents, one of whose duties is to be protective, he will find it in fantasy.

All children possess strong sexual feelings—this is the start of the instinct that insures the perpetuation of the human race. If a parent responds too intensely to the child's feelings, the child will be overwhelmed, resort to vivid fantasies that focus on his sexual feelings.

Parents no longer in love with each other sometimes fantasy as love substitutes the children, who are younger, handsomer versions of their mates, to remind them of the person they once fell in love with. Or a parent unconsciously will love a child who reminds him of a brother or sister he loved. Conversely, he may hate a child who reminds him of a brother or sister he hated. Or he may love or hate a child who reminds him of himself as a child.

Apart from any seduction in which the parent may engage, a child, even the child of the best possible parents, will feel a measure of rage when his sexual desires are frustrated. The wrath of the son spurned by the mother, and the daughter denied by the father, is a fantasied one but nevertheless a wrath that may eat away all through life unless the natural desire is faced and accepted as normal to everyone at a certain time of life, then relinquished.

As we consciously accept the "idea of incest," we will no longer feel guilty. We know our desires spring from the natural need for love. It is a need that, if intense, may give rise to the delusion of incest and, in less extreme degree, to the illusion of finding the perfect parent in one's partner in love.

When we are children, we do not see our parents as they really are. To a little girl, her father is a combination of Sir Galahad and Prince Charming, while a little boy may think of his mother as fairy godmother, the most beautiful, kindly woman in the world. This is fantasy spun on fantasy. It becomes a wonderland of wishes that eventually must be acknowledged for what they are—the impossible dreams of childhood, hiding repressed sexual wishes.

When infantile sexual wishes and fears are carried into adulthood the result is apt to be an unhappy one. Reuben Fine in *The Healing of The Mind* described an attractive girl of twenty-eight, convinced she was unattractive to men. He wrote, "The fact she had lots of men after her, and had since her teens, meant nothing. She was so convinced of her unattractiveness that she would not even talk about it in therapy. Repeatedly, however, she tied it up with the envy of other girls. 'If I were prettier, all the girls on the beach would look at me because I would attract the attention of men,' she said. With this fantasy brought to the surface, her homosexual penis-envy and exhibitionistic wishes could come to the fore. The deepest fantasy of all was her wish to be a man."

As fantasies, dreams and memories are pulled into a coherent whole during a psychoanalysis, the person has a chance to view his life more objectively and understand both his own conflicts and those of his parents. Fine points out that both men and women are often confused as to what is reality, what is fantasy. He says: "The overemphasis on reality is by far the most common of all resistances. In one sense, it may be said to be the core resistance of all, since it is common to every defensive process. The patient always insists he *is* dealing with reality, while the analyst is always trying to help him to see that he is dealing with fantasy."

The patient who responds best to therapy is the one who has "the optimal guilt-fantasy combination," that is, has a strong sense of guilt about his fantasies, Fine believes. He says, "As long as the patient harps on reality, he cannot feel much guilt or responsibility for what is happening to him. Accordingly he becomes reluctant to bring up his fantasy material. Reality consideration must be overcome before he can be led to deal with his fantasies."

Women and men in therapy are expected to have sexual fantasies about the analyst as they repeat their early childhood fantasies about sexual desires for parents. If the therapist reacts to such fantasies with a sexual affair, he will cause the patient irreparable harm. He violates the Hippocratic oath, which holds there must be "no sexual relations" between patients and doctors.

The oath contains the words: "I will follow that method of treatment which, according to my ability and judgment, I consider for the benefit of my patients, and abstain from whatever is deleterious and mischievous. . . . Into whatever house I enter I will go into them for the benefit of the sick and will abstain from every voluntary act of mischief and corruption: and further from the seduction of females and males, bond or free."

The analyst who carries out the tabooed incestuous act, instead of rescuing the patient from inner misery, will cause him everlasting harm, inflicting greater torment. He will hinder his patient to a devastating degree from gaining emotional understanding of his conflicts. To promote and permit a patient to act out a fantasy—a wish—has never proved helpful in easing psychological pain.

Minnesota recently passed a law, the first state to do so, making it a crime for any therapist to have sexual contact with a patient. Other states are expected to follow.

Because the therapist neither judges nor condemns the man or woman for their most repulsive, villainous, obscene thoughts, the patients are given permission to recall fantasies they have pushed into the unconscious during childhood and since. As the analyst provides a safe environment for the fantasies to unfold, he can then understand and assist his patient in becoming aware of the cause of his anxieties.

If we have not repressed too deeply the sexual fantasies of childhood we will be able to form an attachment to and trust someone of the opposite sex. We will want to cooperate with our sexual partner, try to help him attain pleasure as we enjoy our own. We can initiate making love without feeling uncomfortable, not threatened by fantasy. This is mature sexuality, free of fearful fantasy—sexuality enjoyed without guilt.

Some forms of sex, called perversions, hold a deep sense of guilt. What sexual practices do they reflect and what fantasies lie behind these practices?

6

The "Don Juan" and Other Fantasies

Every child goes through a natural stage of sexual development in which he becomes what Freud called "polymorphous perverse." He wants to be held, hugged, kissed and fondled by either man or woman, for he does not as yet know the differences between the sexes. Freud did not use the term "polymorphous perverse" in a derogatory way but only to point out that this normal phase of infantile sexuality was part of everyone's childhood psychosexual development.

Sexual perversion in an adult shows that some childhood sexual fantasy, appropriate to the earlier stage of sexual development, has not been outgrown but because of some intense fear has persisted. The fear usually is connected with threatening emotional experiences in childhood between parent and child that arrested and fixated the sexual aim.

Whether we admit it or not, we are all attracted to descriptions of what we call "perversions"—sadism, masochism, fetishism, exhibitionism, voyeurism, sodomy, transvestitism or perversion in its most minor form, promiscuity. Our interest in perversions occurs because, as Freud said, the average person still fantasies what the pervert performs in reality. All the activities we call "perverse" have been fantasized by us in the earlier stages of our sexual development.

Our childhood sexual fantasies remain in the unconscious part of our minds—the reservoir of our earlier wishes and memories. The pervert has become fixated at an earlier stage of sexuality because the next, or more mature stage, appears too threatening in an emotional sense.

As a rule boys experiment sexually with boys and girls with girls before they are prepared to try with a member of the opposite sex. If the relationship with a parent has been too sexually threatening, the adult may remain "fixated" at the earlier stage, not daring sexual activity with a member of the opposite sex.

Promiscuity is a borderline perversion, on the edge of what we think of as abnormal sexual practice. The fantasy of indulging in sex with as many partners as one wishes, rather than a newfound sexual freedom is an expression of hostility toward the opposite sex. Real sexual freedom, far harder to achieve, is enjoyed in growing exploration of and attachment to one person in more ways than sexual.

The young single man and woman and the teenager, before the AIDS epidemic, were as promiscuous as their elders. A twenty-three-year-old taxi driver, looking for a wife, asked a customer in despair, "What's a 'good girl' today? One who has slept with twenty men? Fifty men?"

Two-thirds of all the women in this country have had sexual intercourse by the age of nineteen, almost all before marriage, according to a recent study of population experts at the Johns Hopkins School of Hygiene and Public Health. One in five has had sexual intercourse by the age of sixteen and one in ten becomes pregnant before seventeen. This cannot be blamed, as in the past, on "uninhibited" ethnic groups because white teenagers account for the largest part of this latest increase.

Promiscuity in women may be in part rebellion against the sexual suppression suffered through the centuries, when they were treated as though they had no right to sexual gratification. Many women have sought the double standard so long denied them, making up for sexual deprivation, as part of women's liberation, along with economic, social and political equality.

But the fantasy that promiscuity brings sexual freedom is a false one. There is vast difference between "sexual license" or sex for the sake of sex, and "sexual freedom." The latter encompasses the ability to combine sexual desire and love for one person in an enduring fashion that brings a sense of fulfillment and self-esteem. On the other hand, sexual license is the use of sexual fantasy for purposes other than love—for momentarily raising a false sense of conquering an enemy, or gaining temporary sexual release as though it were urination.

Sexual license based on fantasy brings in its wake increased unhappiness, a sense of a demeaning of the self and the partner. It represents the acting out of infantile conflicts and is followed by the depressed feeling there is no hope of inner security as sex fails to solve the problems of life.

As one promiscuous woman wailed to a friend, "Somehow sex alone is never enough to bring peace of mind. All I feel after a sexual encounter is a sense of guilt."

The promiscuous possess a hungry need for sex, which they gulp as a starved infant does food. They cannot look on the other person as a human being, capable of and due affection, respect and friendship, but as a sexual "object" soon to be discarded. And it is always "soon," for the promiscuous person flees great guilt over his promiscuity—a guilt he projects on his sexual partner. He *must* abandon the partner after sex because he cannot tolerate anyone who arouses his guilt.

Why the guilt? According to psychoanalysts, promiscuity conceals among other feelings the repressed childhood fantasy of love for the parent of the opposite sex, an intense erotic wish carried from the days of the first stirrings of the oedipal conflict. The promiscuous have never resolved their oedipal dilemma. Because their incestuous wish is taboo, guilt torments them as they project it on the victim they "conquer," then flee forever.

There appear what may be called the "Don Juan" and "Donna Juanita" fantasies. They exist in the men and women who flee from one sexual partner to the next. But in the unconscious fantasy, the many stand for the one. The Don Juan defends against his unconscious fantasy of loving only one person, the forbidden idol of childhood—the parent of the oposite sex. He embarks on promiscuity as though the many will make up for the loss of the earlier "one and only," and at the same time protect him from his incestuous desires.

At the other extreme stands the man so afraid of his feelings he cannot trust himself even to part with semen. Impotence may be strong denial of urgency, just as urgency is often denial of feared impotence. Impotence usually holds the unconscious fantasy of the destruction of the other person and/or the self by the sexual act.

Otto Rank, a disciple of Freud, in *The Don Juan Legend,* says that the ancient story of Don Juan "is more profound than the frivolous breaking of hearts," that unbounded sexuality was not the principal motif of the legend. Rank maintains that the characteristic Don Juan fantasy of conquering countless women, "which has made the hero into a masculine ideal," is based on "the unattainability of the mother and the compensatory substitute for her." It involves the "deeply rooted" biological wish for the exclusive and complete possession of the mother, as once experienced in the pleasure of the early years of life and forever after "sought as the highest libidinal satisfaction."

The repeated sexual conquest of women remains unsatisfying because "the infantile tendency to regress to the mother can only be partially fulfilled," Rank says. He calls the Don Juan "one who has foundered on the mother complex." The promiscuous woman, in fantasy, is still tied to her adored father, seeing his image in each man with whom she has sex, then flees in pursuit of the next.

The many sex therapists, including Masters and Johnson, do not take fantasy into consideration when it comes to sex but concentrate on the body as a machine. This can only prove a temporary solution for underlying conflicts that cause the sexual difficulties to remain. It takes the facing of the inner self to become sexually free.

The man who seeks sex as though it were a "fix" is often called a Don Juan, who was a mythical character, or a Giovanni Casanova, an actual philanderer who wrote several volumes describing the hundreds of women he seduced. Psychoanalysts call such addiction in men "satyriasis" and in women, "nymphomania." They speak of sexual addicts as "compulsively driven" by fantasy rather than exercising choice as they flit from partner to partner in unending search for what they believe happiness.

Many an inhibited person envies the sex addict, as Emerson said, "All mankind loves a lover." This universal fantasy is based on the illusion the Don Juan feels fulfilled as a man. Rather, it is because he lacks the ability to be sexually potent consistently with one woman that he must become promiscuous. He is not a hero but a tragic figure, to be pitied. He is victim (or, in the case of a woman, she is victim) of a fantasy that can never be satisfied, that prevents him from knowing real and lasting love. Ahead of him lies only greater addiction, more unhappiness and the likelihood he will never know the pleasure of mature love unless he faces up to the reasons for his addiction.

Most of us learn to control our sexual desires to a certain extent, to relate to one person, or at least try to. We accept the frustration of not being able to indulge in sex with everyone who arouses our passion. But the sex addict lacks such control. He feels he desperately needs sex with many partners, the way some desperately need alcohol, cigarettes, drugs or food. The sex addict is consumed by his desire, escapes into sexual addiction as defense against many hidden fantasies and feelings he considers dangerous.

He may be a supposedly happily married man with children. Or he may never have married. Or he may have married many times. Whatever his marital situation, he is possessed by an *intensity* of sexual hunger and an inability to withstand the inner fantasies that drive him constantly to different sexual partners. He becomes in effect a sex machine. Sex to him is not pleasure but tormenting need. If he does not find sexual release, he almost goes out of his mind. He glories in his conquests, boasts of them. To him the conquest is the thing, not the woman.

When Ethel Merman discussed her marriage to Ernest Borgnine, which lasted twenty-eight days, she was quoted in a column by Sheilah Graham as saying, "Some men are only interested in the conquest. Then they show the other side. The real personality."

The man interested only in the conquest rarely reveals his hidden feelings, which have many facets destructive to himself and the one he professedly loves for the moment. For one thing, he is usually a very lonely person, seeks the solace of another body to appease a physical and psychological craving. To be deprived of sex means the threat of death.

He has learned seduction as a way of dealing with life's conflicts. He searches for woman after woman to appease what he feels to be emotional starvation. He needs to touch and be touched, to hold a feminine body close, enjoy a sexual climax and then flee. He lives, so to speak, in a sexual climate.

But his excessive sexual hunger does not necessarily make him an expert lover. According to his sexual partners, the Don Juan is not the greatest lover; sex for him is over in a few seconds, the woman often left unsatisfied. Casanova was an exception—he wrote he was proud of always giving a woman several orgasms before he allowed himself to have one. But as a rule, after the woman has been briefly possessed by a Don Juan, she is tossed aside like a used condom.

Those driven to have sex with many lovers or who, in marriage, demand their partners have sex with them whenever they wish it, use sex to fulfill many unconscious fantasies. For one, sex on demand is used to fight homosexual desires. The sex addict is obsessed by love of self, which prevents him from accepting and resolving his feelings about members of the same sex, let alone members of the opposite sex. He defends his secret wish to have sex with a man by pointing to the hundreds of women he has conquered, as though saying, "See how many women I have had sexually, how could I possibly want a man?"

Because early sexual development has been blocked, the male sex addict feels he is not a man, fears castration, and the woman sex addict feels unfeminine. The nymphomaniac believes that if she is alluring to man after man, if she can feel a penis inside her much of the time, this proves she is a woman. It is also her way of conquering and castrating a man as, in fantasy, she momentarily possesses the penis, taken from the man. She is both envious and contemptuous of men. She also feels guilty because in fantasy every man represents her loved-hated father of childhood.

Sex can also be used to combat a deep depression. In the case of a number of Hollywood's men and women who rise to sudden fame and also are noted for promiscuity, it can be seen, as they talk of their lives as children and adolescents, that they may be fleeing a deep depression and fantasies of suicide. Marilyn Monroe, who committed suicide at thirty-six, is an outstanding example.

The excessive use of sex may also be a result of very seductive parents who either act out the seduction or, as is more often the case, are subtly seductive around the child. Such a child, as adult, may try to master the earlier erotic experience. He may also have either a promiscuous mother or father whom he has unconsciously imitated. All children use their parents as sexual models.

Sex may also be used to express hatred. There is no tenderness, no caring for the partner, but only the need to release a passion composed of consuming hunger from the oral stage, a sadistic controlling attitude from the anal stage and a fear from the phallic stage that one is not a man (or a woman).

One husband, when furious at his wife, insisted they have sexual intercourse. He used sex as an assault, to hurt her physically and psychologically. Other husbands will flay a wife with obscene words, taunting and degrading her with epithets. Or they may insist she have sex when they want it, refuse her when she feels aroused.

Sex can also be used as a defense against fear of frigidity or impotence, or the fear one will kill the self or others, or the fear of madness. Excessive sex may be used as defense against any feeling that terrorizes, Freud said, any feeling in us may become "erotized."

Sex should be *part* of our lives, not the *whole,* as it is with the promiscuous person, says Dr. Hyman Spotnitz, author of *The Wandering*

Husband. "It is not either-or with sex," he explains. "But the addict cannot see this. He pursues sex as though it were a matter of life and death. Each act of sex is a crisis which he must somehow survive."

Wholesale indulgence in sex, just as addiction to alcohol or drugs, may eventually take a toll on the body. One husband went to a psychoanalyst because he was suffering severe abdominal pains for which doctors could find no physical cause. On the surface he appeared the typical American success, partner in a large legal firm. He lived in a spacious home in Westchester with sixteen acres of trees and flowers; he had a beautiful, intelligent wife he loved and two gifted children in private schools.

He told his psychoanalyst, "I'm here because of damned abdominal spasms that doctors say are emotionally caused. I've been x-rayed to kingdom come but nothing shows up on the plates."

Then he muttered, "I guess I'm here, too, because I feel that, while I have more than enough money, something is wrong with my life. Much of the time I feel very depressed."

At first he talked only of his severe abdominal pain. Then slowly he revealed details of his supposedly conventional life which turned out to be not so conventional. He told the analyst, "Every Friday I go away for the weekend with some of the boys. We know a series of resorts where we play golf in the summer, or cards in the winter, and then pick up women who are staying at the resort and looking for sexual partners. I spend Friday and Saturday nights having sex with some strange woman, then go home Sunday to the family."

It was a different woman each weekend. He said, "I don't want to get tied to anyone. I'm still in love with my wife and don't expect to leave her. We have sex either Wednesday or Thursday nights. It seems to be enough for her. I need more."

As a bachelor, he had been promiscuous in the same way. He thought marriage would halt the promiscuity but it served as safeguard only for a year, then he was out prowling again. He even had affairs with women clients in his office, locking the door while they had sex on the couch. He also slept with some of the young maids in his home. Occasionally at night he would slip downstairs, ostensibly to enjoy a raid on the refrigerator but actually to have a brief sexual interlude with the maid, who slept near the kitchen. He did not think his wife suspected anything, at least not consciously, for she had never shown any awareness of the real purpose of his midnight meanderings. He tried not to have sex with his secretaries, he told the analyst, because he did not think it was good for the firm's reputation.

During his analysis, his picture of himself as a successful husband, father and business man changed drastically as he began to understand why he was suffering the abdominal pains and why he felt so depressed. This man, who had earned more than a million dollars, was terrified to go places alone, afraid to go out on the street at night by himself. The fantasy that some danger might befall him went back to a deep childhood dependency on his mother, a dependency he had denied over the years, along with a repressed rage at her overprotectiveness. He had been thirteen years old before she allowed him to walk the city streets by himself, so strong her fear a car would strike him.

His father had died when he was seven and his mother had run the large department store owned by her family. He was her only child and he became her whole life. She never married again, often reminded him she had given her entire life to him. When he fell in love and married, she went into a deep depression, as though he had forsaken her and she had nothing left for which to live. He had felt very guilty at falling in love but was determined not to let his mother keep him by her side all his life.

His sexual escapades started early. When he was fourteen, an older girl had enticed him into her bed when he was visiting her house after school, and ever since, on and off, he had been having sex with some woman or other. He told the analyst he felt sexually repelled by men but the analyst pointed out there was a strong homosexual craving in his desire to go away weekends with the "boys," when they all engaged in sex with strange women, sometimes exchanging bed partners of the night before. The analyst explained this was a way of diverting homosexual yearnings vicariously expressed in sharing the woman another man had just possessed.

He also masturbated, he said, to fall asleep on those nights he did not have intercourse with his wife, a maid, a client at the office or a pickup over the weekend. Here was a man who indulged in all the sex he wished, yet was not happy with any woman or himself. He was an addict who engaged endlessly in the sexual act, but with little pleasure and much guilt. His abdominal pains cleared up during the first months of analysis as he started to talk about his sexual activities and realized how much of an obsession they were.

He started to understand his need for continuous sex was an addiction, that he could not claim he loved any of the women and was not even sure he loved his wife. He admitted she was a rather physically and emotionally cold woman, like his mother. His wife seemed not to care whether she ever had sex, but only that he supported her so she could buy elegant clothes and give lavish dinner parties.

As this husband understood the many reasons for his addiction stemming from childhood fantasies and experiences, he was able to stop the weekend trips, the escapades with clients in his office and the seducing of maids. He asked his wife to see an analyst so she might understand her sexual frigidity. Neither wanted a divorce. They were able eventually to give more to each other and to their children, as they could face fantasies and feelings they had denied over the years.

Compulsive sex, like any other addiction, is used to cover a multitude of feelings that are painful and dangerous to self-esteem. It seems easier for the addict to escape into the addiction than take on the difficult task of finding out why he must resort to such extreme measures to get pleasure out of life.

In discussing the promiscuous woman, Dr. Helene Deutsch, in her two-volume *Psychology of Women,* declares that one unconscious reason behind the compulsive drive to be promiscuous is that the woman wants to be a man. She identifies promiscuity with masculinity, since over the ages it has seemed man's right to be promiscuous if he wishes, without allowing this pleasure to women. The promiscuous woman in her fantasy becomes what she believes the independent man is as she refuses to become emotionally involved with one sexual partner.

"Some women boast of this coldness as a proof of strength, others complain of it without realizing that their emotional poverty is a prerequisite for the masculine component of the psyche, which they have accepted," explains Deutsch.

She cites as "an extraordinarily clear example of a conflict between femininity and masculinity" the life of George Sand. Born Aurore Dupin, she married and became Madame Dudevant, but assumed the masculine name "George Sand" as a writer, dressing and acting in masculine fashion. As George Sand she led a promiscuous life and, according to Deutsch, "ruined many men," choosing as lovers "the so-called feminine men." Chopin was one of her "victims."

Deutsch claims that the prostitute, in fantasy, also lives like a man in her aggressive attitude toward society and men. Women traditionally have been expected to respond to the advances of men, rather than initiate sexual activity. But the prostitute initiates, is the aggressor and thus the masculine one in sexual intercourse. (This ties in with the large number of prostitutes who have been molested sexually by men as children and young girls, for "identification with the aggressor" is one of the chief ways of mastering an early trauma, according to Anna Freud. The feeling of being in control, "master of the situation," is a defense against feeling helpless and overwhelmed as in childhood.)

Karen Horney describes the promiscuous woman as in "a flight from womanhood," unable to take on the responsibility of marriage and motherhood. Horney maintains that, to the promiscuous person, sexual relations means "not only the release of specific sexual tensions but also the only way of getting human contact."

If someone has developed the conviction that for him to obtain lasting affection is practically out of the question (because he received so little love from parents), then physical contact may serve as a substitute for emotional relationships. "In that case, sexuality is the main, if not the only, bridge leading to contact with others, and therefore, acquires an inordinate importance," Horney says.

In some men and women the lack of discrimination shows itself in regard to the sex of a potential partner—they will seek relations with both sexes, or passively yield to sexual demands regardless of the sex of the partner, Horney states. Sex distinctions become comparatively unimportant—all the person seeks is emotional contact with "any body" so starved is he for affection, so "bitterly needed" is the brief, affectionate touch.

Horney and other analysts say that promiscuous sexual activity is more an outlet for "psychic tensions" than a genuine expression of the sexual drive. Horney puts it: "Sex is to be regarded more as a sedative than as genuine sexual enjoyment or happiness." It is an expression of what she calls "the neurotic need for affection."

There are different forms of sexual addiction. One wife felt deprived whenever her husband missed a night of sexual intercourse, no matter how tired he was. For twenty years she considered sex part of the evening's routine, like brushing her teeth or combing her hair. She was making a demand he passively accepted, fearing he would lose her if he did not gratify her compulsion. But he expressed his anger in other ways, often castigating her for the unhealthy food she served, the unattractive clothes she wore, the lack of cleanliness in the house, though never about her sexual demands.

Addiction to sex, or anything else, is no accident, stemming from many fantasies. It can be overcome only by a long, hard look at the self and at the purposes addiction serves. It helps to realize that the addiction will only lead to more intense craving, more depression and the likelihood you will never experience the true pleasure of mature love in the sexual act.

There is something unique about sexual desire—it has fascinated, confused, delighted, troubled and obsessed mankind throughout recorded history. No other aspect of human life has given more joy or caused more misery. No other natural bodily and emotional function has been subjected to more divergent means of regulation, given such a profusion of expressions or inspired more powerful fantasies.

This is probably because sexuality in one form or another is a part of every human relationship from the most intimate to the most casual. It affects self-esteem and sense of identity. It is essential to the survival of man and of cultures. Total and permanent sexual anarchy would cause chaos in society, therefore regulations are needed.

Sexuality does not have to be the object of bizarre and destructive fantasies for it is a natural expression of healthy drives. Sex should be approached with pleasure and wisdom even though potentials for limitlessly distorted expressions exist if the early parenting, as we have seen, is harmful.

Sadism, the physical abuse of the partner during the sexual act, is a perversion. The sadist acts out fantasies of hatred in his unresolved mother-infant relationship. He is a frustrated child displaying rage, contempt and a wish to murder toward an ungiving mother. In marriage or sexual affair, the sadist chooses a partner willing to be an object of brutality—abuse the sadist felt but could never inflict back on his mother because as a child he needed her and could not risk alienating her. The one abused in the sexual act, in turn, fantasizes the beatings as punishment for his guilt at his own sadistic wishes. He acts the role of the powerless child he felt he became at the hands of harsh, condemning parents.

There exist what have been described as "sadistically humiliating" parents. Dr. Arnold Rothstein, in his article "Fear of Humiliation," speaks of "the seduction of the humiliator" as a defensive process observed in masochistic characters. He says that "identification with the humiliator" of childhood may be a "central emotion-laden fantasy" in certain people. They possess "fantasies and actions deriving from identification with a humiliating introject"—how the person, as a child, experienced his parents, now images within.

A newly wed woman of twenty-three observed that her handsome husband of thirty was unduly sarcastic in his remarks to his friends and siblings. She also noticed his father showed the same caustic approach to life, realized her husband unconsciously identified with the father who had humiliated him in the same way as a boy.

One act of sadomasochistic sex can be seen as relating to the anger of the anal stage. Some sadists must defecate on the partner before they can be aroused sexually and some masochists must be urinated or defecated upon before they can feel desire. These fantasies are traced to the anger at a mother who harshly tries to control her child's first toilet training. She is the child's original object of desire and if he feels too much anger at her, it will be shown in later life in a fairly direct way.

The sadist defends himself against an assault he fears as he becomes the aggressor. He causes pain on the theory that the best defense is attack. The submissiveness of the masochist masks his unconscious identification with the cruel partner who inflicts the suffering he would like to inflict on those who have hurt him. As punishment for his evil thoughts, he allows the pain to be inflicted on him instead.

One woman told a friend, "I'm bored with the nice, pleasant man who makes no demands on me. I only feel alive when I'm with a man who makes psychic mincemeat out of me. Then I feel at home."

For her, sex had to be tinged with danger and suffering; the men who hurt her turned her on. During her psychoanalysis she realized she felt very guilty because as a girl her father obviously preferred her to her mother and his two sons. As she grew to accept her conflicted feelings about both her father and mother, she avoided sadistic men. She no longer had to punish herself for guilt unknown.

Cruelty and sex are often intimately connected in childhood fantasy. Children at first possess little capacity for tenderness, often express sexual feelings through violence as they slap and hit each other. This is one of their ways of getting close, of establishing contact, even though in an angry way. When adults use cruelty as part of their sexual life, either physical or psychological, they have not advanced beyond childish ways of expressing a need for closeness.

The masochist provokes brutality, placing himself in the role of innocent victim, denying his own drives and thoughts and wishes. He arranges his life so he always appears victimized, not daring to admit he seeks out those who are only too eager to victimize him.

Masochism is strong in women who wish to be men. It is their way of whimpering to the world, through their humiliation, shame and suffering, of telling of the fantasy, "See, I am castrated." One woman remained with a sadistic husband who got drunk and beat her for three years. Then, after therapy, she left him, realizing his brutality was punishment for her many fantasies, including the wish to be a man and have the power that seemed to go with masculinity, as well as for her forbidden incestuous desires.

The sadist must be brutally aggressive, overexaggerating what in normal sexual desire would be manly superiority, because he feels so unmanly. On the other hand, the masochist must play at being passive because he feels his inner rage will destroy him. The sadist is so little a man in his real feelings that he must deny his great dependency on the mother of his childhood. He is unconsciously afraid he will be destroyed by the hated woman who has thrown him off her breast, who has made him feel insignificant, castrated. He feels he will give up what little masculinity he possesses if he does not assert himself to the point of beating her.

He feels he must take whip in hand because he feels so impotent. He can feel like a man only when armed with two penises. The symbolic one he bestows on the woman through the beating, making her in fantasy the phallic mother of childhood. The sadist has never given up the fantasy that his mother lacks a penis since she once had one and it was taken from her because she was "bad" and the same thing may happen to him.

Those who must get sexual release in any other form but heterosexual activity are avoiding the challenge of mature love, too afraid of it. They do not feel psychically strong enough to take responsibility for sexual intimacy with someone of the opposite sex. They are so uncertain about their sexual identity that they feel they cannot cope with the demands, spoken and unspoken, that a person of the opposite sex might make, sexually and emotionally.

Fetishism is another form of denial of fear by the use of an unconscious fantasy. The fetishist harbors a strong fear of and aversion to the female genital—a genital without a phallus. He is uncertain about his own manliness. Thus he reacts with fear at the sight of the female genital. This fear he alleviates by holding on to the fetishistic object that represents the missing female phallus and thereby making himself capable of performing the sexual act without having to be confronted with his dread of castration.

For some men who are not fetishists, the unconscious fantasy of a woman with a phallus seems to fend off the castration anxiety but for the fetishist it becomes necessary in one way or another to make this unconscious fantasy more real. They are compelled to think, see, smell or hold in their hands a symbolic representation of the female phallus of their unconscious fantasy, which represents the fantasied penis.

Freud said the fetish symbolized the penis, not just "any chance penis but a particular, quite special penis that had been extremely important in early childhood but was afterwards lost." The shoe, fur piece, corset, or brassiere or slip, whatever was used as the fetish, necessary for erection and ejaculation, was used, Freud said, to preserve the fantasy that the mother of childhood had a penis. The fetishist had been brought up in such fear of castration that he could never accept the fact that a woman had no penis, and if she could be thus mutilated, then his own penis was endangered.

Often the object that is the fetish is put on the body with foot, finger, penis or nose thrust into it. While retaining his fantasy that a woman has a penis, the fetishist lessens his fear of castration as he uses a compromise object, the fetish, as substitute for the woman's genitals, at the same time holding on to his hatred and fear of female genitals.

Freud suggested that possibly the fetish selected was the last object perceived before a boy's discovery that the woman lacked a penis, such as panties pulled off by the mother before she stood naked in front of him, the final moment in which he could regard her as possessing a penis. Fur pieces, a popular fetish, symbolize pubic hair, Freud said, for it is difficult to tell whether pubic hair conceals a penis. Fetishes may also have an anal quality in that they are often objects that have been used and possess a distinct odor.

The transvestite indulges in a form of fetishism as he dresses like a woman in order to achieve sexual release with either man or woman. When he wears women's clothing, he fantasies he is a woman with a penis and momentarily loses his fear of castration.

The man who can only gain sexual release through rape and the woman who is frigid except under fantasies of rape, both imagine sex to be an act of violence, degradation and shame. This is due, Freud said, to the child's fantasy, as he either watches or hears his parents in sexual intercourse, that his father is assaulting his mother.

The rape of children, a particularly heinous crime, is indulged in by men afraid of their masculinity, who fear the mature woman. Every rapist is afraid of and hates the mother of infancy and inflicts this hatred on his victim, sometimes murdering her so she cannot tell on him. The rapist is often copying the father of his childhood, or other men he saw acting viciously toward his mother, his first image of masculinity.

Certain children respond more easily than others to seduction by a stranger. These children may either have been neglected, long for attention, or they may have been sexually overstimulated by parents and in an effort to release intense, aroused sexual feelings will go easily, even willingly, with a stranger intent on rape.

In some instances of rape, a child could have screamed for help, run away or fought instead of yielding. Dr. Karl Abraham described two different kinds of behavior in little girls who were sexually assaulted. One had been sent into the cellar of her house to get the cellar key back from a workman who had come to fix a water pipe. Before she knew what was happening, the workman tried to sexually attack her. Terrified, she ran upstairs and told her mother what had happened. The mother called the police and the man was arrested.

Another little girl was enticed by a neighbor into the woods. She followed willingly. He attempted to rape her but she managed to break free. She ran home but said nothing to her parents.

Abraham explained the difference between the behavior of the two girls. The one, taken by surprise in the cellar, found herself in a situation she had not sought. The other, yielding to the attraction of doing something forbidden, something she had fantasied, felt guilty, thought of the attack as her fault and thus could not tell her mother. Similarly, the child who is hurt in a game his mother has forbidden him to play will not speak of the hurt or go to the mother for comfort as he normally would.

Some women may have a strong need to be sexually attacked, an unconscious or even conscious wish to be molested, as they deliberately expose themselves to danger. Others do not leave themselves open to attack but imagine it in the privacy of their rooms. They look under the bed each night, fearing a burglar. They are still caught in the childhood wishful fantasy of wanting to possess the forbidden father, steal him from their mother. They project their sexual wish on the man and his desire to seduce them—another example of the projection so dear to the heart of many of us.

Scopophilia, the act of sexual gazing indulged in by a Peeping Tom, is a perversion, as is its opposite, exhibitionism, the desire to display oneself sexually, now a large part of big business in porno movies.

Voyeurs seek a repetition of scenes that once in their fantasy aroused excitement and anxiety—either sexual acts between parents or the sight of the parents' genitals. The voyeur tries to defend against his fear and fascination by endlessly viewing others in sexual acts so he can become aroused. He usually obtains sexual release through masturbation, a childhood form of sexuality.

The exhibitionist tries to reassure himself against fear of castration by showing his penis to the world, as if reassuring himself, "Look, ma, I've got one, you haven't taken it from me." He lives in the days of childhood when, as a little boy, he wanted to show his penis to his mother, for her admiration and approval.

In sublimated form, both voyeurism and exhibitionism are responsible for much of the world's progress and culture. The desire to look, to investigate, leads to scientific advances, journalism and all the professions where curiosity is a necessary quality. The desire to exhibit the self is a motive of those who appear onstage and onscreen, as well as all artists and writers.

Freud pointed out, in discussing the nature of perversions, that the heterosexual uses certain acts in foreplay that could be considered perverse were they not the proper prelude to the act of intercourse rather than an end in themselves. He cited the kiss. The mild "love bite" is another example.

A child's sexual satisfaction is achieved in partial, incomplete gratifications—touching, looking, smelling, exhibiting his body, kissing. But even the kiss may later become what Freud called a perversion if kissing is all two adults do, for fear they cannot go beyond the kiss.

Over the centuries homosexuality has been thought of in most cultures as a perversion but today it is accepted as caused by psychological and/or biological factors. Homosexuality may show a man's fear of the sexual act with a woman, perceived as a castrator.

Freud declared, "Nothing that lies in man is alien to me," and studied the fantasies behind homosexual desire. He described homosexuality as caused by early intense fantasies of the man or woman which had prevented him from reaching the final, or genital phase of psychosexual development. These fantasies drive the homosexual to seek a member of the same sex; he cannot trust anyone whose body is sexually different from his.

One of the fantasies of the male homosexual may be that if he puts his penis into a vagina, it will be cut off. He imagines the vagina as having teeth, dreads what Freud termed the "dentate vagina." The lesbian may be deathly afraid of the fantasy that if the man puts his penis into her vagina she will be killed or maimed by what she believes a murderous weapon.

In the words of Dr. Ludwig Eidelberg, a psychoanalyst: "As a result of traumatic experiences at the first stage of sexual development, the homosexual represses his oral wishes, and the female breast, a powerful sex stimulus for the normal man, then becomes an object of unconscious hate and envy, sometimes hidden by a mask of disgust." This would explain why the homosexual feels the need to caricature women in his walk, gesture and sometimes dress, especially the Mae West type with large bosoms.

To exclude the painful memory of the early lack of love, homosexuals displace the erotic feeling they normally would have for the breast to the penis. "In this way, sucking the penis comes to represent an unconscious satisfaction as well as a denial of the original oral wish, while to have the penis sucked fulfills the urge to play the role of the active, giving, pre-Oedipal mother," explains Dr. Eidelberg.

The homosexual may tell himself, "It is not true that I suffer because I was robbed of love at my mother's breasts. The truth is that I have no interest in breasts and that I get all the pleasure I need from the penis," denying the terrifying earlier unmet need.

Dr. Eidelberg also makes the point that the homosexual, among other fantasies, playing two roles at the same time, selects a partner who represents himself. He can then fantasize he is both himself and the mother with whom he still feels merged. The strong need to act as both the caring mother and the neglected child is clearly seen in each partner of a homosexual relationship.

The power of the unconscious fantasies, first the fantasy of merging with the mother sexually, then the fantasy of being castrated, is such that many a man will be driven to homosexuality in spite of his conscious wish to be heterosexual. Men marry, have children and then, in spite of attempts to deny their homosexual wishes, are driven to homosexuality where they find gratification in the infantile sexual pleasure on which they have remained fixated. Maturing sexually is difficult to do when one has had a complex and conflict-ridden relationship to parents.

Many homosexuals insist they receive greater sexual pleasure than those who indulge in normal sexual intercourse. They defend their way of sex strongly, as they also defend against the emotional torment in their life. They caricature the various stages of sexual development as they make distorted use of mouth, anus and penis. The very caricature tells of the rage within.

Because the homosexual conceals intense anger, he often tries to destroy or humiliate the man to whom he is atttracted. What he believes to be love is often overwhelmed with hate and rage. The injuries inflicted by homosexuals on each other are terrifying, as emergency rooms in city hospitals attest. Rectums are torn with instruments such as broken bottles, bodies beaten and, in extreme cases, the partner is murdered.

The psychoanalysis of homosexuals reveals they are more interested in release of genital desire than in loving anyone and often discharge a far greater hatred against their partners than heterosexuals do. It is paradoxical they use the word "gay" to describe themselves, for their lives are anything but gay—tortured, if examined carefully. This was eloquently depicted in the popular play *The Boys in the Band* where, at the end, the leading man cries out in despair, "Why do I hate myself so?"

Transsexualism, where a man undergoes an operation that removes his penis so he looks more like a woman, "is a keystone for understanding the development of masculinity and femininity in all people." These are the words of Dr. Robert Stoller in *The Transsexual Experiment.*

To lose a penis is not the whole of the threat to castration, Stoller says, for "the penis is only the insignia, the repository of that fundamental of identity, one's sense of maleness. The danger in castration is not organ loss but the far more profound loss of one's sense of existing." He calls the dread of the homosexual as "dread of loss of self," says homosexuality "is not really concerned with what we commonly recognize as genital, erotic homosexuality but with something more primitive—change of sex."

He explained that the "true transsexual" has had no period of masculinity in his life; from infancy on, he has from the start "never prized maleness or masculinity." If we do not separate the purer form of femininity seen in the transsexual, we miss understanding in all males, as Freud did. Stoller says: "the full significance of the symbiosis with the mother and its tidal pull, not just to regression to 'the good breast' but to *being the same as mother,* which would be the destruction of masculinity."

He asks, "Why is there no fear at all of changing sex" in the transsexual? And answers that the change of sex is a threat for any male who has achieved masculinity but no threat for the transsexual in that he has remained emotionally merged with the mother.

Stoller suggests we ought not to define heterosexuality and homosexuality anatomically but rather "according to identity." He maintains: "Anatomy is not really destiny; destiny comes from what people make of anatomy. For the little boy is only anatomically, not psychologically, heterosexual in the first period of his life; that heterosexuality comes only after a massive piece of work, performed with some difficulty and pain. We know of that struggle—separation and individuation—especially from Mahler."

For a boy to advance to the heterosexual state which then becomes the origin of the oedipal conflict he must break from the original, primal symbiosis in which he and his mother are at first merged. He must, as Dr. Ralph Greenson once put it, "dis-identify" from his mother.

"If he and his mother do not set up a reaction in which both willingly (even if at times reluctantly) decide that they will relieve each other's bodies and psyches from the oneness of the womb and the early months of life, then the boy will remain enfolded in his mother," Stoller says. "This will occur not only in a manner that may cripple the development of the usual ego functions, but also the two will be found in a linking of gender identity: the boy will feel himself to be a part of his mother's femaleness and femininity."

He adds there is a conflict built into the sense of maleness that females are spared in that "core gender identity in males is not, as I have mistakenly said, quite so immutable. It always carries with it the urge to regress to an original oneness with mother." The male transsexual does not try to change gender—he has always felt like a woman—only sex, "so that his body will conform to his psyche."

Stoller concludes that homosexuality poses such a threat to males because "deep within, unless well protected by good parental care, the pull toward merging again into mother's femaleness terrifies and enthralls men; it is the Siren's Song." He concludes that transsexualism, "rather than being taken only as a bizarre oddity, is the key test, in fact, the paradigm for Freud's theories of sexual development in both males and females."

The lesbian has received far less study than the male homosexual, possibly because psychoanalysts have treated fewer lesbians than homosexuals. The woman who turns to other women for sexual acts is frightened of men, seeks the safety of the penisless creature, the woman, who is like her mother, with whom she is emotionally merged. She may have the fantasy that she is the man in her mother's life, in her use of some sexual instrument, or her finger or tongue, as symbolic of the penis during sexual acts.

The mother of a lesbian may have encouraged a deep dependency in her daughter, made her feel her mother needed her erotically. The little girl, when an adult, still yearns for a mother to protect and love her even as she may act the part of the man.

The lesbian has never come to terms with her oedipal fantasies. Often her father has left home when she is a baby or growing child and there is no male with whom she can fall in love, shifting love from her mother to her father. She has not learned to play a daughters's role in competing for her father as part of natural sexual development. Since her oedipal conflict remains unresolved she is still a rival with her father for her mother's love and will continue to seek women as love objects, competing with the man, visualizing herself in fantasy as a man among men.

As an adult, she feels it less dangerous to have sex with a woman than a man. Also, many mothers of lesbians dislike and fear men and this comes across clearly to their daughters. The latter receive the strong impression men are to be hated and feared—they are the enemy.

A father may create lesbianism in a daughter if he shows no interest in his daughter and basically ignores her existence. She may then denigrate her femininity, doubt she will be attractive to any man. She identifies with her father's rejection of her and in turn rejects men. Another situation that may promote lesbianism occurs if the father wishes she were a boy. Or if he is overpossessive and intensely jealous of her boyfriends, feels threatened by their presence. This may enhance her fantasy she will lose his love if she dares admire another man.

In turning to women she appeases her father as if saying, "See, I love you alone. Have no fear, I will never, never love another man." By this act she also defends herself against the fear of her sexual desire for her father by regressing to earlier feelings of desire for her mother.

If a mother, out of jealousy, shows extreme disapproval of her daughter's natural yearnings for her father, the girl may give up the idea of desiring a man. On the other hand, a mother, unsure of her husband's love, may provoke her little girl into being seductive to the father, as though to say to him, "See how lovely a daughter I have given you? She is part of me, she came out of me, so you must love me and never leave me." The daughter's guilt at her own natural seductive feelings may be so great she will turn to women later in life for sexual release.

Little girls who sense that their parents never wanted them may have the fantasy that if they only had been born with a penis this would bring love. A little girl who realizes her mother loves her son more than she does her daughter may wish desperately she had a penis and unconsciously act the role of the man in her later sexual relationships with women.

Fathers who wish a daughter had been born a boy unconsciously stimulate in the little girl the desire to be a man, as eloquently pictured in the first book to appear in this country about lesbianism, *The Well of Loneliness,* by Radclyffe Hall.

We could call pornography a perversion. The sexual fantasies in pornography portray the fantasies of childhood, says Dr. Charles Socarides, an authority on homosexuality, in *Beyond Sexual Freedom.* Declaring that pornography ranges from the "mildly suggestive" to the "absurdly exaggerated," he sums up the recurring themes: incest, seductive parental figures, a profaning of the sacred, "supersexed males," "nymphomaniac females," homosexuality (especially lesbian activities), scenes of flagellation in the context of sexual relations, the use of children and animals in sex relations, and the sexual abuse of individuals seen as "low caste," such as blacks and foreigners.

Describing pornography as "the rape of the senses," Socarides says in all defloration scenes there is usually a sadistic element and incestuous relations are portrayed as "frequent and guilt-free." He explains that because pornography encourages sexual relations between members of the same family by removing the barrier of guilt, this is an attempt "in essence to destroy the family." He explains further:

"The incest barrier is the product of thousands of years of evolution culminating in the family unit. Aside from preventing inbreeding of potentially unhealthy genetic combinations, its purpose is to promote family stability, group cohesion and cooperation. It protects children from sexual exploitation, adults from the overwhelming envy of the young, and the young from a wish to destroy parental authority and seize adult privilege.

Freud's brilliant psychoanalytic study *Totem and Taboo* uncovered the profound unconscious significance of incest prohibitions and their vital function in preserving family life and promoting later normal healthy mental functioning."

Socarides maintains that underlying the chronic use of pornography, be it in films or books, lies fear of sex. Fear of sex is not innate behavior, but is a learned behavior that leads to adult inhibitions. Fear arises in earliest childhood, aroused by the prohibitions and intimidations of parents. It results in the development in children of anxiety and fantasies of guilt. On reaching adulthood the person is unable to function in a sexual situation without feeling frightened and guilty.

He seeks ways to circumvent his fear and guilt and simultaneously obtain sexual release. He may gratify his fantasies through pornography to achieve release of sexual tension. Though this in no way solves his sexual problem and may make it worse "in that stronger and stronger doses of pornography may be required to bring about orgasm, with an ultimate failure in performance."

Pornography cannot successfully function as a harmless psychological release or safety valve. It lies in the same category as alcohol and drugs, where deep-rooted fantasies about sex remain strong in the unconscious.

Pornography may portray young women in sexual acts with animals such as dogs or horses. One of the depths of self-degradation is to engage in sexual acts with animals. Kinsey in his famous studies found this occurred quite often in rural areas. During wars overseas our soldiers described how some men from remote regions of our country would seek goats and other animals at night rather than rape children or women.

One man who became a physician confessed that when he was a boy growing up on a lonely farm in Wisconsin he had sought animals rather than seduce his younger sister for whom he felt strong sexual desire.

The sexual urges of childhood normally lead to mature sexual life but they may wind up as permanent way stations along the road to sexual maturity if early childhood fantasies have been too threatening because of cruel or thoughtless parents.

If we wish to know our deepest impulses and fantasies there is no better way than to study our dreams at night. They reveal the memories we have repressed over the years that have led to our most agonizing obsessions and fears.

What can a dream tell us about our fantasies that will enable us to live more at peace with ourself? What kind of fantasies do we find in our night dreams, as distinguished from our daydreams?

7

How Dreams Reveal Our Fantasies

A daydream is defined in Webster's *New World Dictionary* as "a pleasant, dreamy thought; a reverie," a "visionary notion or scheme." There is only one quotation about daydreams in John Bartlett's famous *Familiar Quotations*. It is from *No Mean City* by Simeon Strunsky, a writer and journalist:

"To renew ties with the past need not always be daydreaming; it may be tapping old sources of strength for new tasks."

This is true, as Freud said, for one of the purposes of daydreaming is to help us plan our lives, choose our careers, our loved ones and friends. We have noted that daydreams may occupy as much as half the time of many people, especially when they grow older and have more free time on their hands.

But daydreams do not reveal the fantasies that haunt us over the years, causing needless terror, anger or sexual maladjustment. These deepest fantasies are found only in our dreams at night. Strunsky's quote about "tapping old sources of strength for new tasks" could also apply to our use of dreams to fathom and bring to the surface of our mind our buried fantasies.

Shakespeare once again described a truth about mankind succinctly, accurately and poetically when he wrote, "We are such stuff / As dreams are made on."

Often we do not want to look at "such stuff" because it may be terrorizing, dangerous to our self-esteem. But if we want to live to the

112

fullest awareness of our thoughts and wishes, our dreams will lead to the "right stuff," right because they allow us to know the truth about ourselves.

Dreams reveal our inner fantasies, ones we have carefully shielded from ourselves and others because they flood us with anxious or guilty feelings. Our dreams mirror moments which, if we can understand them, are free of rationalizations and defenses—the shining, if often forbidden, primitive self.

Freud called dreams "the royal road to the unconscious" as he discovered the path that led down that royal road. If we tread that path we may face fantasies we have hidden from the world and ourselves because they do not conform to what civilization expected of us.

We have to be a sort of Sherlock Holmes of the psyche to follow the clues in dreams to our fantasies, for they lead to the revelation of conflicts that have haunted us over the years. In extreme instances, buried conflicts have at times caused men and women to commit murder or suicide.

The idea that fantasies exist in a part of the mind of which we are unaware, a part far more important than the conscious one, has been denied, usually with fervent hostility, by most people ever since Freud showed it to be true. He realized he had dealt the world "a severe blow" because, in effect, he concluded we are *not* masters of our mind. Today a growing number of men and women accept the unconscious as the repository of fantasies deemed dangerous to our self-esteem and sense of identity.

The essence, the purpose of a dream, is the partial outlet of some forbidden wish relating to a sexual or aggressive conflict we believe dangerous. In a dream we may freely express our fantasies of sexual desire and murder, though usually in disguised form so we will not be too horrified or alarmed upon waking.

Our psyche has provided subtle ways of protecting us from consciously knowing the fearful acts and thoughts we dream of. As Arlow says, "It would not be possible to tolerate the strictures placed on the pleasures of our primitive wishes were it not for our ability to abrogate those strictures symbolically at night in our dreams. The dream enables us to get on with living."

A dream is a message from our unconscious, a message that before it reaches our awareness has been censored somewhat by the preconscious, the pathway between conscious and unconscious. The preconscious stands on guard to prevent too shocking a wish from gaining consciousness—a wish such as incest, vengeance on those who have hurt us, or uncounted numbers of sexual partners.

A dream is set off by something we have seen or that has happened to us or we have thought during the previous day which, in our memory, arouses fantasies of earlier years we prefer to forget but which still lie strong within. A dream contains symbolic clues to what still troubles us.

A thirty-two-year-old woman dreamed of a large bright blue rose, woke puzzled as to why she would dream of it. She recalled that the day before she had stopped in front of a department store window, looked wistfully at a shimmering blue satin evening dress, wished she could buy it but thought the price too high. She also noticed a vase of red roses on the floor of the display, thought how beautiful they were.

Her analyst listened to her dreams, helped her interpret them, so she knew if she allowed thoughts about the blue dress and the red roses to surface she would uncover the hidden meaning of the dream. She remembered nostalgically her first party dress in high school: it was bright blue taffeta. She also remembered the excitement with which she had put it on, walked downstairs to show it to her mother and father.

Her father had stared at it, particularly the low-cut neckline, then ordered, "Take it off. I won't have my daughter dressed like a prostitute."

"But daddy, all the girls are wearing low-cut dresses, it's the fashion," she had protested.

"I don't care. You march right upstairs and find another dress."

She wanted to protest, but dared not, fled to her room and burst into tears. She selected a more conservative dress, furious inside, wanting somehow to get even with her father. When her date arrived, he brought her one red rose, her first gift of a flower, and she remembered tears again coming to her eyes. But tears of gratitude, not shame, as she had felt when her father scolded her.

Eighteen years later, the sight of a blue dress in a store window and the red roses had aroused memories of that conflicted evening: one in which, she realized, she wanted to kill her father for his cruelty and also felt love for the young man—she had long forgotten his name—who had shown affection. She had never dared display one moment of anger at her supposedly beloved father but the rage had simmered within over the years. She also realized it was not just this one event but the many times he had not allowed her the freedom to think for herself, made her feel like a wanton, stupid infant. She had never dared stand up for herself and at this too she was angry—at herself for lacking the courage, always feeling the victim.

A dream may hide fantasies of violence and/or sexual desires for the parent of infancy, or a sibling, or a childhood friend. The unconscious sexual cravings that naturally occur during stages of our psychosexual development are the source of fantasies thought wicked or evil instead of accepted as normal for that time of life.

The highly regarded English psychoanalyst, Ella Sharpe, in *Dream Analysis,* describes two typical fantasies that underlie dreams. In one, "The patient dreamt she was a child walking slowly along a corridor in a great mansion. She had heard a great hero had returned from the wars. He was in her bed in one of the rooms. She slightly lifted up the latch of the door and peeped into the room, a palatial room in which the bed was at the far end. She could see the hero sitting up in bed looking very fine and noble. She must get nearer and nearer, and slowly and quietly she tiptoed across the room until she stood at the end of the bed and gazed through the bars at him with adoration."

During the analysis the patient revealed the actual setting of this fantasy came from her memory of a picture in a story book of childhood. The dream showed her as a child struggling with the oedipal conflict, a little girl's love for her handsome hero father, a conflict that needed to be worked on in analysis to be more fully resolved. This fantasy, as reflected in the dream, was the memory of a wish—the girl's desire to possess her beloved father, the man in the bed. The repressed memory slowly came to consciousness many years later: unresolved wishes may reoccur in dreams until the conflict is resolved.

Another dream illustrated not just the wish but also how a current event may act as stimulant for a dream and the fantasies within. A male patient dreamed he stood in a room face-to-face with a wizard. The image of this wizard stemmed from the memory of a childhood book. The man felt the wizard come alive as he told his dream, described the wizard as threatening. He called the wizard a constant enemy of the "prince" and reported that the wizard was finally killed.

The conflict again is of a sexual, oedipal nature, triggered by an incident that occurred the previous night. The man, in helping his wife undress for bed, on impulse lifted up her dress, said playfully, "Hello, bogey." Asked by the analyst what "bogey" meant to him, he replied, "I never thought about this but to a boy a bogey is a spirit, a ghost. I think of my father. I expect he was the wizard in my dream I wanted to kill."

Another man, about to marry, accompanied his fiancée to a department store to find pillows for their new home. That night he dreamed he sat at the kitchen table opposite his late grandfather who sat stooped over, his head on a red pillow. When this man woke, he felt extremely upset.

During his analytic session he thought of a repressed memory as he recalled a painful event in his early life, the details later confirmed by relatives. His father, a member of the Mafia, one evening was called out to the garden for what seemed an innocent meeting with another Mafia member. Instead, his father found himself face-to-face with a hired assassin who promptly shot him in the head. Someone in the family placed a white pillow that turned red under his bloody head, as they all stood in horror watching him die, among them the dreamer, at that time a boy of four.

This was the age he struggled with his oedipal conflict. Part of him wished his father would disappear forever, as he now actually had at the hands of the assassin. The patient at that tender age had been particularly vulnerable to the loss of his father; his fantasy life up to then was filled with the thought of taking over the role of husband to his mother. When he realized his father was dead, he felt terrified, stricken with grief and guilt that his wish had come true. His father had been very important to him, he loved him, recalled days of playing ball with him, riding on his father's shoulders as a boy, temporarily feeling like a king.

Sometimes reality imposes itself and the fantasy of the child comes true with detrimental consequences as he grows up. He tries to resolve a conflict based on a wish that could never be safely relinquished to fantasy. The real event—the killing of the father in an accident, for instance—occurs at a time the boy's thinking is still connected with magically powerful aspects. It is hard for him to shake off the feeling that his father's death had nothing to do with his own wishes.

Commenting on the rapid organization of a dream in response to some external stimulus of the day or night before, Freud noted that there must lie in our mind readily available unconscious fantasies that can be woven instantaneously into the structure of a dream. Psychoanalysts then probe a patient's "screen memories," those that give clues to the painful truth and buried thoughts.

"Although there is much forgetting that is simply forgetting, a rule of thumb is that the more psychodynamically important a memory is, the more prone it is to warping or forgetting altogether," Dr. Theodore Shapiro, psychoanalyst, told Daniel Goleman, columnist in *The New York Times*, for a story on "Memory" published June 23, 1987.

A study of fifty-three women who, as children, had been victims of incest, conducted by Judith Lewis Herman, psychiatrist at the Women's Mental Health Collective in Somerville, Massachusetts, showed that the "earlier, longer and more violent the incest, the more it had been forgotten," Goleman reported.

"Not surprisingly, people's memories are better for the out-of-the-ordinary, special moments of their lives than for the mundane, according to new data on which events survive best in memory," Goleman pointed out. But those "special" moments, if they held fear, anxiety or terror, are the ones deeply hidden in the unconscious, revealed only in our dreams.

The deeper memories are stirred by what Freud called the "day residues," an experience or thought that leads to the ancient conflicts because they stir certain memories clustered around an important fantasy—as the blue dress and red roses awakened the woman's hidden rage at her father.

One woman in analysis spoke of a dream that reflected an authentic memory of a specific event that struggled to reach her consciousness. She described frequent episodes of anxiety when she was hugged or held in place by a seat belt. Her reactions of panic could not be explained by actual events in her current life. Friends and relatives made fun of her strong emotional reaction, called her "silly" to let her fantasies run away with her. It seemed obvious an important memory was forcing itself to the surface of her mind.

To the woman, her feelings while in a car seemed particularly urgent since the new traffic laws required drivers to wear seat belts and she felt this unbearable. She went into a panic when she could no longer get away with not using the belt.

One day she told her analyst of a dream in which a little girl, with whom she felt very identified, was restrained in the arms of a woman in white. A man in white approached, holding a knife. The little girl struggled in vain to get loose. At this the patient woke up from her nightmare in a cold sweat, screaming in fear.

She asked her father if something similar had ever happened to her in childhood. He nodded, confirming her suspicions. He told her that as a three-year-old she had to undergo an operation to remove polyps in the passage of her nose. The anesthesiologist had trouble placing enough ether on the mask over her face for her to inhale. Old-time medical practice did not include preparing children for what they had to go through and he did not explain the purpose of the ether. She tried to elude him, thrashed around until he had to call a strong, powerful nurse to take the little girl on her lap, hold her down with an iron grip until he had finished his task.

As an adult she experienced the fear of what she believed an assault, as well as her own desire to destroy the doctor and the nurse as defense in a situation in which she felt endangered and utterly helpless. It was natural for her to want to "attack" adults who had shown a lack of empathy and understanding of what she endured.

As a result of analyzing the dream, she could now get in touch with her feelings of complete abandonment by her parents who, in her fantasy, were uncaring and unprotective since they allowed her to go through the painful procedure without coming to her rescue. It is difficult for children to perceive frightening and painful medical treatments as helpful. The experience may leave emotional scars or express itself in symptoms when the conflict is impossible for the child to resolve—in this case the conflict of being "a good, submissive little girl or a fighter for her life." The analysis of this dream led to complete recovery from the symptoms of anxiety this woman suffered most of her life. She lost her fear of being hugged (in fantasy, restrained by the powerful nurse) and she could now fasten her seatbelt without fear.

Dreams not only serve the purpose of revealing fantasies and wishes we think taboo but also function to prolong sleep, Freud said. Grotjahn points out in *The Voice of the Symbol* that the dream "also tries in a symbolic way, almost playfully, to offer solutions to conscious and unconscious conflicts with the help of the symbol."

He calls "our nightly regression into sleep and dreaming," a "kind of mental death and rebirth. With the help of symbol formation and its creative integration, we lay the groundwork for the solution of our conflicts. The symbol stands in the middle, between unconscious wish and conscious integration."

As Grotjahn puts it: "In our dreams we return to the unsettled questions of the day, which are connected with the unsettled conflicts of former days. In the dream we try to solve them. . . . The dreamer will return to this dream problem repeatedly until it is solved; this repetition is not masochistic—it is an attempt at symbolic mastery. It is the model example of symbol integration which demonstrates the use of the symbol as a technique of integrating outer and inner world."

People of the prehistoric past tried to deal by magic-mystic rituals and symbols with the uncertainties of their lives, with the struggle among themselves and within themselves, and with the cosmic events in their natural environment, he pointed out. He added that the child and the adult of our time try to do the same in sleep.

If we observe a child during sleep, even during the first year of life, he seems to be experiencing many fantasies and feelings. He smiles, he cries out, he shows satisfaction, joy, frustration, anxiety, "and sometimes even horror," Grotjahn says. He adds, "It is not surprising to see an infant so hard at work in his sleep. A whole new world has to be mastered slowly."

To understand the voice of the symbol, "we must listen to its expression in the individual dreamer and to its unifying theme in the course of the history of human ideas," he maintains. He calls the analysis of the myths of mankind "the road to the symbolic language of mankind through the ages."

A dream is an important message to ourselves which we have to decode if we want to understand it. Reuben Fine in *The Development of Freud's Thought* says *The Interpretation of Dreams,* published in 1900, is universally regarded as Freud's greatest work. Freud later wrote that the book contained "the most valuable of all the discoveries it has been my good fortune to make. Insight such as this falls to one's lot but once in a lifetime." (This appeared in his special preface to the English edition of 1932.)

On the first page of the book Freud challenges his colleagues: "Anyone who has failed to explain the origin of dream images can scarcely hope to understand phobias, obsessions, or delusions, or to bring a therapeutic influence to bear on them." In a chapter, "The Analysis of a Specimen Dream," he uses a dream of his own to show how to interpret a dream. He explains that to understand a dream the dreamer's "associations," or thoughts in connection to the content of the dream, are needed. They lead to the hidden meaning of the dream.

In the chapter, "A Dream Is the Fulfillment of a Wish," (and if there is a wish, there is a fantasy, or several fantasies behind it) Freud says: "The more one is concerned with the solution of dreams, the more one is driven to recognize that the majority of the dreams of adults deal with sexual material and give expression to erotic wishes." He was later to add the aggressive wishes as equally important.

In another chapter, "Distortion in Dreams," Freud makes a distinction between the "manifest" and the "latent" content of the dream. The manifest content is the story of the dream as it appears to the dreamer. The latent content is the deeper meaning of the dream as revealed through the person's free associations. Between the manifest and the latent content "is seen the interplay of two forces, the *wish* which is striving to break through into consciousness and the *censorship* which seeks to restrain this wish from doing so," Fine explains. This contrast constitutes elaboration of Freud's first fundamental hypothesis about neurosis involving a defense against unbearable fantasies.

During psychoanalysis, men and women find that as they can understand the meaning of a dream they are slowly able to face an undercurrent of repressed wishes and fantasies for which they have felt guilty. Subjected to the light of reason these fantasies then are seen as part of normal childhood feelings.

Hallucinations and visions that occur in waking states also are linked with repressed memories that break through openly. Fine remarks, "This suggests that in dreams too the transformation of thoughts into visual images results from memories. Hence arises the view that the dream is a substitute for an infantile scene modified by transference to recent material. The infantile memory can not be revived directly, and must therefore be satisfied to return as a dream. Thus dreaming is a regression to childhood, a revival of the instinctual impulses which dominated childhood, and of the methods of expression that were then available."

Freud wrote that "all the material making up the content of a dream is in some way derived from experience, that is to say, has been reproduced or remembered in the dream" but that dreams "yield no more than *fragments* of reproductions." He added that there are exceptions in which a dream repeated an experience with as much completeness as is attainable by our waking memory. He cites as example how one of his university colleagues reported a dream that reproduced in all its details a dangerous carriage accident he had once endured, with an almost miraculous escape.

It may happen, Freud explains, that some fantasy or memory occurs in the content of a dream which, when we awake, we do not recognize as forming a part of our knowledge or experience. We remember dreaming about the event but we cannot recall when or even whether we experienced it in real life. We feel in doubt as to the source that has been drawn upon by the dream, are tempted to believe "dreams have a power of independent production." But then, often after a long interval, some new experience recalls the lost memory of the event in the dream and reveals the source of the dream, the fantasy it has protected. "We are thus driven to admit that in the dream we knew and remembered something which was beyond the reach of our waking memory," Freud says.

He cites the example of a Swiss colleague, a philosopher, who, in a dream, saw the courtyard of his house covered with snow under which he found two small lizards half-frozen. As a lover of animals, he picked up the lizards, warmed them, carried them back to the little hole in the masonry where they belonged. He also gave them a few leaves of a small fern that grew on the wall, which he knew they were fond of eating. In the dream he knew the name of the plant: *Asplenium ruta muralis.* The dream then returned to the lizards, He saw to his astonishment two new ones busy eating the remains of the fern. He looked into the hole in the wall; it was filled with a procession of lizards, all moving in the same direction.

When he awoke, he thought that though he knew the Latin names of very few plants, *Asplenium* was not among them. To his great surprise he confirmed the fact that a fern of this name actually existed. Its correct name was *Asplenium ruta muraria,* slightly distorted in the dream. He wondered how he had acquired knowledge of the name of the fern.

He forgot the dream until sixteen years later when he visited a friend. He saw a small album of pressed flowers, sold to foreigners in parts of Switzerland as mementos. He suddenly remembered his dream, opened the herbarium, found a picture of the *Asplenium* of his dream. To his amazement he saw its Latin name written underneath the picture *in his own handwriting.* He then recalled that two years before his lizard dream, the sister of his friend had visited him on her honeymoon carrying the album, as a gift to her brother. The philosopher had taken the trouble to write the Latin name under each dried plant at the dictation of a botanist.

Returning home after his visit, he looked at an old volume of an illustrated periodical to which he subscribed, found a picture of a procession of lizards similar to the ones appearing in his original dream.

Freud does not go into further associations by the philosopher that revealed the hidden meaning of the dream. We do not know the event or thought of the day before that stimulated the fantasy behind this dream.

But the fact that the dreamer recalled his friend's sister, who visited him "on her honeymoon" so he could write the Latin name under each dried plant, is one clue. He may have had thoughts about this young woman, perhaps wished it were he going on the honeymoon with her, possessing her sexually. The two small "lizards" in the dream, then a procession of lizards eating up his fern, might refer to new babies that would soon be streaming out of her, and he may have wished he were the father of these "hungry" creatures. Little animals often symbolize babies or siblings.

Describing how swiftly a dream floats away in the morning after waking, Freud said, "the world of the senses presses forward and at once takes possession of the attention with a force which very few dream-images can resist. . . . Dreams give way before the impression of a new day just as the brilliance of the stars yields to the light of the sun." But even if a dream seems instantly forgotten, it may be recalled during the day if its content is touched upon "by some chance perception."

Our dreams appear essentially in images, though words may be spoken. We create ideas in dreams, as we do when awake. One woman of forty-eight, about to change jobs, dreamed she was lost in a desert, her car and her money stolen. In a panic she plowed through the sand looking for help. She came upon two tough-looking men, was at first frightened, thought they might kill her. Then she appealed to them, saying, "I have lost my car, my wallet, everything. Will you help me?" She had the feeling that this was her last resort, there was nothing else she could do but beg them to return her to civilization. She woke as the two men started toward her in what she thought a friendly approach.

She was in therapy, told the dream to her analyst, saying, "I was in deadly fear of these two villainous men. I was afraid they might be bank robbers and would hurt me. I had no way to fight them off but if they didn't help, I would die."

In thoughts connected to the dream she spoke first of feeling the day before a mourning for her father, who had died four years before on that very day. She laughed as she said to the analyst, "I always felt about my father that I had no way to fight him back, as I felt about the robbers in the dream, but also that if he hadn't helped me out in life I would have died." She also remembered on the day she had learned of his death telling her best friend as tears streamed down her cheeks, "Now who is there left who will love me?"

She had felt abandoned, as she did in the dream, by everyone. The dream contained her wish and fantasy that she would find not one but two fathers as she felt lost, deprived of car, of money, of the strength to find her way home. She felt so emotionally destitute without her father that she even risked death to try to find some solace, some solution to her loneliness and sense of abandonment now that he was gone forever.

As Freud said, dreams "hallucinate." They replace normal thought by hallucinations, both visually and in the words used. The transformation of ideas into hallucinations is not the only respect in which dreams differ from thoughts in our waking life. Dreams may construct a "situation" out of images, overdramatize an event in our life that happened to us as children, that seemed catastrophic at the time.

We seem in a dream, as Freud put it, "not to *think* but to *experience;* that is to say, we attach complete belief to the hallucinations. Not until we wake up does the critical comment arise that we have not experienced anything but have merely been thinking in a peculiar way, or in other words, dreaming. It is this characteristic that distinguishes true dreams from day-dreaming, which is never confused with reality."

Plato in his *Republic* said that the best men are those who only *dream* what other men *do* in their waking life. In a sense what we are forbidden to do in waking life—have sexual intercourse with our first loves (our mother, father, siblings), murder anyone we hate—we may dream without paying the price of punishment. In dreams, no matter how viciously we act, how many taboos we break, how much we may hurt those we supposedly love, we are never punished, though we may wake feeling guilty.

Dr. Hyman Spotnitz in *Psychotherapy of Preoedipal Conditions* calls dreams "the royal road to the preoedipal conflicts." He maintains the fantasies in our dreams stem from the earliest years of our life, they are the well from which we draw all dreams.

He says: "Psychoanalysts now find it easy to define the unconsciousness as the repressed content of the mind and tend to forget Freud's early definition of the unconscious as the sum of the preverbal period," meaning the "cognitive functions that use thinking to process the early infantile visual impressions."

Spotnitz points out that while in Freud's self-analysis he concentrated on his oedipal conflicts, a closer examination of Freud's dreams corroborates his theory that later conflicts appearing in dreams "disguise the emotional experiences of the first three years of life that provide the impetus for creating the dream." These experiences contain many fantasies about the mother, the father and the siblings.

Spotnitz maintains that when analysts tackle the disguised meaning of dreams, they encounter the same difficulty Freud and other psychoanalysts encountered "in taking the giant step from repressed verbal memories to never-verbalized early impressions." He explains, "It is understandable why analysts as well as patients find it so difficult to look at the hidden meaning of dreams."

In an early (1898) letter to his close friend, Dr. Wilhelm Fleiss, Dr. Spotnitz says, "Freud described his own unconscious as ugly. But, as he pointed out, he was not unique: if everyone could get in touch with the wishes that hide within the depths of the unconscious, we'd find out that people aren't really evil, but that this material does come from a period of life when we're helpless and dependent and are feeling that we cannot cope with the experience we are having."

Spotnitz also reports in *Treatment of the Narcissistic Neuroses,* written with Phyllis W. Meadow, psychoanalyst, that patients will recall directly, or in the symbols of the dream or fantasy, the unconscious craving of early childhood for the parent of the opposite sex. He says it is important for analysts to help patients recognize their destructive fantasies and wishes for "as their terror of speaking of destructive urges gradually diminishes they lose their toxic quality." When someone allows himself to voluntarily dwell on outlawed feelings, such as thoughts of violence and revenge, and finds he may do so without needing to act on them, he loses his fear of these feelings and thoughts and the "toxoid responses" end.

If we want to understand the fantasies of the deepest layers of our personality, the most direct route is to study the complex content of dreams, revealing the ancient conflicts and fantasies. Spotnitz points out one of Freud's earliest discoveries was that through condensation a number of wishes may be combined in one dream. This layering of wishes led Freud to the theory that our earliest wishes—those predating rational thought—provide the driving force for the creation of dreams and that unraveling the mystery of dreams required a method by which visual imagery could be translated into language. As Freud began to understand the structure of the dream, he realized the dreamer could condense wishes from various times of his life into one wish, many situations into one situation, or reverse an emotion into its opposite.

Freud's self-analysis revealed the conflicts that later developed from emotional experiences during his first three years of life. He traced the train phobia he suffered throughout life to the traumatic separation from his homeland at three. Spotnitz noted, "It is interesting to speculate whether Freud's death by cancer of the jaw could have been averted if he had fully worked through his depression and its connection with his early history. For example, we know from his associations that his brother Julius, born when Freud was a year old, died a year later. We also know that shortly after Julius' death, Freud fell from his chair, splitting open his jaw, and that this injury led [in later years] to major surgery."

One of the most important fantasies in our life is the "rescue fantasy," often appearing in dreams. Phyllis Meadow, coauthor with Spotnitz of the book mentioned earlier, described a twenty-two-year-old attractive young woman patient as characteristic of someone traumatized during "the preverbal attempts to acquire the necessary maturational experiences for growth," which occur in the first year of life. This woman seemed "physically tense and inhibited, somewhat sullen and accusing." She reported feeling controlled by others, complained that this confused and frightened her.

She told Meadow she would like to be in control of what happened to her, she wanted to be with people without pretending or trying to live up to an image. She stated she usually avoided involvement because it was too difficult, saying, "When I can't be perfect, I just go around all day trying to disappear." She confessed she was frigid in sexual relationships though she had repeatedly achieved orgasm in masturbation since the age of twelve.

She revealed her first years had been spent in a midwestern city with a brother three years older, a mother who worked and a father who left his family when she was two-and-a-half-years old.

She remembered she always had an active fantasy life, spent many hours every day making up exchanges between two imaginary characters, "bad Mary" and "good Carol." Mary teased and tormented Carol, who tried to think of ways of rescuing herself. At the age of five, she started to listen to the Lone Ranger, a radio serial about a masked hero. His voice came through an echo chamber that sent a chill down her spine as he asked the listener to return with him to yesteryear.

Her new fantasy expressed all her longings for someone she could love, all her fears were expressed in the dangers that befell the Lone Ranger. In her rescue fantasies, she saved him from death and disaster. As Dr.

Meadow put it: "With herself in the role of the good mother, life was tolerable." The young woman's striving for perfection in fantasy put her above and away from others and it was a way of saying, "I can shake off bad thoughts."

We all have fantasies, both in night dreams and daydreams, of being rescued from the pain of the past. The rescuer acts out his own rescue fantasies, telling of what he wished someone would do for him. Those who try to save others from death and disaster reveal their longing for mothering. Many a child also becomes a rescuer in later life because his mother in fantasy expected him to rescue her from her unhappy existence. As an adult he plays the role of the nurturing mother.

Many seek the reverse, hope they will find someone to rescue them from the pain of the past, a substitute for the fantasied mother or father of childhood (symbolized in the title of the famous Gershwin song, "Someone to Watch Over Me.") As soon as such a person succeeds in finding someone he believes a rescuer but no rescue takes place, he feels cheated, disillusioned and breaks off the relationship.

Psychoanalysts have to guard against their fantasy of rescuing a patient from his torment. The patient in turn arrives with fantasies of cure, expecting the analyst to rescue him immediately, an impossible goal. The patient rescues himself, using insights the analyst provides as the patient learns to trust someone for the first time in his life.

Psychoanalyst Dr. Harold Searles has written extensively on how the patient at times wishes to rescue the analyst, sensing his conflicts. Dr. Sander Abend in "Unconscious Fantasies and Theories of Cure" maintains patients frequently have their own thoughts about how psychoanalysis works, based on unconscious wishes and fantasies persisting in the patient's mind since childhood. These fantasies of cure stem from the very conflicts that caused the symptoms for which the patient seeks relief, he explains.

Another psychoanalyst, Dr. Herman Nunberg, points out that while the patient consciously wants relief from unconscious conflicts that have caused him to suffer, at the same time he wants the treatment to fulfill the fantasies and wishes underlying his conflicts. Fantasies and wishes that have been strong over the years die hard, only after an awareness of the unreality of their powerful influence.

Arlow, in "Theories of Pathogenesis," cites one man, an only child, whose analysis clearly showed "the pervasive and destructive effects of an unconscious fantasy that he was responsible for the fact that he was an only child." As a boy, when he saw other families with many children, he congratulated himself on the good fortune of being an only child, not having to suffer the competition and deprivation siblings bring. But when no other child appeared, he felt it was the magic of his wishes that had destroyed the potential siblings, developed "a tremendous burden of guilt" and much of the torment he later felt stemmed from this unconscious fantasy.

In a study of the theories of the production and development of the individual's personality, Arlow noted how often the mother was blamed for a person's later unhappiness and difficulties, saying, "she is the current version of the villain in pathogenesis," blamed as the cause of all fantasies that make him suffer. He added it was not his intention to "minimize the true trauma that mothers can inflict upon children in the earliest phases of life," such as the totally detached mother or the depressed mother who neglects a child, fails to feed it, permits it to cry incessantly, or the battering mother. But he warned, analysts may "fall prey to the temptation of sympathetic rather than empathic identification with the patient."

He explained that the strong instinctual drives of the child and the developing relationship to his mother are "inextricably intertwined," that there is a "multiple determination of psychopathology, including factors which, to this day, we probably appreciate much too little." He mentioned Freud's statement that neurosis is part of the fate of man as a member of civilized society, "as a fundamental contradiction between his biological nature and the demands of culture."

Sharpe's words about the importance of coming to grips with the significance of dreams show how vital it is that we gain clarity about our conflicts so we may function in the most constructive way throughout our life. Sharpe advises: "Analysis of dream content, liberation of affect, [emotion] and conscious understanding render possible the operation of these innate processes over wide tracks of the psychic life to the advantage of the psychical ego in reality. Only by effective displacement and symbolization on the external world is sublimation possible.

"The breaking up of dreams in the process of psychoanalytic technique is one of the processes that enables the inner psychological forces to bring about a new synthesis. In calling the technique psychoanalysis we lay stress upon the technician's art. Tacitly, however, we acknowledge that the new synthesis is brought about by the forces within the psyche itself. The recuperative powers lie within. The technician by analysis removes whatever stultifies them."

She tells us eloquently how understanding the fantasies expressed in our dreams can be helpful until the end of our life as a way of coming to terms with our inevitable death. An eighty-one-year-old woman who had suffered most of her days from various illnesses had a dream three days before she died that proved a consolation to her in facing death. It reflected her hopeful, positive attitude in life. After relating the dream to her daughter, she did not regain consciousness. She had said, "I saw all my sicknesses gathered together and as I looked they were no longer sicknesses but roses and I knew the roses would be planted and that they would grow."

What are the fantasies of fury and revenge that can become so intense they go beyond mere dreams and drive some to actual murder? And the fantasies of distorted sexual impulses from earlier stages of development that can lead parents or other caretakers to seduce a child sexually?

8

The "Revenge" Fantasy

Our society is not as permissive of the expression of fantasies of rage and vengeance as it is of fantasies of an erotic nature, and rightfully so. Seldom does an erotic act, even if inflicted against a person's will, end in his death, except in certain rape cases.

Most men and women carry on their daily work, live in fantasy without exploding in the fury that ends in the death of a real or imaginary enemy. They consign their rage, along with those fantasies they prefer to forget, to the caretaker of forbidden thoughts and feelings—the unconscious part of the mind.

But unfortunately there are those who act out their fantasies when they become unbearable. For instance, three days before Christmas, 1987, Edward Brenta, a construction worker, forty-two years old, shot his wife Judith and his two young daughters in the head, killing all of them. He then set the house he once shared with his family in Long Island City on fire, killed himself with the .25-caliber handgun. His estranged wife, living in the house they once shared, was seeking a divorce, had taken out a protection order against her "troubled" husband.

Three months earlier the nation was shocked by the murder of six-year-old Elizabeth Steinberg, ostensibly the adopted daughter (though there never had been a legal adoption) of Joel Steinberg, a New York City lawyer. It is alleged he had been physically abusing the girl for years before he struck her head with a fatal blow. She had lived from birth in his Greenwich Village apartment with him and his live-in woman friend, whom, it is alleged, he also physically abused over the years.

We all have to cope with what Freud called the two opposing forces in the mind—the life instinct, or love, and the death or destructive instinct of hate. Love, operating under the drive of our erotic fantasies and feelings, at times became fused with the destructive instinct but, by and large, opposed it. When the destructive instinct became too fused with the sexual, the result was the perversion he called sadism. If extreme erotic feelings were present in violent acts, this he called "sexualized aggressiveness." If violent feelings were present in sexual acts, this was "aggressivied sexuality."

Freud admitted in 1930 in *Civilization and Its Discontents:* "I can no longer understand how we could have overlooked the universality of non-erotic aggression and destruction, and could have omitted to give it its due significance in our interpretation of life."

He also wrote: "The afflictions of mankind flow *not* from the frustration of his sexual drive . . . as I, at first, thought—but from man's ineradicable aggressiveness, his destructiveness, his persistent malevolence. I have called it malevolent and destructive, and so it certainly appears when not sufficiently cloaked or fused with those loving and constructive tendencies, the love of human beings for one another and for their children, homes, pets and hobbies and possessions as manifestations of a fundamental constructive force."

Theodor Reik, who was analyzed by Freud, quotes Freud as stating that if we are judged according to our unconscious fantasies and wishes we are, like the primal men, " a gang of murderers." This appeared in Reik's book *Curiousities of the Self: Illusions We Have about Ourselves.*

We all have fantasies of killing those who hurt us in any way. Some are conscious fantasies, others, unconscious. The wish to kill when we are attacked, physically or psychologically, is a wish over which we have no control as the unconscious reacts automatically in the interest of self-preservation. What Reik describes as "murder by thought."

He adds, "The man who has never had murderous thoughts in his life should be on display in Macy's window."

The first law of our unconscious is undoubtedly: "Protect thyself, body and mind, from any assault, this before all other considerations." This unconscious law, under which we all operate in childhood (and many in adulthood unless they know themselves well), holds "the wish is the same as the deed," as pointed out in an earlier chapter. This law causes us to feel unnecessary guilt until we consciously can realize the wish is *not* the same as the deed.

The murderer lives in a world powered by early fantasies of hate. He is obsessed by thoughts of getting revenge. We all use our aggressive drive in temperate form for our activities; it is the motor force of our behavior. But the murderer's aggressive drive overwhelms all feeling of caring, love, tenderness as they propel him on his strongest mission in life—REVENGE.

This mission is launched in childhood when he feels hatred in strong doses administered by his mother or father or both. The hatred of a parent for a child and the effect on the child was mentioned by Freud in 1931 in his paper *Female Sexuality*. He described the early attachment of a daughter to her mother as closely connected to the cause of the daughter's neurosis and speculated that excessive dependence on the mother held "the germ of later paranoia."

He described this "germ" specifically as "the surprising, yet regular, dread of being killed (?) devoured by the mother" (the question mark is Freud's). This dread of the mother may, he said, arise from an unconscious hostility on the mother's part which the child senses.

If we develop normally, our fantasies of parricide or matricide as part of the oedipal phase do not possess us as they do the child whose fantasies may later lead to the killing of others. The murderer has suffered extensive emotional and/or physical abuse in childhood and never had a chance to accept his rage and use it as a positive force in his life. Most murderers as children suffered an overwhelming fear of parents who felt murderous toward them. This is shown not only by many studies but by such books as Truman Capote's *In Cold Blood* and Norman Mailer's *The Executioner's Song*.

Professor Flora Rheta Schreiber also captures this early trauma in her eloquent book *The Shoemaker*, the story of a man who, as a child, was tortured physically and emotionally by his foster parents. As an adult he heard the voice of God instructing him to kill mankind—his fantasies as a child that encompassed the way he believed his parents felt toward him and his wishes of vengeance toward them.

Because our conscience is partly unconscious, it is apt to demand punishment even for a guilty wish not carried into action. If we become aware the fantasy is not the act, we can free energy attached to the guilt, use it for love, work and creativity.

Our guilt runs high when a parent dies. The child, no matter what age, blames himself for the death of a parent because of his many earlier wishes related to competition or revenge. One man of forty, at his father's death, moaned, "It's all my fault. I could have kept him alive if I had been nicer. Didn't hate him at times because I thought he was too dictatorial."

At certain times in our development we are particularly sensitive to the loss of a beloved one, as during the oedipal phase where the fantasy of wishing the parent of the same sex were gone forever predominates. We fantasize how wonderful it would be to do away with the competition in our love for the parent of the opposite sex.

A woman, depressed, forlorn and at a loss what to do with her life told her analyst in a trembling voice about a childhood trauma. Her mother had died from cancer. As a young girl she had witnessed her mother withering away for three years, fighting a losing battle. The daughter had been deeply attached to her father and when her mother was ill, the daughter dressed in her mother's clothes, fantasized she was enjoying her father's company as a wife would. In the dark of night she had even ventured out of the house in her mother's high-heeled shoes, imagined she was going to a party with her father.

When her mother died she was overcome with guilt not only because her oedipal wish had come true but also anger at her mother for dying—a mother is supposed to take care of her children, not abandon them. She walked the streets searching for her mother, so engrossed in fantasies of finding her and bringing her home that she even approached a few women, thinking they were her mother until she quickly realized they were strangers. She recalled how, as a child, she would dream she visited a strange house where her mother lived but her mother would not return home with her. She then ran home to her father, begged him to bring her mother back but he would not grant her wish. She slowly accepted her aggressive feelings toward her mother and the fact that they did not cause her mother's death.

Reik alludes to the ancient superstitious belief in the omnipotence of evil wishes, such as the fantasy of the "evil eye." Reik asks, "Do we not speak of 'shooting glances' at someone, and of 'murderous glances'?" He quotes from Oscar Wilde's *The Ballad of Reading Gaol,* one stanza of which starts, "Yet each man kills the thing he loves," and ends, "the coward does it with a kiss / The brave man with a sword!"

Reik also refers to the fantasy of death in the expressions "He made a killing in the stock market" and "killing time." He says it is undeniable such phrases reveal the undercurrent of some violent fantasy that pertains to the stock market and to time.

Let us recall that Freud theorized that the roots of murder lie "in the nursery." The child first becomes terrified of the person in authority who frustrates his wishes and needs. The child feels and is, in reality, helpless, not equipped to cope with what he perceives as an annihilating adult.

As he grows, he may have a destructive mother who brings out destructive fantasies in him. A thirty-five-year-old man recalled he had been beaten by his mother when she caught him masturbating at the age of six. He told his analyst, "When I felt sexually aroused as a boy I imagined my mother would cut off my genitals. The way I felt when she beat me for masturbating. She didn't want me to get pleasure from my body. I hated her for this, I thought it was evil of her for making me feel that way."

This fantasy made it difficult for him later in life to feel sexually free with a woman. He could have an erection but not an ejaculation. As during the analysis he understood his murderous rage at his mother because of her abnormal fear of anything sexual, he felt more of a man, fell in love, married.

A young child does not know a fantasy is just a fantasy and lacks the power to cause damage to anyone. A child believes in the power of the magical wish; his ability to judge reality is somewhat shaky. Therefore, a fantasy can cause intense guilt. But as the child grows he realizes fantasy can be a safe way of dealing with aggression—both his own and that of others.

There is vast difference between assertiveness, which we need even to rise from our bed in the morning, and aggression fired by hatred which, in the extreme, can lead to murder. Even Freud had difficulty explaining the various aspects of aggression. He wrote Marie Bonaparte, psychoanalyst and close friend, in 1937, saying he would "try" to answer her question about the nature of aggression.

He started off explaining, "all activities that rearrange or effect changes are to a certain extent destructive and thus redirect a portion of the [aggressive] instinct from its original destructive goal. Even the sexual instinct, as we know, cannot act without some measure of aggression. Therefore in the regular combination of the two instincts there is a partial sublimation of the destructive instinct."

He added we may regard "curiosity, the impulse to investigate," as a complete sublimation of the aggressive or destructive instinct: "Altogether in the life of the intellect the [aggressive] instinct attains a high significance as the motor of all discrimination, denial and condemnation."

We all repress aggressive impulses such as the wish to maim or murder. Primitive man gave in freely to these impulses but we pride ourselves we have come a long way since the day when, at the mere thought of destroying an enemy, man did so.

When we have a destructive fantasy or feel a destructive emotion one of three things may happen. The fantasy or emotion may remain as it is, wholly or in part, and we act on it, even unto murder. Or it may change into anxiety as we repress the fantasy in an unconscious act. Or we may become aware of it, then consciously suppress it so it no longer troubles us.

The emotion or wish that we repress does not die, it remains alive in our unconscious where its repression demands the constant expending of energy. Psychic energy holds back the original emotion, preventing it from bursting to the surface of the mind. As we succeed however in bringing a repressed idea to consciousness—one of the goals of psychoanalysis—we no longer need to waste psychic energy as guard for the repressed idea. Which means we have that much more energy left for living and loving.

Repression is a child's way of trying to handle an unpalatable, intolerable feeling or fantasy. A child hurls a dangerous wish out of consciousness without thought, not yet capable of reason. The adult is supposed to be able to accept or reject a fantasy or wish after thinking it over, using intelligence and judgment to reach a conclusion. If a child has either repressed destructive fantasies too severely too early in life because of punitive parents, or not learned to repress enough because of indulgent parents, the development of reason and judgment is apt to be impaired.

Repression includes both the denial of the fantasy or dangerous wish, and also the thoughts that surround the fantasy. If, for instance, a child has been brutally beaten by a father, he first fantasizes revenge—the natural reaction to brutality—then is apt to forget his powerful wishes for revenge so he can keep his father's love, such as it is, which is better than no love at all.

Repression proceeds from the part of our mind, our ego, that deals with self-respect, Freud explained. One man's repression may be another man's deed in that one man may kill his wife when she threatens to leave him while another may repress his wish to kill her and turn to drinking or another woman.

An extreme result of repression is seen in the act of a little boy who choked his cat to death, much to the horror of his parents. They took him to a therapist and the boy at first spoke enthusiastically of how much he idolized his mother and father. But after a few months, murderous fantasies against what he felt were abusive parents, started to escape from the boy's lips in the therapist's office. He had repressed violent wishes to kill his parents, who had physically and emotionally abused him as he grew up, locking him in a closet when he misbehaved, humiliating him in front of his peers. He carried out his murderous wishes on the unfortunate cat. In their behavior toward animals and insects, children often betray how they feel about their parents.

This satisfaction of a fantasy, even the impulse to kill someone who has hurt us, is pleasurable. Our first wish is always to satisfy an impulse. But if we did, we would often come in conflict with parents and society, so we learn to repress the fantasy, the wish and the deed, especially the aggressive ones.

The repressed impulse then gains illusory power. This is a result of the extra energy required to dam the impulse in the unconscious and the lack of satisfaction of the impulse, which keeps crying out for satisfaction, if not fully, then partially, or in indirect manner.

Some resort to suicide as an expression of their rage against a parent. This became clear in a case in Miami reported by Jon Nordheimer in *The New York Times* on October 23, 1987. An expert on suicide testified that Theresa Jackson, forty years old, the defendant in an unusual trial, accused of mentally abusing her daughter in ways that led to her suicide, had created a psychological climate that forced her seventeen-year-old daughter, Tina Mancini, to take her mother's .57-caliber Magnum pistol, place it in her mouth and pull the trigger.

The psychiatrist, Dr. Douglas Jacobs, director of the Suicide Education Institute of Boston and an authority on suicide, told reporters he knew of no other criminal case in which a "psychological autopsy" of a suicide victim was introduced in court.

"I determined," Dr. Jacobs testified, "that had it not been for this young girl being the victim of an exploitative relationship with her mother, feeling powerless and hopeless, she would not have suicided."

The mother, found guilty of child abuse, was charged with procuring a sexual performance by a child, mental abuse and forgery, falsifying her daughter's birth certificate so she could dance naked in bars. The prosecution contended the mother compelled her daughter to work as a stripper in seedy "joints" in Fort Lauderdale and that the mother failed to seek treatment for Tina after she made a former suicide attempt. Dr. Jacobs told the jury Tina found nude dancing "degrading," felt trapped in "a psychological straitjacket," forced to bring home money to support her mother.

Tina felt her mother valued her only for the money she turned over to her and "a murderous rage built up inside her that was literally painful," Dr. Jacobs explained. She was earning up to $500 a night, working sixteen hours a day and when her mother demanded she work seven days a week, they had a violent fight.

Tina left a note saying, "I love you, Mom. Love, Tina," then reached for the gun. The prosecution described the mother as "a very emotionally disturbed woman," said the relationship between mother and daughter was "like sisters, not a daughter-mother one."

This was a case where a child preferred to kill herself rather than "identify with the aggressor," a phrase first used by Anna Freud in *The Ego and the Mechanism of Defense*. Through this defense, we try to conquer our fear of someone who threatens our emotional survival by fantasying we are the aggressor, rather than the victim.

A classic book about a murder, *Dark Legend*, written in 1950 by Dr. Fredric Wertham, psychoanalyst, eloquently reveals the unconscious fantasies behind one horrifying act. Wertham spent several years uncovering the fantasies of a young killer to show the motives for the murder.

He used as preface for his book the Greek myth that described how in Mycenae, Greece, after the close of the Trojan War, a young man of high birth and noble appearance murdered his mother. The youth told the citizens of Mycenae he had committed the brutal act because his mother had dishonored his family; she had, he said, indulged in adultery and killed his father. The young man said Apollo himself had instructed him to kill his mother. Apollo was the Sun God, son of Zeus, a tribal father-god.

The son was brought to trial in Athens. The question before the court was not whether he was guilty of murder but whether he was guilty of un-Greek activities. The jury of twelve was divided, six for acquittal, six against. Athena, the Goddess of Wisdom and the protectress of Athenian society, sided with the six for acquittal, settling the deadlock. She called off the Furies who had been pursuing the young man in vengeance for his awful deed. The young man was Orestes.

Wertham's book is based on a true Orestes-like story. A young boy of seventeen, living in the crowded tenement district of New York's Lower

East Side, approached a policeman one day in the 1940s. The boy was about average height, slim, with black hair and expressive brown eyes in a handsome face. The policeman noticed the boy wore no shoes, just socks.

The policeman was about to comment on this when he saw that one of the boy's hands, wrapped clumsily in a white handkerchief, was bloody.

"Cut yourself?" asked the policeman.

"I just killed my mother," the boy said.

Later that day Wertham was making his rounds in a city hospital ward when he came across an intern treating this young boy for a deep cut in his hand. The boy gave Dr. Wertham a quick, shy smile as he walked past. He asked the boy, "How did you cut yourself like this?"

"The knife slipped," he said, added, "It was while I was killing my mother."

Thus Wertham met Gino, felt a liking for the boy, who was "direct and simple and honest . . . a charm in his dark eyes and shy smile, that made him very attractive."

When he asked Gino why he killed his mother, the boy replied quietly, "Because she dishonored my family." Wertham, interested in why Gino had taken a bread knife and stabbed his mother thirty-two times in what must have been a violent fury, decided to set out on what he called "a kind of intellectual detective adventure."

Gino was charged with murder and Wertham testified before the Lunacy Commission as to Gino's state of mind. Wertham told the Commission he thought Gino was not "normal" but Gino disagreed, insisted he was sane. The Commission accepted Wertham's opinion, committed Gino to a state asylum for the criminally insane.

But Wertham felt he had answered none of the questions which seemed to him the heart of the problem; the mystery remained unresolved: "For to say that a man is insane, and therefore he has committed certain acts, is to explain nothing at all. Such an evasion of real causes for human behavior may well be the result of a dim feeling that they are too near our own thresholds. Often a criminal is a man who does what other people merely think."

Wertham set out to uncover the fantasies in Gino's mind that had driven him to murder his mother. Murder interested Wertham, he said, particularly the murder of a mother by her son, because as a psychiatrist his work brought him "the problems of many neurotics who express hostility or real hatred against those nearest to them. . . . Family hates constitute one of the most fundamental problems of psychiatry."

An act such as Gino's throws light on one of the darkest places in psychology, Wertham wrote—the psychology of action. When and how are thoughts translated into action? When does a desire, an impulse, leave the world of fantasy and enter the world of reality? If, in the fantasies leading to the crime of murder, we can distinguish some that differ from the fantasies of others who did not murder, we may learn much about the difference between the "neurotic fantasist" and the man driven to kill.

Gino killed his mother late at night when she was asleep, wielding a knife with "the greatest ferocity," Wertham noted. Gino's first impulse after the slaying was to soothe his frightened siblings, his second, to confess to the police.

Knowing family conflicts cause more murders than "gangster killings," "revengeful feelings" and "insanity" put together, Wertham set about to gain more of Gino's story. He visited Gino in the asylum, took down his words, later checked details with Gino's friends and relatives.

Gino described how his father at eighteen traveled from Italy to America, set up a bakery in which he made bread at night, delivered it by day. He was fourteen years older than Gino's mother, who was sixteen when they married. Gino remarked, "He and my mother, they were like when a fellow and girl make love to each other." Gino's father died at forty-four after fourteen years of marriage.

Wertham's book is rich in the presentation of Gino's inner life through the young man's own words. What emerges among many fantasies was that after his father's death Gino felt deprived of the love of his father, with whom he identified. And soon Gino was also deprived of the love of his mother as she brought into the house as lover a friend of her late husband's, a local bootlegger. He wanted to marry her but she refused. But when she began sleeping regularly with her late husband's brother, Gino's uncle, Gino became emotionally incapable of coping with what he thought her unfaithfulness to his father and, in fantasy, to himself.

Gino had always been closely attached to his mother, felt "love in abundance" for her, Wertham noted. He added that the death of Gino's father served as an incentive "to the fantasy of the baby-mother relationship, when, for the baby, there was no father."

Gino told Wertham he also imagined himself standing in front of his mother, covering her with a revolver and "telling her not to talk or move, then telling her the whole story, making her realize how bad she was." He was giving expression to his sexual reveries but in a negative way. In one fantasy, he saw his mother "being kissed and intercoursed" and hated her for making love with other men.

Wertham discovered that through Gino's fantasies ran "a red thread" that enabled Wertham to correlate two seemingly divergent elements: incest and the dread of incest. He concluded that in Gino's mind there was evidently "the closest connection between sex and death, and no clear distinction between one woman and all women."

"I felt it was very significant when Gino told me, 'If a woman doesn't want it, a man can't do anything. The only thing he can do is kill her,'" Wertham said.

This was the "red thread": his fantasy of having sex with his beautiful, young mother and his fantasy that if she refused him but slept with other men, he had to kill her. He wanted to take his dead father's place but instead other men did, leaving him without his mother's love which he needed, and without her body, which he unconsciously desired. Orestes in lower New York, so to speak.

Gino had never resolved his oedipal conflict, he did not, as other boys his age did, date girls. He writhed in the thrall of an incestuous love for his mother. Wertham explained that a son, in his earliest years, feels a tender and sensual affection for his mother which, when genital strivings become strong, he suppresses, relegates to fantasy and symbol.

As long as his father lived Gino knew his place, entitled only to maternal love. But when his father died, as long as his mother remained unmarried, he felt like a suitor. Wertham's final clue came through the only dream Gino remembered. It occurred following his father's death and his mother's intimacy with his uncle.

He dreamed his mother held a baby tightly in her arms. He asked if he could hold it. She said, "Get out. It's not your baby." His father suddenly appeared, said to him three times, "See your mother? See what she is doing?" as though to make a strong point. At this Gino woke up.

The fantasies in this dream reveal the core of Gino's conflicts, Wertham asserts. Gino in reality had noticed his mother was pregnant with his uncle's baby, though his mother tried to conceal the pregnancy. In the dream, Gino expressed the underlying wish to be the baby's father. Wertham explains, "The words, 'Get out. It's not your baby,' are the axis of the dream." They show Gino's unconscious fantasy—his wish to have a baby with his mother. In the dream his mother tells him contemptuously, in effect, "You can't make a baby. You are just a little boy, you are not grown up"—death to his most ardent wish over the years, to possess his mother as his father had done.

The appearance of his father in the dream satisfied a wish, a yearning in Gino for his father's return. When the image of his father says to Gino, "See your mother? See what she is doing?" this to Gino was accusation of his mother's unfaithfulness—producing a baby by another man. Since the man was the brother of Gino's father, he also symbolized the father and how Gino must have felt originally toward his father each time his mother gave birth to another baby, unfaithful to her first one. In the dream, his father's words were an invitation to Gino to punish his mother, kill her.

These fantasies were repressed from Gino's awareness but they darkened his life until he finally exploded, no longer able to bear them. Consciously he justified the killing in his words, "Because she dishonored my family." She brought lovers into the home, bore an illegitimate child, instead of accepting Gino as husband or remaining without a husband so he could in fantasy continue imagining he possessed her.

Wertham noted this hostility against the mother based on a son's excessive attachment to her is called the "Orestes complex." He pointed out that this complex and the Oedipus complex are not mutually exclusive though they differ in certain aspects. The emotional conflicts based on the Orestes complex can exist independent of jealous rivalry with the father in that the complex shows itself not only in excessive attachment to the mother but hostility against her and women in general, indication of potential homosexuality.

This was a case of actual murder but there exists another kind of murder, the slow murder of a person's psyche. The term "soul murder" was first used by Daniel Paul Schreber, a judge in Vienna, who lived from 1842 to 1911. He became a distinguished juror in the former kingdom of Saxony, now Leipzig. He was promoted in 1893 to the high office of president of the kingdom's Superior Court of Appeal.

Shortly after he assumed this presidency he fell ill with a mental disease diagnosed as "paranoia" and spent almost nine years in mental hospitals. During the last years of his hospital stay Schreber, who kept copious notes on his mental and physical states, wrote a book about his illness, *Memoirs of a Mental Patient,* published in 1903.

Freud's analysis of Schreber became the forerunner of studies on paranoia. A more recent book, *The Schreber Case,* appearing in 1974, written by Dr. William G. Niederland, gives a fascinating portrait of Schreber's childhood with a sadistic, sex-ridden father, a physician, clinical instructor in the medical school of the University of Leipzig. Dr. Schreber forced his two sons (Schreber, Jr.'s brother three years older, would kill himself at the age of thirty-eight) to undergo at an early age orthopedic exercises, restrained by tortuous apparatus. Straps, belts and other forms of mechanical restraints that were his personal inventions (obviously devised from his own pathology, Niederland points out) were part of the father's violent, sadistically tinged methods of body control.

Dr. Schreber was a very emotionally disturbed man and his fantasies were clearly seen, Niederland pointed out, in advising his readers that they should never forget to compel the child, when it needed to be punished, "to stretch out his hand to the executor of the punishment." He also warned parents about "dangerous, hidden aberrations." He referred to masturbation as one of them, calling it "an insidious plague." He warned that masturbation made youngsters "stupid and dumb . . . very soon makes them impotent as well as sterile." Niederland cited the medical report that accompanied the *Memoirs* as stating one of Schreber's fantasies was that "he thought he was dead and rotten, suffering from the plague, all sorts of horrible manipulations being performed on his body."

Dr. Niederland also notes the important fact that it was only when Schreber was called upon to assume a prominent "father" role as president of the judicial court that fantasies of sexual and aggressive origin, repressed for thirty-two years, broke through his conscious mind. He fell ill on the very date his father died at the age of fifty-three of intestinal obstruction. Schreber's mother lived to be ninety-two. One of Schreber's sisters remained unmarried. Schreber married Sabine Behr, fifteen years younger, but they had no children though she endured a series of miscarriages.

For every 10,000 preschool children, almost ten percent were sexually abused in their homes each year, while of every 10,000 school children enrolled at day care centers, five and a half per cent were sexually abused—half the number abused at home. These statistics, based on confirmed cases reported to the United States Government, were the findings of the most comprehensive study of sexual abuse of children ever conducted, financed by the Federal government.

The study was described in *The New York Times* of March 22, 1988. The statistics were revealed by the University of New Hampshire's Family Research Laboratory, which undertook the three-year study, costing

$200,000. Cases of 1,639 children at 270 day care facilities across the country were examined, as well as the national statistics reported on child abuse in the home.

This country appears to have seen a recent increase in the sexual abuse of children by parents but is it not that we have become aware of acts that have always been carried out but never reported or publicized? In addition it is estimated that today there are between half a million to one and a half million battered children in this country and that two out of every thousand die from the physical violence inflicted on them. The types of violent acts most likely to lead to serious physical injury for the child include kicking, biting, hitting with a fist or knife or gun, beating the child with a belt or heavy object.

Therapists who work with children who have been sexually abused and adults abused as children find it makes a vast difference whether the sexual experience took place in reality or was fantasized. When the seduction is real the damage to the self-image is intense, may even feel like annihilation. The child was not able to go through the natural oedipal period but bound by his guilt and wish for revenge to the earlier period when the seduction occurred, particularly if the seducer was someone the child once trusted, which is often the case. Many concerned psychoanalysts emphasize that the actual experience has more of a devastating effect than the fantasy that accompanies a particular developmental phase.

Therapists who have dealt with women seduced as children by their fathers or other relatives report that the depressive symptoms that have not yielded to any other treatment are lifted after the women feel free to talk about experiences and are believed, not waved off, as often happens, with the comment, "that is just a fantasy."

The child who has been seduced blames himself because at this time in life he is self-centered, sees himself as the cause of everything that happens, good and bad. He feels the seduction as an attack on body and psyche, affecting his image of himself as "a bad person" deserving assault as punishment for his incestuous wishes. The child will also have persistent fantasies of vengeance because of the attack.

A daughter's tragic revenge on her father occurred when eighteen-year-old Cheryl Pierson, a high school student in Seldon, Long Island, was accused in a court trial with paying $1,000 to eighteen-year-old Sean Pica, a classmate, to kill her father, a forty-two-year-old widowed electrician, because he refused to stop subjecting her to sexual acts.

She told a packed courtroom that her father, whom Pica had shot in the driveway of the father's house as he left for work, had sexually abused her since he started fondling her at eleven as her mother, Cathleen, fell ill with terminal kidney disease. At thirteen, he forced her to have sexual intercourse two or three times a day, she said, after the death of her mother. Sometimes the abuse took place in the shower, sometimes in bed, sometimes in his car, where, she commented, she often "prayed we would crash and die." She finally decided to kill him when she feared he would sexually abuse her five-year-younger sister, JoAnn.

Cheryl spoke of a rift in her life between reality and fantasy, according to a report of the trial in *The New York Times* on September 15, 1987. Dr. Jean Goodwin, professor of psychiatry at the Medical College of Wisconsin, a national authority on sexual abuse, testified that Cheryl was a victim of sexual abuse and, as such, suffered from "post traumatic stress syndrome." This condition explained her fantasies of revenge which, Dr. Goodwin said, were common with victims of sexual assault, as well as the fact Cheryl was often unable "to tell what was really real."

Dr. Goodwin maintained that such a fantasy world was part of the coping process and when Cheryl, as part of her fantasy, approached Pica to ask him to kill her father their discussion made her "feel better." To accuse Cheryl of being the "engineer of the crime," as the prosecution put it, was to "misunderstand her basic sense of unreality."

Pica is serving a twenty-four-year prison sentence, eligible for parole after eight years. Cheryl was sentenced to six months in prison as a youthful offender with possible parole in three.

Today psychoanalysts believe that a number of patients, especially women, are not engaging in fantasy, as Freud believed, when they speak of fathers sexually seducing them at a very early age. Analysts are finding though that some patients will not mention "incest," or even remember it, at the start of an analysis, as psychoanalyst Elizabeth Thorne points out, "But if you listen receptively the patient will gradually develop an awareness that something unbearable happened in infancy."

She cites the case of one of her patients, a woman in her fifties, who moved to another part of the country and continued her analysis by letters in which she began to write eloquently of early memories. There emerged a completely unexpected breakthrough of memories about sexual attacks by her father starting when she was two and continuing until she was five. She recalled terrifying rides alone with him, mysterious physical pains and even "the smothering panic of something stuck in my mouth." Thorne helped her piece together the panic-ridden confusions of her very early life which she had buried deep because they had been too emotionally overwhelming to bear consciously.

When someone commits murder we may be sure his fantasies of hatred and revenge are intense and started in childhood. Unless we kill literally to save our own life, no matter whom we murder, even though it be a stranger, the rock-bottom fantasy is that we are killing someone vital to us in childhood whom we suspect frustrated or betrayed us, and in doing so wounded us emotionally beyond repair. That person might either be our mother or father or a sibling or someone who took care of us—such as a foster or adoptive parent, or a cruel grandparent or aunt and uncle.

A man who murdered his wife, such as the one mentioned at the start of this chapter, when she took action to divorce him, is in fantasy murdering the mother of childhood who threatened to abandon him because he was "bad." His wife's threats reawakened his deeply buried earlier fear when a child. Any later threat of abandonment was tantamount to his death, like the earlier one had been. In his fantasy life, he was still a terrified infant, fearing for his life.

A woman had difficulty tearing herself away from the sight of three bears in a cage at the city zoo. She spent hours staring at them, fantasizing the two big ones would try to devour the little one, then the little one would snap at them, slowly eat away at them until nothing was left. In her fantasy the little bear would then regurgitate its parents and the cannibalism would start over. Such obsessional thinking often prevented her from carrying out her daily tasks. During her analysis she was helped to understand that this fantasy expressed her unconscious wish to take revenge on her father, who had been excessively abusive, and a mother who did not protect her during her childhood.

What happens when the wish to murder is turned on the self instead of the one who is loathed? Then, instead of releasing murderous feelings, a deep depression ensues that may lead to schizophrenia, in which the conscious mind loses complete control: or the person may commit suicide.

9

The "Cruel Mother" Fantasy

O ur mental hospitals and many of our city streets are crowded with
homeless men and women who are so deeply depressed and distressed that they cannot take care of themselves. They are unable to hold a
job, lack money to pay for food or rent. They need mothering, a mothering
they never received or they would not be in such plight.

One homeless woman in her mid-forties wandered daily along West
Fifty-Seventh Street in Manhattan, angrily arguing with a phantom: "You
God-damned bitch, why can't you see how much you hurt me?" She was
cursing her mother, who had died but was still living within her. This
woman was calling out for help, under the control of her angry childhood
fantasies and in the grip of deep depression.

If we live too deeply in a world of obsessive unknown fantasy, ignoring
reality, we may pay the price of a deep depression. We may find ourselves
unable to give or receive love, to work, to enjoy life. We may exist in a
vacuum, depend on others to take care of us, to shelter and feed us.

The depressed person uses fantasy as too much of a safety valve. He lives
in terror of his fear and rage, feelings he dares not consciously admit.
Some even retreat so far into fantasies that take over the orbit of the
conscious stream of thoughts that these persons are labeled "insane."

Though depression may seem to stem from a vague feeling of despair
and anxiety, dozens of specific fantasies underlie it. The fantasies that
cause depression formed part of one of the most momentous discoveries of
Freud.

He found that the roots of depression flourish on real or imagined hurts
at which we dare not express anger for fear of losing love. The repressed

feelings, denied their natural outlet, cause depression. The real world appears so tormenting that the person retreats to a world where fantasy reigns supreme. He believes that only in the world created by his fantasies can he escape agony, frustration and fury.

The severely depressed—the schizophrenic, the catatonic, the autistic child—retreat to the world of fantasy. They are unable to relate to others in love or friendship; it takes all their energy just to exist for themselves. Often a schizophrenic cannot speak coherently; he disguises his thoughts in garbled words so no one will know his murderous fantasies. Sometimes he will not speak at all, his overwhelming anger and wish for revenge on those he feels failed to love and protect him render him mute.

The depressed feel, as Tennyson wrote in *In Memoriam*:

> And Time, a maniac scattering dust
> And Life, a Fury slinging flame.

And also, as in that classic poem:

> But what am I?
> An infant crying in the night:
> An infant crying for the light:
> And with no language but a cry.

Such feelings in a child led to the concept of "soul murder" described by Judge Schreber and since written about poignantly by Dr. Leonard Shengold. He speaks of the soul murder of a child as psychological destruction in many forms, including neglect, abandonment, seduction both overt and subtle, and physical cruelty.

Schizophrenia may in some cases be a defense against parental behavior of such overwhelming destructive nature—physical assault or mental cruelty—that it leads to wild distortions of the natural unfolding of fantasies. A raging mother is terrifying enough to another adult but to her baby she is fantasied as a maniac. He fears annihilation, usually through the fantasy she will devour him, since his mouth is the chief focus of his feelings at this earliest stage of life. One result of Freud's theory of the power of the aggressive drive is that some psychoanalysts, such as Dr. Frieda Fromm-Reichmann and Dr. Harold Searles, developed ways to enable the severely emotionally disturbed to get in touch with early feelings of anger toward a mother.

One of the first books to describe the role fantasies play in schizophrenia is *Symbolic Realization* by M. A. Sechehaye, a Swiss psychoanalyst, published in 1951. She wrote of her treatment of a seventeen-year-old girl, Renée, whom numerous psychiatrists had given up as doomed to live in madness because of "progressive deterioration." This moving account of psychoanalytic treatment describes the process of therapy with the deeply emotionally troubled. Few psychoanalysts have devoted so many years to a very disturbed patient and written so eloquently of their experiences and the results.

Mrs. Sechehaye first saw Renee when she was in a mental hospital and then treated her for nine years, by which time Renée had regained her sanity. The experience allowed her to indulge in the feelings of possessing a new mother, a "good mother," one she could love and who loved and protected her. As a result of this mothering, she slowly gave up her world of fantasy, moved into reality.

Renée, who wrote her account of the treatment in a second volume, *Autobiography of a Schizophrenic Girl*, stated, "I loved Mama for herself and not in relation to my need to possess all of her." She was helped to leave behind the insatiable child within, stand on her own, after Mrs. Sechehaye allowed her to regress in fantasy even to the womb, as she described what it felt like to lie inside her mother. Through "symbolic realization" of her need for emotional nourishment never offered as a child, she could embark on her way to a normal, mature adulthood.

During therapy her deepest fantasies emerged. Mrs. Sechehaye gave her a balloon and Renée wrote on it the word "Mother." She fantasied the balloon as her mother's breast, would not let go of it. Mrs. Sechehaye also gave her a plush tiger which Renée loved, and kept close to her. One day she drew a picture of her guilt feelings in the form of immense eyes in a little girl lying down, wrote the words "He lies in terror" as a description of her life.

Her fantasies were based on a terrifying early reality. The first few years she slept in her parents' bedroom. On waking she would feel starved, ask for food, but her father laughed at her, made her wait, threatened to withhold all food if she cried. He said he would also take her mother away from her permanently, announced he would beat her mother and devour her, then pretend to bite her mother hungrily.

Her father was an industrialist who studied Russian, Chinese and the violin, for the pleasure of it. He earned enough money to keep the family in lavish style. Her mother was descended from an aristocratic family from southern France. Both parents, Mrs. Sechehaye discovered, were cruel to their children in open and subtle ways.

Renée recalled the day her little playmate, a white rabbit she adored, was killed by her father in her presence—a lasting emotional shock. He also indulged in other cruelties. When she was eighteen months, while the birth of a second baby absorbed her mother's full attention, he was sexually seductive, would lift the skirt of her dress, tease her about her nakedness. A servant girl once said to her, "Someone must have cut something off of you," meaning her fantasied penis. Renée imagined her father had done this, in line with his other cruelties.

Her father did not always tease or threaten but occasionally showed a deep depression. One day as they walked along a beach, she remembered, he suggested renting a boat and drowning themselves at sea, saying, "We don't care to live, do we?" This was to him, at least consciously, a jest but the little girl of seven by his side felt the aura of death. She feared her father wanted to kill her.

Mrs. Sechehaye pointed out that Renée, as a little girl, felt abandoned from the start of her life. During therapy, "the slow passage from the feeling of abandonment to inner assurance proves there was an actual defect of evolution and not only an after-shock regression to a previous stage." It was necessary, she said, that Renée's evolution had to be upheld by someone living, that she had to be "connected emotionally to a being who gives . . . who is another reality." Whenever she gave Renée food or protection or love, "that which her instinct demanded," Mrs. Sechehaye furnished proof of maternal love and the aggressiveness Renée felt against her mother diminished. At the same time the aggressiveness against herself (she hated herself, as she took in emotionally the hatred of her father and mother) also lessened.

Mrs. Sechehaye explained she had to find something other than the verbal method of psychoanalysis because Renée's initial conflict occurred before she developed the ability to speak and because she had regressed to the stage of "magic presymbolic participation." The mode of expression had to be "more primitive, and had to correspond to the stage at which the trauma had taken place," one "suitable to a baby: expression by the symbolic signs of features and movements."

She added that if asked what role the Oedipus complex played in Renée's illness, she would reply that since Renée's conflict started before the formation of her ego and related primarily to the nursing mother, the role of the father was essentially to Renée that of a rival for her mother's love. The salient points in Renée's case did not relate to her fear and guilt in wishing to take her father from her mother but "to magic and moral realism."

Dr. Edith Jacobson, who for many years studied depression, concluded that oral frustration, the feeling of severe and lasting hunger in the earliest years, seemed the first forerunner of profound disappointment "such as comes about later by being hit by the loss of a most valuable object." In the state of severe disappointment, she wrote, "one finds the feeling of blank, empty hopelessness, of nothingness, often accompanied by the sensation of physical emptiness which certainly goes back to what Sandor Rado describes as the hopeless despair of the baby that is craving for the mother's breast."

Disillusionment in parents may play a significant, painful part in the child's detection of and adjustment to the realistic world, Jacobson points out. After losing his belief in his own omnipotence the child is convinced of and takes part in the fantasied magical omnipotence of his parents. He loses this new belief in godlike parents as he matures, uses reason.

Whether this process of disillusionment has a constructive or destructive effect on the development of the child's ego and sense of reality depends, Jacobson says, less on the severity of disappointments in the parents than on the stage at which the disappointments occur. The child disappointed early cannot profit from his disillusionments. Instead of acquiring a solid realistic picture of the world, "the child may swing from an optimistic to a pessimistic illusion which again distorts reality."

If an extreme deflation of the parental images sets in early, the ego of the child is deeply affected by it, according to Jacobson. The magical power of the parents is, at this stage, the child's chief source of narcissistic support. Any deflation of his parental images tears down his infantile ego; in fantasy he is still partially fused emotionally with his parents. As he experiences the downfall of the godlike parents, their destruction becomes identical with his self-deflation and self-destruction. The child responds from then on to disappointments and frustrations with a narcissistic hurt, feels depressed.

With the start of the genital stage, fantasies and feelings of the earlier oral and anal stages and the new genital, aggressive impulses fuse in the child's reaction to his devaluation of his parents and himself. The disappointing mother appears "empty, disgusting, dirty and destroyed, castrated." Jacobson refers to the preoedipal disappointment in the mother as inducing "the female castration conflict." For the little boy, too, "it seems to be the genital disappointment in the mother which makes him aware of her castrated genital that reflects and substantiates his own castration fears."

She adds that severe disillusionment in parents during the first years of life "crushes the infantile ego, on one hand, and on the other, may start the superego formation at an earlier stage than normally." This premature shifting of infantile conflicts into the inner mental stage establishes a pseudostrength and pseudoindependence of the ego but its relationship to the conscience retains characteristics of the earlier dependence on the omnipotent mother. In discussing the effect of the oedipal conflict in the development of depression, Jacobson points out analysis of the manic-depressive person "reveals a fixation" on the powerful ambivalent, oral and anal fantasies.

As an adult, such a person may be driven by a strict conscience rather than a flexible ego. He may feel emotionally impoverished at times, inflated at other times, capable of extraordinary achievements, Jacobson observed. He still clings to a magical power which, by gaining its favor, can be changed from "bad" to "good" as it promises support and projection (like the good parent). Such extremes in behavior appear markedly in the personalities of depressed persons, she adds.

One of the first to describe a type of schizophrenia as "rage turned on the self," Spotnitz describes the defense of psychosis as operating unconsciously to protect the person "from the release of what is felt as volcanic aggression and thus serves to disrupt his psyche." He maintains that through therapy that takes into account the preoedipal rage by releasing the impulse to love from the "impossible task of blotting out the impulse to hate, and by taming hate into personally and socially desirable forms of human expression," the psychoanalyst "diminishes the destructive potential of the hate and frees the love urges for creative service."

The latest research by psychoanalysts who have treated the very emotionally disturbed shows there is a critical phase of development in early infancy that reflects a failure in mothering, as Mrs. Sechehaye showed. The mother is incapable of an adequate emotionally protective attitude toward the child; her enjoyment of her baby is a diminished one because of her conflicts over having a baby. The seeds of future mental illness may be sown in this early failure in the mother-child relationship.

Ideally, the infant needs to experience a close dyadic relationship to become a healthy human being. Mahler describes how the mother-infant dyad forms a symbiotic unit—two persons joined in "homeostatic equilibrium." She explains, "Beyond a certain, but not yet defined degree, the immature organism cannot achieve homeostasis on his own." Whenever there is "organismic distress," a forerunner of anxiety, the mother, with her special ways of relieving her child from distress, must be on hand. The infant at this early age has no way of achieving relief of tension on his own.

Mahler elaborates further on the concept of "symbiosis." She explains that "images of the love object (mother), as well as images of the bodily and later the psychic self, emerge from the ever-increasing memory traces of pleasurable ('good') and unpleasurable ('bad') instinctual, emotional experiences, and the perceptions with which they become associated. Even the most primitive differentiation, however, can only take place if a psychophysiological equilibrium can be attained. This depends first on a certain matching of the discharge patterns of the mother and the young infant, and later, on their interactional patterns, behaviorally discernible in mutual cueing, as well as in the infant's earliest adaptive patterning and in his receptive capacities with the 'good enough' holding behavior of his symbiotic mother."

Dr. Judith S. Kestenberg describes how the mother's attunement to her infant's needs is a necessary ingredient in his healthy development. Complete attunement is based on mutual empathy; there is not only a sameness of needs and responses but also a synchronization in rhythms—in the way the milk flows and the baby sucks, in the way the mother holds her baby in her arms and the way the baby molds into her body. But, Dr. Kestenberg warns, if such an attunement persists too long it may lead to a prolongation and intensification of the symbiotic phase, reflected in the growing child's inability to enjoy his awareness of being separate from his mother, and inhibit his capacity for independent functioning.

Too much attunement, for example, when an infant is constantly over-stimulated, will lead to distress because he receives little relief; the methods by which he is soothed are too stimulating. Such a child later in life may react oversensitively to environmental changes, unable to face reality. As a general statement, the seeds of psychological problems and severe mental illness are sown early in life.

Winnicott remarked there is no such thing as a baby, there are only babies with mothers. To become capable of enjoying life, the baby has to be loved and cherished, not hated or thought a burden or a nuisance. Without such maternal love, a love that overcomes the mother's occasional feelings of hate, the child will have a difficult time overcoming his strong feelings of hate.

W. R. D. Fairbairn, another prominent British psychoanalyst, who first trained in philosophy and theology, then worked with schizophrenic patients, was also impressed with the importance of an early mothering relationship of quality. He believed serious depression in later life developed from the mother's failure to give the infant an adequate experience of "being loved for himself." The foundation for healthy emotional development depended on imparting to the infant that he is "a person" valued and enjoyed by his mother. When deprived of this experience, despite his longing for love, he later becomes too frightened to express love lest it be rejected, instead lives in a world of fantasy.

In place of Freud's "developmental" process of "object relations" (relating to the mother and father) centering on the erotic zones, Fairbairn speaks of the concept of being governed by the quality of dependence. He sees infantile dependence at the start characterized by primary identification with the mother as the baby starts to incorporate her attitudes.

The gradual emotional separation from the mother throughout childhood and adolescence constitutes, he says, a transitional period from which the healthy person emerges with the capacity for mature dependence—in which "giving" is as important as "taking." There ensues the growing ability to differentiate between the self and the loved one as a separate person with an identity of his own.

By the time oedipal fantasies are stimulated at the age of four or five, the child may already possess a divided self. It is the extent to which these divisions are present, along with the intensity of their activity, that determines the outcome of the oedipal conflict, Fairbairne says.

As more studies are carried out in this very early relationship between mother and baby, it will probably become even clearer how important a time this is in the development of depression and the fantasies inherent in it.

A depressed little boy, Ivan, over the years had experienced the slow, oncoming death of his fatally ill mother. He was preoccupied with her condition almost all his waking hours but in part found substitutes for her absence in his daily life. She had been an accomplished singer and Ivan treasured his songbird. Outside her room stood a low-growing tree and

Ivan would sit hidden in its branches, fantasize the branches as his mother's arms sheltering and shielding him from the hardships of life. Through the change of seasons and their impact on the tree, Ivan experienced the life cycle, "after death, life comes back again."

His mother died when Ivan was seven and he killed his songbird in fury and despair over his own lack of power to cure his mother. The killing of the bird symbolized in fantasy her death. At least through this act he had a sense of control of death, he was no longer the passive victim to whom the catastrophe of losing a beloved one had occurred. At the funeral he heard the minister's words about the possibility of uniting after death with our beloved ones in heaven. He subsequently made a serious attempt to drown himself so he could join his mother, undo the loss and cope with the guilt that followed his hatred of his mother for abandoning him. His father took him to a therapist who helped him mourn his loss.

The need to imitate what has happened to the parent because of guilt is elaborated on by Dr. Phyllis Greenacre who wrote about the life of the Russian author, Nikolai Gogol. She describes his childhood experiences of an almost endless succession of losses through deaths of siblings, losses that were traumatic and left pathological scars within Gogol, contributing to his later suicide.

When he was sixteen he lost his father and at that time he wrote his mother: "True, at first I was terribly stricken by this news; however, I did not let anyone notice that I was saddened. But when I was left alone, I gave myself up to the power of mad desperation. I even wanted to make an attempt on my life." Gogol starved himself, died at the same age as his father, forty-three. Just before he died, he spoke of his father's dying "of the same disease."

Jacobson suggests this deep an identification with the parent may occur when the child experiences himself as the parent, in a narcissistic almost total identification with the loved one.

If the person does not commit suicide but feels deeply depressed, the depression may be lasting or may occur primarily around the anniversary of the death of the parent. Dr. George H. Pollock has carried out extensive research on the mourning process and adaptation to the loss of a loved one. He studied the incidence of losses during childhood among a group of adults and found that when the loved one is not completely mourned there occurs a significant amount of "anniversary reactions." Pollock for instance noted that a specific day, season of the year or holiday could serve as trigger for the appearance of a strong emotional reaction, a symptom related to the anniversary of the death.

In his historic article "Mourning and Melancholia," published in 1917, Freud compared the normal emotion of grief as expressed in mourning the death of someone loved, and depression. In mourning, the bereaved person soon recovers from his grief and anger, finds another person on whom he can displace his love.

But in depression, there seems no recovery; the person does not know why he continues to be depressed. He only knows he feels a loss of identity, the world seems "poor and empty"; he reproaches himself continually for a world he cannot fathom.

In Freud's words, the person feels "a profoundly painful dejection, abrogation [abolishing] of interest in the outside world, loss of the capacity to love, inhibitions of all activity, and a lowering of the self-regarding feelings to a degree that finds utterance in self-reproaches and self-revilings, and culminates in a delusional expectation of punishment."

He thus distinguished between what he called "mourning," which occurs when someone we love dies, and "melancholia," the word he used at that time for "depression." He was well aware of the impact of the death of a parent upon a child, for he reached his important discovery of the power of the Oedipus complex immediately after his father died—partly perhaps as an unconscious attempt to regain the lost, loved-hated father.

The one who mourns the death of a loved one is expected to take time to come to terms with his sorrow. A year's grace is what society allows a mourner. Freud called this a time of external tears and "internal bleeding." But the strong emotion that grips some after the death of a parent may not be caused by the loss alone. The survivor clings to the fantasy that he wants to die also, that without the parent he believes there is nothing left to live for. This kind of mourning, Freud pointed out, holds deep depression.

The depression may permeate the whole of living or occur primarily at the time of each anniversary of the death of the parent. One man in analysis suddenly realized he felt depressed the first week of each October. As he spoke of this mysterious depression he remarked to the analyst he was only four when his mother died.

"Do you remember the month?" asked the analyst.

"No, but I'll ask my father," he said.

When he returned for his next session, he said in surprise, "My mother died on October third. I never knew that."

"Not consciously," the analyst said, "but your unconscious remembered and mourned."

Many sons and daughters go through a period of mourning for a dead parent, then resume life as it was before the death, though the loss remains as a sadness. But some never recover, their grief too intense for them to assimilate. One reason the horror movie *Psycho,* based on the book by Robert Bloch, mesmerizes so many of us (some viewers have seen it a dozen or more times on television) is that the son is unable to let go of the body of his dead mother (even though he has killed her) because he does not want her out of his sight. As a child, we all feel that way about our mother (both the wish never to let go of her and the occasional wish to kill her when she enrages us).

A brilliant, beautiful woman, forty-nine years old, wife of an advertising executive, had a reputation for humor and cheerfulness until her mother died. Then she sank deeper and deeper into an unexplained depression, made three attempts to kill herself. Finally she succeeded with an overdose of barbiturates.

"Why? Why?" her friends demanded of each other, searching for an explanation of her despair. On the surface she had everything—wealth, beauty, brains, a devoted, successful husband, two married sons. But she had lost the only person who really mattered, her mother; without her mother nearby she had the fantasy she too wanted to die and join her in heaven, enjoying the same closeness she had as a child. She was tied tightly by emotional chains from which she had never broken free. Most of us do not react this drastically to a parent's death though some feelings of devastation usually occur during the first year of mourning.

Originally Freud linked depression to sex, believed that repression of the sexual drive was the sole cause of depression. He noticed that women who suffered from depression were often sexually frigid though they had "a great longing for love in its physical form." He believed at that time (1894) that if the "physical erotic tension" accumulated and remained unsatisfied, depression would result. Here we see the start of Freud's theory that fantasies caused depression, as he mentioned "physical erotic tension," for the psyche is the birthplace and storehouse of fantasies.

He spoke at this time of "gaps in his theory" about depression which "sorely need filling." One was "filled" in his vital discovery of what he called "the great secret." This was the existence in the human mind of the countless fantasies that made up what he named "psychic reality." This encompassed an inner reality as contrasted with the objective reality of the world outside.

Then in January 1895 Freud drew a connection between depression and masturbation, still tying depression to erotic feelings. He said depression could arise as an intensification of neurosis because of masturbation— many of his depressed patients spoke of masturbating frequently. He noted that a number of young girls suffered a tension that seemed like depression, occurring when sexuality was undeveloped. Such a girl, he said, often explained she had not eaten "simply because she has no appetite and for no other reason." Then he added, "Loss of appetite—in sexual terms, loss of libido." (His colleague, Karl Abraham, was later to say of depressed persons who overate that "food has taken the place of love.")

Freud concluded, "So it would not be far wrong to start from the idea that *melancholia consists in mourning over loss of libido*" (italics his).

He noted "striking connections" between melancholia or depression, and sexual frigidity in women and impotency in men, saying that depressed men and women often appeared uninterested in sex. He added that the depressed person usually had difficulty all his life becoming sexually aroused. That proved the foundation of all future scientific discussion of depression. He declared that hostile impulses against parents, the wish that they die, were an integral part of all neuroses. They came to light consciously in the form of obsessional ideas. In paranoia, the delusions of persecution—supposed murderous threats by unseen and unknown enemies—stemmed from the person's own wish to kill his parents in turn projected on others.

The impulse to kill a parent is repressed at times when pity for the parent is paramount, such as when he falls ill or dies, when one of the signs of grief is to reproach the self for the parent's death, to become depressed—or to punish the self in a hysterical way by putting the self in the place of the parent as punishment for the death wish.

Depression could also be the reaction to the loss of a loved one who had not died, Freud observed. He cited the example of a bride deserted at the altar. In other instances, a depressed person had the fantasy of loss and yet did not know exactly what it was he lost. In still others, the person knew whom he had lost but not what in him he had lost. This would suggest, Freud said, that depression was in some way related to an unconscious loss of someone you love, as contrasted to mourning, where you are conscious of whom or what you have lost.

Freud noted as he listened to the fantasies and accusations of depressed men and women patients about themselves that the fantasies and accusations seemed to fit someone else, someone the depressed person "loves, has loved, or ought to love." He concluded the self-reproaches were really directed against the "someone" who was loved, then shifted onto the self.

Depression holds a condition absent in normal grief, a condition that may become part of normal grief thus transforming it into "a pathological variety," Freud said. This condition comes about because of one factor— the conflict inherent in ambivalence. The mixed feelings of love and hate "casts a pathological shade on the grief, forcing it to express itself in the form of self-reproaches, to the effect that the mourner himself is to blame for the loss of the loved one, i.e. desired it," Freud stated.

He maintained that the person incapable of mature love, who can love only in a childish, narcissistic way, when threatened by the loss of the parent is apt to regress to the primitive stages of his psychosexual development, primarily fantasies of rage at the parent, then feelings of guilt. He reacts to the loss with feelings of hate but dares not admit them. He turns the hate on himself and this causes the depression. He acts as if he had taken in something bent on destroying him but does not know what it is or how to fight back.

Freud also studied fantasies underlying suicide. He stated, "We have long known it is true that no neurotic harbors thoughts of suicide which he has not turned back upon himself from murderous impulses against others, but we have never been able to explain what interplay of forces can carry a purpose through to execution."

The analysis of depression now showed, he explained, that the ego could kill itself if, owing to the power of the loved one "as retained within as image," it could treat itself the same as it did the loved one, directing against itself all the rage it felt for the other person. Self-hate may overpower self-love as hatred of others may overpower love of others.

Many a time an act as extreme as suicide has its roots in infancy. The suicide is killing the "bad" mother within himself. The baby who feels unloved believes his mother "bad" but, needing her desperately, turns this around, accuses himself, "I am bad, she is good." The more frustrating the mother, the less love she gives, the less she knows what her baby needs and the "badder" she becomes to him. This badness he then takes unto himself and the hatred within may simmer over the years, then explode in suicide.

A baby believes he is merged with his mother; he does not differentiate between himself and his mother. If the depressed person has been unable to separate emotionally from his mother, he still feels somewhat merged. If he is so depressed he must kill himself, in fantasy he kills the part of his mother with whom he feels fused. In his unconscious, it is death to both. In a sense the depressed person, who has taken in psychically much of the "bad" mother, punishes her in effigy when he commits suicide.

One of the goals of depression is to get rid of, by denial, the "badness" in both the self and the love-hated person in order to regain the mutual love that supposedly existed in infancy. In some instances suicide is the last-ditch attempt to do so, a fantastic attempt, an attempt straight from the cradle, when the self and the mother are completely merged.

Suicides often have a fantasy of revenge just before they kill themselves, and think of the loved-hated one as an enemy with whom they are finally getting even as they commit a deed they believe will make the enemy feel as guilty as they do. They express the wish to destroy, with guilt and remorse, the life of the one who has so deeply hurt and disappointed them. The notes they leave speak of a desire for vengeance and the hope their death "will haunt" the person to whom the note is addressed.

The suicide shows primarily the sadistic aspect of the oral stage (biting) and of the anal stage (spite and anger) with which he combats a loss, according to Freud. It is "this sadism which solves the riddle of the tendency to suicide." The neurotic harbors thoughts of suicide that he has turned back upon himself from the murderous impulses he first felt against parents, Freud maintains. He added that the analysis of depression showed the ego could kill itself if it treated itself as the loved one, directing against itself all the rage it felt for the other person for, in essence, abandoning him or in other ways showing cruelty toward him.

In Freud's words, "the shadow of the object," the loved one, falls upon the ego so that part of the latter can be criticized as though it were the forsaken one. He pointed out that in the two opposite situations of being intensely in love and of suicide, the ego is overwhelmed by the loved one, though in totally different ways.

If Freud's theory of suicide is applied in lesser degree to depression, the latter is seen to stem from the wish to kill someone toward whom we hold intense feelings of mixed love and hate. We believe we want to kill him because, in the unconscious, hate automatically carries with it the fantasy of death.

Another fantasy also haunts the depressed person, that the wish is the same as the deed and therefore he must punish himself for guilt over the wish to kill. Depression for most people is a turning inward of murderous wishes not intense enough to drive to suicide but intense enough to cause torment at times.

In a way, depression is death to the self administered in small psychic doses. Depression signals death to love and being loved, for it is difficult to love a depressed person. His hatred is easily sensed, not only in his self-pity but in his hopelessness, his lack of energy, his inability to relate to others.

Depression is, in Dr. Sandor Rado's words, "A cry for love"—a cry that starts in the cradle. Abraham, a pioneer in the study of depression, traced adult depression to what he called the "primal depression of infancy." He theorized that if someone became depressed as an adult, he had first gone through a "primal depression." This earlier depression preceded and set the pattern for adult depression. The latter, he said, "in the last resort . . . is derived from disagreeable experiences in the childhood of the patient."

Abraham also held there was pleasure in depression in that the depressed person seems to take delight in suffering and continually thinking about himself. When the pleasure changes to too much pain, he will either pull himself out of the depression, kill himself or seek a psychoanalyst, Abraham concluded.

Dr. René Spitz coined the phrase "anaclitic depression," to refer to an infant's feelings when he sensed his mother did not give him enough love. Spitz noted that the symptoms and facial expressions of depressed children resembled those of adults suffering depression. If a child remained deprived of his mother, for instance, without an acceptable substitute for longer than three to five months, he became even more depressed, whimpered continually, Spitz discovered. The disturbance "will leave scars which will show in later years," he added.

The total absence of a mother's love equaled "emotional starvation," in his words. It led to a progressive deterioration that engulfed an infant's personality and eventually led to his death.

If a child lives in the aura of a parent's depression he may react to what otherwise might not be crippling crises as though they were a matter of life and death. In a depressed atmosphere the child is forced to endure not only the normal traumas of life—the appearance of a rival brother or sister, weaning, toilet training—but also his mother's depression, for which he will feel responsible, out of his natural sense of omnipotence. He will also have difficulty separating from her emotionally for she is unlikely to encourage him to become independent, wanting to keep him by her side.

Anna Freud discovered that the depressed mother generates in her child depressive fantasies. This process is not just imitation, she added, but a response to the emotional climate that infects his psyche as a germ would his body. The hostility the child senses his mother feels will further depress him, as well as arousing his rage.

Dr. John Bowlby, a British psychoanalyst, later helped define what Freud named "the mourning process." In observing children separated temporarily from their mothers, Bowlby concluded the children went through three phases—protest, despair and detachment. In each, the child was prone to tantrums and episodes of destructive behavior, often of a "disquietingly violent kind."

In Bowlby's words: "At first with tears and anger he demands his mother back and seems hopeful he will succeed in getting her. This phase of Protest may last several days. Later he becomes quieter, but to the discerning eye it is clear that as much as ever he remains preoccupied with his absent mother and still yearns for her return; but his hopes have faded and he is in the phase of Despair. Often these two phases alternate: hope turns to despair and the despair to renewed hope. Eventually, however, a greater change occurs. He seems to forget his mother so that when she comes for him he remains curiously uninterested in her, and may seem even not to recognize her. This is the phase of Detachment."

In relating this behavior to adults who are depressed, Bowlby observes: "There is, indeed, good reason to believe that the sequences of responses—Protest, Despair and Detachment—is a sequence that, in one variant or another, is characteristic of all forms of mourning." In other words, our fantasies change with each sequence.

Following an unexpected loss there occurs a phase of protest in which the bereaved strives, in fantasy, deed, thought or feeling, to recover the lost loved one. At the same time he reproaches the lost one for the desertion. During this time and during the following phase of despair, feelings of love and hate are mixed. Mood and action vary from an immediate expectancy, expressed in an angry demand for the person's return, to a despair shown in "subdued pining" or not expressed at all. Though alternating hope and despair may continue, eventually there develops some measure of emotional detachment from the one who is lost. Then follows acceptance of permanent absence.

This is healthy mourning when it occurs in an adult. It becomes unhealthy, or pathological, in a child because it occurs when he is too young to handle his deep feelings of loss at a time he needs a loving attachment.

The depressed mother is unlikely to encourage her child, who starts off being totally dependent on her, to become independent. When he tries to separate, he will be frustrated by her wishes to keep him close, will hate her with a vengeance that far exceeds that of the less dependent child. This hate brings fantasies of retaliation, then guilt, then depression as he turns the hate inward. When she eventually dies, no matter at what age, he is apt to punish himself through even deeper depression.

Part of us as an adult fantasies, "If I ever let go, I will destroy myself and everyone around me. I will steal, use profane language, rob, have sex with everybody—man, woman and child—kill my wicked mother and father and sisters and brothers, mate and children, best friends."

This is the fantasy of uncontrolled violence, the monster fantasy. Who is the monster? Our own unbridled, primitive fantasies and passions.

Dr. Joseph Rheingold, a psychoanalyst, asks, "Why is man the only species whose behavior is so forcibly motivated by hate—by hostile protest and rebellion, by domination and exploitation, by recrimination, vindictiveness and revenge? Why is homicide-suicide a basic potential of human life?"

He answers: "It is because of the hurt inflicted upon the infant, the unbearable fact of human existence that the person who bestows life and upon whom the child is helplessly dependent also wishes to extinguish life and suppress its spontaneity."

The crueler the parent, the more painful the childhood and the greater the need for the child to live in fantasy and depression. His parents may be brutal but they are all he has to love and he will fight their loss with his whole psychic might.

Some children suffer depressions so deep they are never able to achieve mature love. But even those who become fairly emotionally mature (goal of goals) find that there remains some feeling of mourning of losses suffered in infancy and childhood. They are able to seek new, appropriate pleasures with suitable substitutes for lost loves.

The depressed person, if he gives up on life, may resort to suicide. In the past few years the fantasies of suicide among adolescents has steadily increased. It was reported on CBS news, August 16, 1987, there had been

400,000 attempted suicides by adolescents during the past year, a three-fold increase since the 1950s.

Just short of suicide, a kind of pseudo or delayed suicide, is practiced by many of all ages to try to ease depression through addictions that momentarily ease their fear, hatred and guilt. They try alcohol, drugs, promiscuity, overeating, starving, overwork, smoking, gambling to alleviate the "down" feelings.

What are the fantasies behind such addiction? Fantasies that are expressed more openly as the threat of nuclear disaster seems to devastate youth and those who believe nations are more eager to wage war than to find the pathway to peace.

10
The "Lottery" Fantasy

A thirty-year old woman, secretary to an executive in a large advertising agency, stood midway in a long line waiting to buy a lottery ticket from a stationery store in mid-Manhattan. The man in back of her, owner of a grocery store nearby, said, "You here again? You expect to win today?"

She smiled, said, "Hope springs eternal. Why not me, someday?"

"Good luck, pal," he said. "I been waiting five years."

The growing popularity of lottery tickets with the chance of winning millions of dollars for one dollar attests to the increasing number of men and women who resort to fantasy in the latest "get rich quick" addiction.

Our forefathers searched for gold in the mountains or sunken treasure ships at sea. Today it is the lottery or the racetrack or betting on baseball, football or basketball games.

Such addictions however are not as detrimental as alcoholism or drugs which kill through AIDS. The number of AIDS-related deaths among intravenous drug users was 150 percent higher than previously reported, far more rampant than believed, according to the statistics at the end of 1987. Homosexuals were no longer "the major group at risk in New York City."

Addiction to drugs, like any addiction, is caused in large part by the conscious fantasy that the euphoria drugs produce will bring peace, happiness, retreat from the pain of reality. Beth Lazarus, a psychiatric social worker with extensive experience in the treatment of drug addicts, wrote in an unpublished paper, "The Psychodynamics of Chemical Dependency and Treatment Implications," that a chemically dependent indi-

163

vidual acts as if any tension were a dangerous trauma—that is, felt as hunger as it once was for him as an infant, life threatening.

The addict, she says, thinks like a child: "I can create my own world. I do not have to work or be disciplined. I can give myself over to all my desires. Stuff or starve. Not be responsible for what I say or do. Live in the limbo of freewheeling thought and deed, no one to order me around. I am my own master, to hell with everyone." Thus the addict reasons, be it drugs, alcohol, food, cigarettes.

In R. D. Chessick's experience, described in "The Pharmacogenic Orgasm in the Drug Addict," the addict uses drugs to satisfy certain oral longings and the effect of the drug rests on the fact that it is felt as food and warmth given by the fantasied nursing mother. Drug-dependent adolescents and adults feel reunited with the idealized, beloved caretaker from the past. They become totally anesthetized by the drug, like the satiated infant asleep at his mother's breast after being nursed.

If there is a great deal of trauma in the early life of the addicted person, he seeks ways of finding the good mothering he never had. He has been left with deep distrust of and ambivalence toward the unsatisfactory mother—the need to "take in" is accompanied with a feeling of spitting out. Studies show that as a result of massive childhood trauma, addicts experience arrests in their emotional development and impairment in their tolerance of emotion. There occurs a fear of feelings and a need to block them. Some drug-dependent individuals repress their rage and destructive wishes toward their mothers. This shows itself in a rigid "walling off" of the person the addict may encounter in the present to whom he becomes attached (the representative of his early object of love, his mother), the "idealized one." By walling off his feelings he is able to protect his fantasies from the destructiveness of his fantasized power.

In general, the addict has limited capacity to tolerate anxiety, depression and frustration. His ability to judge reality is weak; he blames his inadequacies on others. He has limitations when it comes to differentiating between past and present, reality and fantasy.

Alcoholism and drug addiction represent ways in which deeply troubled men and women try to escape painful fantasies and feelings of loneliness, depression, guilt, anger. These addictions also unconsciously serve as rationalization for those who either want promiscuous sex or because of their fear of sex, an excuse from refraining from sexual activity. Addictions also furnish the excuse to carry through on homosexual relations as inhibitions fall: "I didn't know what I was doing because I was so drunk."

If we cripple ourselves physically and psychologically through drug addiction or alcoholism, we are trying to flee painful fantasies, not realizing we add new anguish to our lives by these destructive habits. Alcoholism may lead to liver and other internal injuries as well as destroy brain cells. Alcohol and drugs have an effect on the fetus a woman bears, often causing birth defects. It is impossible to keep pouring drugs or alcohol into the body without in some way harming vital organs.

For the last fifteen years Dr. Denise Kandel, professor of public health in psychiatry at Columbia University, has been engaged in a major study of 1,200 young people. She has explored such questions as who uses drugs and why, the history of drug involvement, the risk factors and the consequences.

What encourages an adolescent to use drugs at a particular developmental stage? Kandel believes it is mainly peer pressure but that the moving on to stronger drugs frequently reveals psychological problems. One significant risk factor is a poor relationship to parents, the feeling of lack of closeness. Studies have shown that parents who have trouble setting limits to their children's behavior cannot discipline them effectively and are the most likely to raise children who act out troubled feelings through drug taking.

Alterations of states of consciousness under the influence of drugs interfere with the capacity of our ego to adapt to reality. Under unfavorable circumstances, such as an emotionally destitute childhood or child abuse, the adult is apt to regress emotionally, which leads to the emergence of primitive unconscious fantasies. Addiction to drugs not only affects the psyche but also the body, sometimes ending in death, as in the case of the actor John Belushi.

From the experience of therapists in general it seems that excessive drinking by one or both alcoholic partners in a marriage ranks high as a contributing cause of broken homes. Among the consequences of such addiction are divorce, financial insecurity, unemployment, illness, preventable accidents, desertion, maltreatment of children, juvenile delinquency, prostitution and minor and major crimes.

This is the opinion of Dr. Ruth Fox, authority on alcoholism in her article "The Alcoholic Spouse," in *Neurotic Interaction in Marriage*. She cites as definition of an alcoholic, someone "*unable* to stop after two or three drinks." For him "it is all or nothing and one drink is usually the beginning of a spree . . . compulsive in nature, once he has started. He is driven by unconscious forces he does not understand and against which rational judgment and will power are helpless." This is an excellent definition of a fantasy that has not been faced.

Tests have shown, she reports, that while different types of personalities are capable of becoming addicted and alcohol may be used to try to solve the most diverse kinds of emotional conflicts, addicts possess many characteristics in common. Among these are: an extremely low frustration tolerance, inability to endure anxiety or tension, feelings of isolation, devaluated self-esteem, a tendency to act impulsively, a repetitive "acting out" of conflicts, extreme narcissism and exhibitionism, a tendency toward masochistic self-punitive behavior and extreme mood swings. In addition, there often appear marked hostility and rebellion, conscious or unconscious, and strong (oral) dependent needs, frustration of which leads to depression, hostility and rage.

She concludes: "The more traumatic the childhood, the more serious will be the personality defect underlying the alcoholism." To the alcoholic, in fantasy "love is rather a desire to be loved and cared for, the primitive kind of loving an infant feels for the mother," rather than the wish to give love.

Underneath what she calls "alcoholic arrogance" lies a desperate attempt to deny and cope with fantasies of dependency, helplessness, fear and impotence. She adds, "The alcoholic's desire to force someone to accede to his wishes and love him in spite of what he does makes him an extremely difficult person to live with."

Fox also describes the alcoholic as full of fantasies of fear of desertion and retaliation, with "a burning desire for vengeance on a world that he feels has treated him shabbily. Those nearest him—the ones he needs most—are usually the chief targets for his venom. Hence wives, mothers, sisters, fathers, employers come in for most of the abuse."

Dr. Karen Horney in *Neurosis and Human Growth* maintains the basic anxiety—an aggregrate of emotions—leads the alcoholic to wish to stifle feelings of inadequacy, hostility, isolation and helplessness. Also, from time to time, he tries out various conflicting maneuvers, each designed to raise his self-esteem. On one occasion he will be ingratiating, charming, even fawning, on another, hostile, grudging, cruel. The unpredictability of the alcoholic is one reason he is difficult to live with.

Studies show that from 40 to 60 percent of all alcoholics come from the disturbed background of an alcoholic family where one or both parents drink excessively. A parent who, when sober, is often affectionate, understanding and fun loving, when drunk, may become morose, demanding, unreasonable, even violent. His child is caught in a variety of fantasies as to what his parent is really (unreally) like. The parent's swing from high hopes in the child to shattering disappointments may build up in the child a basic mistrust and all later intimate relationships become distorted.

The alcoholic tries to overcome his basic feeling of helplessness, according to Dr. I. Portnoy in "Psychology of Alcoholism," through building the unconscious fantasy "he *is* whatever he *wishes* to be." Since he wants to be a "grandiose" person, he deludes himself into thinking he "is this glorious person." The arrogant pride, the inordinate claims for special and unlimited privileges, the feeling of being entitled to unconditional happiness and love, the conviction he should be free of responsibility for his actions, all these unconscious fantasies exist.

Overeating stems from fantasies connected to the oral period of our lives. For a baby his only weapon is his mouth and teeth, he is a little cannibal. The fantasy of cannibalism permeates the person who still feels he is a baby using teeth for revenge. The overeating in which so many of us indulge is a remnant of this cannibalistic stage in our lives.

The mouth is also part of our first sexual experience and the kiss of adulthood retains this early erotic sensation. There is sensuous delight in eating, which originated in the first foods we tasted. Many also hear the voices of mothers saying, "Eat, eat, eat," to be a good child meant to overeat to please mother.

On the other side of the coin of overeating exists the widespread problem of undereating. "Anorexia Nervosa" has been in the headlines as more and more young women indulge in it. Dr. C. Philip Wilson, who has studied "the fear of being fat in female psychology," says the symptoms of anorexia are caused by the ego's attempt to defend itself "against an overwhelming terror of being fat which has been caused primarily by an identification with a parent or parents with a similar, but less intense fear." He claims there is a general fear in our society in most women of becoming fat, no matter how "perfect" a woman's figure may be. That "if she is told she looks fat, she will have an emotional reaction out of all proportion to reality," and if she is told she looks thin or has lost weight, she usually will be "inordinately pleased."

Anxiety and the affects of shame, guilt, humiliation and fear, associated with the fear of being fat, are defended against with denial "which in certain cases reaches an almost psychotic intensity," he states. As this primitive defense of denial is analyzed, a number of fantasies clustering around conflicts emerge, including: displacement of sexual-moral conflicts, displacement of heterosexual and latent homosexual conflicts, displacement of anal conflicts, displacement of aggression, displacement of oral impulses, loss of impulse control, the wish to be ethereal, the fear of a disfiguring pregnancy, displacement of menstruation fears, penis-envy conflicts and body-phallus fantasies.

Fantasies and conflicts from every developmental phase can be repressed and displaced onto "the fear of being fat," Wilson says in his book of that name. The fear is a denial of neurotic and normal dependency needs, he adds.

Anorexics have a harsh, punitive conscience and the anorexic's "rage with the mother, which was initially rooted in repressed, sadomasochistic oral conflicts has been displaced onto food." Wilson muses that twenty-five years of experience in the analysis of anorexic patients and their parents "has shown me that the predisposition to develop anorexia is established in the mother-child relationship in the earliest years of life." The mother uses food to control the child and the child's fantasies center around her anger at being overcontrolled in the area of food, as she refuses to eat.

A seventeen-year-old anorexic, on leaving home for college, told a friend joyfully, "Now I can eat whatever I want. What a pleasure that will be." But the habit was so instilled in her of being careful about what she ate that she found herself even stricter than her mother—as though to deviate from her mother's control meant loss of her mother's love.

Another youthful anorexic grew up with a mother who kept herself fanatically thin and the daughter went her mother one better, was even more vigilant about her diet. She fell so seriously ill she had to be hospitalized. A doctor helped her understand why she did not eat normally.

Wilson says that it is no accident young girls in the adolescent stage become anorexic, for this is when they separate physically from their parents. Becoming emaciated is a plea to return home and be taken care of. They are overwhelmed by the fearful fantasy of being unable to cope with a hostile world.

The bulemic anorexic, who goes on food binges, then vomits up the food, is the other side of the coin of the *Anorexia Nervosa,* Wilson points out. The underlying fantasies and emotional conflicts are the same.

Usually anorexic women "vehemently deny their conflicts," he maintains, but unhappy parents bring them to therapists for consultation. Since the adolescent anorexic girl is in a situation of realistic and neurotic dependence on her family, changes in the parents' behavior and attitudes toward her can be crucial for therapeutic success. Parents may need therapy themselves to accept the emotional changes in their daughter and to understand certain destructive interactions with her on their part.

Gambling, including the lottery players, is another addiction that arises from fantasies of both conscious and unconscious nature. Conscious fantasies include the desire for sudden wealth and to "beat the odds." Estimates place "pathological gamblers" in this country between two to four million, according to a release from the American Psychiatric Association on August 31, 1987.

The Association reported on the Gambling Treatment Team at South Oaks Hospital, Amityville, New York, which has developed "a consistent, quantifiable, structured instrument" enabling the early identification of pathological gamblers (according to the September issue of the *American Journal of Psychiatry*). This early identification is important because the "disease" of gambling may have severe consequences, including suicide, according to the authors of the article, Henry R. Lesieur, Ph. D. and Shiela B. Blume, M. D.

Associated problems include separation and divorce, large debts, loss of assets such as property, depression, lost time at work and school, court appearances, suicide attempts by the gambler's spouse and medical problems in the gambler.

In his book *The Psychology of Gambling* Dr. Edmund Bergler described what he called the "classical gambler's neurosis" as "centering around infantile impotence and its masochistic elaboration." Characteristically the gambler is distinguished by "the mechanism of orality, made up of three parts: unconscious construction of defeats; retaliative fury, seemingly for the purpose of self-defense, and self-commiseration." The gambler appears to want proof he is loved, just as he apparently wants to win when he gambles. But unconsciously he remains unsatisfied unless he receives his "daily dose of injustice," Bergler stated.

One patient told Dr. Bergler, ironically, "For me, gambling is a question

I ask of Fate. The question is simple: 'Am I your favorite?' It's a constant fight between me and my competitors—the other two billion people on the earth. When I'm winning, my feeling is that I'm the favorite; when I'm losing, I feel that my prayer for love will be heard some time."

Dr. Bergler asked, "You believe that gambling is a way of testing Fate. But how do you explain your not being satisfied when you win? Why do you pester Fate for constant confirmation?"

"A repeatedly confirmed statement is more foolproof," the patient replied.

Dr. Bergler did not accept this evasion. He asked, "Can you explain why your pleasurable emotion when you win is never as deep as your unhappiness when you lose?"

He replied, "My capacity for suffering is greater than my ability to enjoy success, that's true. I'm just made that way."

Dr. Bergler said, "Isn't it more likely that under the disguise of wanting to be loved, you want exactly the opposite?" He meant wanting to be punished for feelings of hate and wish for revenge on the parents of childhood.

Within the gambler's personality, in a state of constant conflict, exist two contradictory forces—the conscious wish to win and the unconscious wish to lose. They are by no means evenly matched and the wish to lose ultimately prevails, Dr. Bergler believed. He explained that the relative strength of conscious and unconscious wishes may be compared with the power of a doorman (the conscious) and the power of the owner of the building (the unconscious). The doorman's "braggadocio may be intimidating" but he has no real power, for that lies in the hands of the owner "even though he is not present in the lobby."

The gambler has regressed to the earliest level of psychic development, Dr. Bergler explains. His conflict centers around the mother of his earliest infancy, whom later—by projection—he "reduces to absurdity as a giving person, allegedly exposing her as bad, malicious, and a refusing 'monster'" (the horses and jockeys who do not win).

A child asks for candy and his mother, for sound dietetic reasons, refuses his request. The normal child overcomes this disappointment, the vulnerable, oversensitive child does not, Bergler says, but interprets his mother's refusal as malice. He lives with thousands of such minor refusals as he grows up. When he becomes an adult, he does not try to compensate for disappointments in a logical way, he does not, metaphorically speaking, eat all the candy he can stomach. Instead, without realizing it, he continues to play the role of the denied, hurt child, feels unjustly treated. He stares hungrily through the window of the candy store but buys nothing though he has money. By masochistically refusing himself, he acts out his fantasy that his parents are "refusers," obviously more satisfying to his wish for revenge than gratifying his original desires.

Dr. Bergler describes the "candy store" of youthful days as the stock exchange in adulthood, or the roulette wheel or poker table: "Every loss serves as corroboration for the inner alibi: 'I am not masochistic. It is my parents who are mean.' *Gambling is thus used to furnish an excuse for the gambler's main inner conflict: the constant reproach of psychic masochism.* Unfortunately for the gambler, this alibi is forthcoming only when he loses. And the need for it is stronger than the conscious wish to win."

Other psychoanalysts who have treated gamblers discover that many, both men and women, were taken as children to the racetracks by their fathers and/or mothers and recalled the excitement felt by a parent during the race. These patients later resorted to gambling to recreate in adulthood this feeling of pleasurable excitement, especially when their lives lacked much pleasure. It brought back the fantasies of being with parents in a "fun" sense, whether or not the aim was winning, though that was preferable, for then the parent seemed pleased, whereas losing caused him to look depressed.

Every one of us is a potential gambler, either of the harmless or dangerous (to self) variety, Bergler declared. He calls this "a shocking statement, and one that many would like to deny" but says scientific evidence shows it to be true.

The person who occasionally will bet on a horse or baseball game, or play bingo, is not a gambler in the pathological sense. It is how deeply a person is involved in gambling that makes him a pathological gambler. In Bergler's words: "The mental energy of the pathological gambler is almost constantly concentrated on gambling, on computing chances and making prognostications. His fantasies and daydreams center around this one idea: the pathologic concentration overshadows everything else—vocation, love, hobbies."

His belief in ultimate success cannot be shattered by financial loss, however large. For he believes the next day he will win, if only he can obtain money to tide him through this temporary run of bad luck. The result of this false fantasy is that the true gambler never stops when he is winning for he hopes to win more and more, become extraordinarily wealthy: "He does not consider his winnings the result of chance; to him they are a down payment on that contract he has with Fate, which guarantees that he will be a permanent winner." This inability to stop gambling while he is still ahead is one of the strongest arguments against the assumption, common to all gamblers, that you can become rich through gambling. This fatal optimism drives the gambler to push his luck too far and ensures the solvency of gambling houses and racetracks, Bergler maintains.

The gambler also seeks and enjoys an "enigmatic thrill" which cannot be logically explained, for it is compounded of both pain and pleasure. "This tension is a mixture, part pleasurable, part painful; it is comparable to no other known sensation," Bergler explains. One of his patients called it "pleasurable-painful tension." It is, in Bergler's words, a "painful uncertainty, but uncertainty is precisely what the gambler seeks." He expects to win and therefore feels elated before the race or throw of the dice or distribution of cards.

Other psychoanalysts have explained that the masochistic pleasure of losing assuages the guilt the gambler feels in risking his money knowing the odds are against him. "I got what I deserve for being a bad boy," he feels as the unconscious, once more, triumphs over reason.

In addictions we clearly see the disastrous effect they may have not only on mind but body. An addiction, in a general sense, arises out of the fantasies that something we take in through our mouth, or other parts of the body, like the injection of a drug in the arm or the inhalation of tobacco, can ease the psychic pain in our life.

There is another way our body tells of our fantasies, in addition to its reaction to alcoholism, drugs, overeating or undereating. What is this very prevalent means of expressing fantasy through our body—a way man has used since he first appeared on earth?

11

The "Body Speaks" of Fantasy

Becoming aware of your fantasies may prevent what physicians call psychosomatic illnesses, such as ulcers, high blood pressure, sinus conditions. Anxiety is a sign of inner fantasies at work, feeling undue pressure as though you are driven by some unknown wild spirit.

A woman of twenty-nine suddenly suffered such severe sinusitis she thought she might have to leave her cherished job as a newspaper reporter. She went to a doctor, he examined her, said there was nothing physically wrong, suggested she see a psychoanalyst.

She took his advice, discovered that for the first time in years she was able to cry, principally at the thought her mother did not love her as a child. She was astounded to find that after a month, in which tears flowed three times a week at her analytic session, the sinusitis completely vanished, never to return. She stayed in analysis realizing she had many childhood fantasies to conquer—the enemy within, according to her overstrict conscience.

Body and mind are inseparable. As the father of medicine, Hippocrates, said in 300 B.C., "In order to cure the human body it is necessary to have a knowledge of the whole of things." He meant the whole of the self, which in large part is governed by our fantasy life and the emotions it provokes.

It was through the symptoms of physical illness that Freud started to understand what he called "the mental apparatus or psyche." His first patients were women who complained of severe headaches, paralyzed limbs, poor vision. He persuaded the women to talk about their physical symptoms. As they did, their thoughts led him to the realization that the symptom expressed a hidden fantasy and wish that had been repressed.

173

This fantasy and wish was usually sexual or aggressive—sexual desire for someone taboo, or aggressive feelings about someone who had wounded their self-esteem or of whom they were jealous, "death to my rival." We all want to be the winner—in sex, in work, in life in general.

The physical symptoms Freud treated had formed as partial expression of the women's submerged fantasies and wishes. The illness was an attempt by their unconscious to cope with some dangerous fantasy, fear or wish of which they were not aware. The symptom vanished when the woman could make conscious its causes by telling Freud memories and thoughts. The symptom served the purpose of partial gratification of the wish. She expressed the wish to hurt someone else by hurting herself as she also eased her guilt by punishing herself through bodily pain.

One woman of forty-nine, who had just undergone a breast cancer operation, asked her analyst, "Why do so many women have cancer of the breast?"

The analyst asked, "What are your thoughts?"

She hesitated, then said, "Maybe it's because as infants they wanted to destroy the breasts of mothers they felt as dangerous and uncaring."

Psychosomatic illness is a way of inflicting suffering on ourself for what we believe evil fantasies. The illness also contains the fantasy of unconscious revenge on those we believe have hurt us. If we are sick we cannot work or function sexually; others must care for us. We thus avoid any open expression of hatred against those we supposedly love, instead receive their sympathy and attention.

One man undertook psychoanalysis to find out if it would help his severe asthmatic condition, since nothing else did. On the couch he recalled many experiences in childhood connected to his breathing, which to him had always been a matter of concern—most of us accept breathing as natural and do not have to worry every moment whether we will be able to breathe.

This man possessed many distorted fantasies about the importance of his breath. He believed success in sexual intercourse depended on maintaining steady, regular breathing. He would try to regulate his breathing at such times, insist his partner regulate hers.

As a boy he had slept in his parents' bedroom until he was five, at times heard his father's heavy breathing during sexual intercourse. To him, such breathing indicated something terrifying taking place between his mother and father. He tried to keep terror from his own life by controlling his breathing during sex and at other times. His father, when he sat around the house, would also sometimes explode in spasms of coughing during which he was unable to catch his breath.

To the son, his own breath became a very precious thing, associated with fantasies of sex and what he imagined was his father's rage. As he could face his fantasies, his asthma disappeared. There were other reasons too for his trouble in breathing, what Freud called "overdetermined." The man also recalled as a small boy his mother would often hold him to her so tightly he felt he would suffocate.

Patients suffering from skin conditions were studied by Dr. Max Schur, a psychoanalyst and Freud's physician. At the onset of his study of men and women in analysis who suffered diseases of the skin he had no idea of the importance of emotional factors in the cause of their skin problems and was doubtful about the potential therapeutic results. Then he noticed these patients rarely had problems with itching during their sessions. He concluded the verbalizing of their fantasies, daydreams and thoughts was an important factor in their ability to stop using the skin as a way of communicating what troubled them.

Schur described one patient of many in his pilot study to investigate various dermatological problems. She was a twenty-two-year-old woman admitted to the skin ward of Bellevue Hospital, New York, diagnosed as suffering from "generalized atopic eczema." She confessed she gained no satisfaction during intercourse, developed attacks of itching each time she saw her husband. She also suffered the obsessive thought she might kill him by stabbing him, felt guilty because, she said, he was "a nice man."

During analysis she disclosed that her alcoholic father had raped her as a child, preceded by a period starting when she was three when he regularly masturbated her. Though he threatened to kill her and her mother if she told on him, she revealed his assaults to her mother. Instead of coming to her daughter's rescue, her mother was afraid of the disgrace this would publicly bring and how it would "spoil the future" for her two sons. Thereafter, the girl hated her mother even more than her father.

As a Catholic, she went to church regularly and often broke out with a rash on her face. She did not tell the priest of her father's sexual assaults nor her obsessive thoughts of killing her father by stabbing him. When she was fourteen her father died of a stroke; she promptly fell ill with severe headaches and a prolonged weakness of her right hand, could not attend the funeral. She told the analyst she resented her father's dying before she had mustered the courage to kill him.

After his death her skin condition worsened. She had periods of amenorrhea and gained weight. She masturbated only once, fantasizing the original practices of her father, followed by her wish to kill him. She felt so horrified at having an orgasm that she never dared masturbate again. At the place where she worked as executive secretary she fell in love with her employer, a young, unmarried man her age, had intercourse, then married him. She found out the marriage proved no answer to her conflicts. In analysis she became aware that her hatred for her mother was as important a factor in her life as the sexual abuse by her father. Her mother had not satisfied her childhood need for love and protection.

Dr. Schur reported that during analysis she worked to understand her conflicted relationship with her mother as well as her sibling rivalry with her two brothers. She envied boys, wished she had been born a male. As she could accept her mother's behavior as a sign of weakness and neurosis rather than viciousness, she was able to forgive her mother and accept her own femininity and motherhood. At this stage of her analysis she enjoyed a normal orgasm and became pregnant.

Her skin also cleared completely. It could have qualified as an advertisement for a "beauty cream," as Dr. Schur commented. She finished her analysis toward the end of her pregnancy and her skin remained clear ever since, he added.

The survivor of someone loved who commits suicide often suffers a sense of helplessness and has the wish that he had some control over his helpless feelings. To cope with his feelings of futility and guilt he may suddenly be possessed by terrorizing fantasies that cause psychosomatic symptoms.

One woman developed guilt feelings after moving away from her mother country, no longer available to her ailing, beloved father to the extent she wished, for he had always been there for her. She also felt guilt about her anger at him because of the deterioration of his health even as she rationally realized how unreasonable her anger was.

Her father had always represented life, energy, initiative and the capacity to make the best of unhappy situations. At the age of seventy he had rid himself of all professional obligations, fulfilled his dream to return to the university, take courses in archeology and art, which he had always loved. At eighty years of age he suffered a few strokes that disabled him. She fantasized how she would push him in a wheelchair so he could more fully enjoy the archeological artifacts and art treasures, a service she was unable to carry out because she was no longer in the country.

Following a swift visit to see him, on her return to her present homeland, she received a call informing her that her father had committed suicide. Intellectually she understood this was a decision he had made after contemplating eventual devastating consequences of more strokes. Since the capacity to function fully had been of vital importance in her father's life, she knew he believed taking his life was for him the preferable solution. He left a letter expressing love for his family, thanked them for the joys they had shared.

A few weeks after the funeral she found herself succumbing to one illness after the other, starting with a cold that turned into pneumonia. Ordinarily a very healthy person, she was puzzled by illnesses that culminated in neurological problems, causing her at one point to fall on the street and hurt herself.

She had remained sitting on the street for a few minutes with her thoughts. It suddenly dawned on her that for some time she had unwittingly imitated her father's way of walking toward the end of his life, when a series of small strokes made it difficult for him to move. She realized she was using her body to act out her need not just to punish herself for having failed to assist in caring for him but also as an attempt to try to understand what made her father take his life. She asked herself, "Can one really be so sick that one feels life ceases to have a meaning and importance?" After this understanding of body-and-mind interaction, she quickly recovered from her ailments and ever since has had no health problems.

Her body had expressed what was, at that point, impossible for her to face and think through. For the duration of the months her illnesses occurred she, in part, became her father in a futile attempt to counteract the loss. In other words, on an unconscious fantasy level he was still alive inside her, a fantasy she promoted by her inability to accept her loss more fully.

Consciously she tried to deal with her overwhelming sorrow by resorting to the idea that her father had followed the tradition of Scandinavian behavior since the time of the Vikings—to commit suicide when the strength of the body ebbs and there is no remedy and only further deterioration in sight. But no rational thought could completely satisfy when it came to accepting a loss where guilt and anger were involved. Her feelings needed to be faced and worked through before her loss could be accepted and she felt entitled to give up her intense guilt and rage.

Some studies show there may be a high risk of cancer within eighteen months after the loss of someone or something of vital importance, such as a spouse, a child, a friend or the loss of a job, if the loss is not sufficiently mourned. Lawrence LeShan studied 152 cancer patients along with a control group. He discovered that 77 percent of the patients had suffered acute losses of persons they loved or a treasured job just prior to the outbreak of the cancer. He concluded that the loss had been a significant contributor to the onset of cancer. He also found an inability in these persons to express hostility, as compared to a control group.

Headaches may be a way of combating inner conflicts. When you suffer a headache, you may be denying certain thoughts or wishes you do not want to think about. You may be trying to repress fantasies that are intense and tormenting. Studies have shown a migraine headache often appears after a time of stress, when fantasies run high. Instead of becoming aware of the fantasies connected to the stress, the person suffers a headache. Dr. Frieda Fromm-Reichmann, well-known psychoanalyst, treated eight patients who suffered migraine headaches, discovered in all of them hostile, envious fantasies and impulses turned on themselves.

This is not so strange when you consider that the headache may serve the purpose of denying dangerous fantasies. It is one way of protecting the self from thinking "bad" thoughts, acting out hostile fantasies. There is truth to the Biblical saying, "None so blind as those who will not see," meaning, "become aware of the truth," the true feelings contained in the fantasies.

The eye is a vulnerable target for the expression of inner fantasies. It is through our eyes, as children, that we see things both violent and sexual, things we are not supposed to see. Through the eyes we also satisfy our curiosity about our body and its functions and the bodies of others. Our eyes not only search for signs of danger that may threaten our lives but also take in the desirability of someone we love. Eyes serve both our self-perspective and procreational urges.

The eyes are also the target of the classical punishment for oedipal desires. Oedipus put out his eyes when he learned he had murdered his father and married his mother, by whom he had four children. Dr. Robert Lindner, in his famous book *Rebel without a Cause*, traced a young boy's eye tic to the time when, as a baby, he lay in a crib in his parents' bedroom observing his father and mother in the act of sex.

Children believe a magical power emanates from the eye—we talk of the "evil eye." That the eye has a sexual power may be seen in the "magic" communication that takes place between two people who meet for the first time and, through an exchange of glances, feel a deep attraction to each other.

Psychosomatic illnesses throughout the body cannot be considered apart from our thoughts since the brain controls the body. Both the conscious and unconscious parts of the brain are directors of our central nervous system. Our whole body is, as it were, "in tune with our brain," as Dr. Paul Schilder, a psychoanalyst who pioneered in psychosomatic theory, put it. The conditioned reflexes of our body are connected to the processes of our psyche. So that when we have fantasies that lead to conflicts between pleasure and pain, physical symptoms may develop.

When we feel threatened, either from the outside world or our own thoughts, our brain is thus affected. A perception, a fantasy, an idea or a memory is either strongly or weakly "cathected," in Freud's word. That is, aroused and charged with psychic energy which demands immediate release in one way or another so balance can be restored to the mind.

Some distressed persons feel they undergo a psychic emergency almost every minute of the day. It is no wonder the steadily reacting systems of the body may become overtaxed and eventually break down. It is not natural to act as though there were an emergency all the time, to live in a constant stage of repressed fear and fury emanating from fantasies of the past. Painful though it may be to become conscious of destructive fantasies, this awareness prevents greater pain in the long run.

The close connection between psychosomatic illnesses and fantasies was eloquently described by Dr. Georg Groddeck. He was one of the first medical doctors to recognize that any treatment of physical illness that ignored the emotional life of the sufferer was one-sided. He claimed, "Diagnosis ought to take into account the entire man and the whole circumstances of his life."

He wrote of his experiences as a physician in *The Meaning of Illness*. He called illness "a creation of the organism," the "It," which he defined as the vital force, the self that tries to express a threatening fantasy through illness. To fall ill connotes the suppression of some terrifying thought contained in the embedded fantasy, he believed.

Groddeck suggested that the person who assists the physically ill man or woman, whether a physician or someone else, understands what the sick one is unconsciously communicating through his illness so his needs

may be appropriately met. For example, a man who had been deserted by
his wife had developed painful sensations in the area of his heart. The
cardiologist could find no evidence of physical dysfunction of the heart.
Through psychoanalysis the man was helped to realize the symbolic
meaning—the fantasy behind his ailment, the intense heartache he felt at
the loss of his wife, a pain he stoically tried to deny.

He also became aware of his unconscious fantasy of wishing to stab his
wife in the heart—a retaliatory fantasy quickly repressed because of the
guilt that followed such a wish. Instead, he meted out punishment to
himself by experiencing his "crime" as a pain in his own heart. When he
could face his psychic pain and aggressive fantasies, the heart symptoms
disappeared. Such fantasies might lead to crippling disease, even cause
death unless the person becomes aware of the essential message he is
trying to communicate to himself.

Every illness has a symbolic meaning in the psyche, Groddeck said. For
instance, constipation is a sign of obstinacy, of withholding something a
person does not want to be forced to give up. If someone suffers from a
sore throat, he may unconsciously be making sure he will not speak words
that might injure himself or someone else.

"It is sometimes better to lose the sight than to endanger the soul,"
Groddeck wrote. "It is sometimes better to sacrifice one's hand than to
steal or to murder. It is sometimes better to flee from life by means of a
serious illness, yes, perhaps by means of death itself, than to live on,
groaning under the burden of repressed guilt. Why should not the It
employ a germ of some sort, or a pebble, or fruit-parings, a drink of cold
water, a fright, a terrible thought, in order to rid itself of all responsibility,
and destroy all its guilt in a fever, in the pain of a broken limb, in a chill, in
a faint or palpitations, or dropsy, and if it is forced to extremities, even
death or madness?"

Dr. Walter B. Cannon showed that the direct expression of psychological states could produce physical symptoms. He proved, through tests on
animals, that emotions, particularly rage, caused profound changes in
blood chemistry. A principal change was a dramatic increase in blood
sugar. The sugar was released from the liver because of the action of the
hormone adrenalin, secreted from the adrenal gland. Disturbances also
occurred in the respiratory and circulatory systems and gastrointestinal
tract.

When a flood of fantasies that cause anxiety pours into the brain's highest cortical centers—those that control our conscious thinking—the anxiety may paralyze these centers. Then the subcortical and spinal centers, our autonomic nervous system, go into action as kind of a substitute director. But this system reacts in a rigid pattern because it is not subject to any "will" but is automatic. It is governed by our primary thinking system, which means it gives symbolic, rather than direct expression as outlet for repressed emotions the conscious has been unable to handle.

Changes that take place from emotional stress thus form independently of what we call "will power." The body's reaction to what Cannon called "fight or flight" from a dangerous situation, occurs whether the fantasy causing the changes is conscious or unconscious.

Cannon's classic book *Bodily Changes in Pain, Hunger, Fear, and Rage,* published in 1929, described his research into the relation between feelings and changes in the body. In trying to find out which part of the brain controlled emotions, he concluded that a structure deep in the brain, the hypothalamus, was concerned with the emotional aspect of sensation and the viscera (our internal organs) were controlled only at the hypothalamic level. But skeletal muscles were governed at both levels, cortical (conscious thinking) and hypothalamic (unconscious thinking).

Cannon's theories have since been extended in that scientists have discovered we possess two higher centers of thought, or cortexes. A neocortex does our thinking (probably unconscious as well as conscious); and a paleocortex, part of what is called our limbic system, which is more primitive, is not capable of complex thought and is found even in very primitive animals like frogs.

The paleocortex may be the source of our feelings, which it communicates to the neocortex for the conscious experience of emotions. The paleocortex also can communicate our feelings to the hypothalamus and then to our autonomic nervous system, to give bodily expression of emotional states. The hypothalamus also controls our pituitary, the control for our various hormones which, in turn, have profound effects on our bodily processes.

Without neocortical processing of the paleocortical output there can be bodily expression of emotions independent of our conscious awareness, which means we may express unconscious thoughts and wishes and be unaware that we do so. The bodily symptom tells of some fantasy at work and the symptom also allows what Freud called "partial gratification," though a distorted one, of the original fantasy, now repressed. The symptom, such as ulcers or headaches, represents *denial* of the fantasy and its accompanying emotions, and protects us against awareness of what we feel is a dangerous wish but at the cost of bodily pain.

In a sense, each time we suffer a psychosomatic symptom our body tells us we are unhappy because of some fantasy we wish to carry out but know is forbidden—such as an illicit sexual affair, or revenge against someone we hate. If we acted on these natural primitive wishes we would be little more than savages.

Much physical illness could be averted if we were more aware of the fantasies underlying our psychosomatic symptoms and realized that they are no longer dangerous because there is vast difference between a fantasy wish and an act. As we become aware of the fantasies underlying psychosomatic symptoms we then release energy for love, for work, for creativity.

What are the ways in which fantasies can serve our creative spirit? Are there means by which we can increase our creativity through our fantasies?

12

The "Great Artist" Fantasy

One of the ways we can use our fantasy in the service of self-esteem is to be creative. Fantasy is the basis of creativity, which flows into many areas—art, music, writing, fashion design, architecture, science.

Fantasy also supplies the connecting link between the artist and audience, as Reuben Fine points out. He describes the creative person as "putting into artistic form the fantasies which the ordinary mortal daydreams about." These fantasies are based on the universal strivings, "a fight for love and glory," and the artist "gets his gratification from a permissable release of his fantasies while the audience gets theirs from the tolerated viewing or reading of them."

A concise summary of Freud's views on the artist's use of fantasy was given by Freud in *A General Introduction to Psychoanalysis:* "There is, in fact, a path from fantasy back again to reality, and that is—art. . . . Like any other with an unsatisfied longing, he [the artist] turns away from reality and transfers all his interest, and all his libido, too, on to the creation of his wishes in the life of fantasy."

Freud pointed out the way back from fantasy to reality "is found by the artist thus: He is not the only one who has a life of fantasy, the intermediate world of fantasy is sanctioned by general human consent, and every hungry soul looks to it for comfort and consolation."

Freud made the first analytic study of a famous artist and the fantasies that lay behind his creativity as he wrote of the life of Leonardo da Vinci in *A Study in Psychosexuality.* To be accurate, Freud studied only one fantasy of Leonardo but delved into the unconscious meanings it held in his childhood.

183

Leonardo's paintings, perhaps the best known of which is the Mona Lisa, hang in the leading museums of the world. He was born an illegitimate child in 1452 in the little city of Vinci between Florence and Empoli. His father, Ser Piero da Vinci, was a notary and descendant of a family of notaries and farmers. Leonardo's mother, Caterina, was a peasant girl, who later married another native of Vinci. Leonardo's father married the prominent Donna Albiera the year of Leonardo's birth. Because the couple remained childless, Leonardo, at the age of five, moved to his father's home until he left to become an apprentice in the studio of Andrea del Verrocchio.

While Leonardo lived in the home of the master artist, he and several other young men were accused of homosexual relations—then forbidden—tried and acquitted. Freud comments, "It seems that he came into this suspicion because he employed as a model a boy of evil repute." He added that Leonardo "only transmuted his passion into inquisitiveness," that he "investigated instead of having loved," and that it was doubtful he "ever embraced a woman in love."

The book centers on a few lines of a personal nature Leonardo interspersed in his scientific descriptions as a communication from his childhood. In a passage where he writes about the flight of the vulture he suddenly interrupts to describe a memory from early years that suddenly arose:

"It seems that it had been destined before that I should occupy myself so thoroughly with the vulture, for it comes to my mind as a very early memory, when I was still in the cradle, a vulture came down to me, opened my mouth with his tail and struck me many times with his tail against my lips."

This memory of Leonardo's, in which the vulture opens Leonardo's mouth with its tail, is not a memory of the period in which Leonardo dreamed it, but a fantasy from childhood, Freud states, formed into the dream at a far later date. Freud explains that because the psychoanalytic technique affords "excellent means for bringing to light this concealed material, we shall venture the attempt to fill the gaps in the history of Leonardo's life through the analysis of his infantile phantasy." Freud illustrates here how a detective of the psyche investigating the content of a dream seeks and finds his clues.

Examining the vulture fantasy with the eyes of the psychoanalyst, Freud explained similar fantasies were found in dreams and could be translated according to the language of dreams. He said, "The translation follows an erotic direction. Tail, 'coda,' is one of the most familiar symbols, as well as a substitutive designation of the male member, in Italian no less than in other languages."

The situation described in the fantasy, that a vulture "opened the mouth of a child and forcefully belabored it with its tail," corresponds to the idea of "fellatio," Freud goes on, a sexual act in which the penis is placed into the mouth of another person. He adds, "Strangely enough, this phantasy is altogether of a passive character; it resembles certain dreams and phantasies of women and of passive homosexuals (who play the feminine part in sexual relations)."

Freud then describes the fantasy as related to the days Leonardo was a child and at his mother's breast, a "pleasure" that would be indelibly printed on his mind. The fantasy concealed nothing more or less, Freud said, than a reminiscence of nursing at his mother's breast which Leonardo, as well as other artists, depicted with the paint brush in the form of the mother of God and her child.

Then Freud asks why Leonardo fantasied his mother as a vulture: "Where does this vulture originate and how does he come into this place?" He then recalls that in the sacred hieroglyphic of the old Egyptians, the mother is depicted as a vulture. The Egyptians worshipped a motherly diety who was vulturelike—the name of this goddess was pronounced "Mut"—and Freud suggests the similiarity to the word mother (Mutter in German) is not accidental.

He also states that the vulture was thought a species of bird that consisted only of females. According to Egyptian myth, impregnation took place at certain times when the birds would stop in the midst of their flight, open their vaginas and were impregnated by the wind. Leonardo was probably well-acquainted with this scientific fable, Freud said, since he was an omnivorous reader in all spheres of literature.

The image of Leonardo's vulture fantasy, Freud maintained, probably occurred following his reading in a book of a church father, or about natural science, that reported vultures were all females and reproduced themselves without the cooperation of a male, and a memory flashed through Leonardo's mind that became transformed into the fantasy. Freud added the fantasy might also express Leonardo's feelings that he was such a vulture child because he had a mother but no father for the first five years of his life.

Freud also ventured the explanation that the image of the vulture's tail in Leonardo's mouth represented "an echo of the pleasure which he had once experienced at his mother's breast." The images in a dream may lead to many fantasies of the past.

According to Freud, the "real content" of the fantasy was the replacement of the mother by a vulture. This indicated Leonardo as a child had longed for his father, felt himself alone with his mother, the vulture: "The fact of Leonardo's illegitimate birth fits in with his vulture phantasy; only because of it was he able to compare himself to a vulture child." For the first five years of his life he must have missed his father, seeing other little boys with their fathers, though he no doubt received his mother's undivided attention and love.

It is this feeling of being "special" in infancy and childhood that inspires many creative people to give vent to their talents, according to psychoanalytic studies. The poignancy in Leonardo's *Mona Lisa* undoubtedly stemmed from his feelings for his mother and the loss he felt when taken from her at five. From then on, he only had fantasies of her to sustain the loss. But as Freud states, in the first three or four years of life, impressions become fixed and modes of reactions are formed toward the outer world which can never be robbed of their importance by any later experiences.

Freud concluded his study of Leonardo's dream: "If it is true that the incomprehensible childhood reminiscences and the person's phantasies based on them always bring out the most significant of his psychic development, then the fact, corroborated by the vulture phantasy, that Leonard passed the first years of his life alone with his mother must have been a most decisive influence on the formation of his inner life."

As a young boy Henry Moore would massage his mother's back with bath oil to ease her rheumatism. When we study his sculpture of large reclining figures crowned by tiny heads, we see in them the little boy's perspective of his mother, her head high above a back of large proportions because all his energy and concentration were once focused on her back. Laurie Schneider Adams, psychologist and art historian, professor of Art History at John Jay College, New York, points out this earlier experience was preserved in Moore's unconscious and later in life given free artistic expression—reflection of his adult creative fantasy.

Moore was quite conscious of his passion for the mother-child motif. He wrote, "I have had an obsession with the Mother-Child theme. I discovered when drawing, I could turn every little scribble, blot or smudge into a Mother and Child . . . I suppose it could be explained as a 'Mother complex.' " (He was quoted in Adams' article, "The Theme of Mother and Child in the Art of Henry Moore," published in *Psychoanalytic Perspectives in Art,* Volume 1, 1985.)

The losses of our lives play a large part in the creativity generated by the need for restitution of a loss, Rochlin points out. He says that a "virtually endless fund of activity stems from the experience of loss or the fear of it," that it is characteristic of all of us to attempt to recoup our losses to restore an inner balance that has been upset. Our resources called on to achieve this may do so through the creative process, a means through which restitution is achieved "either in fact or in fantasy."

While perhaps the greatest and most continuous creative way in which we seek restitution is through our dreams, Rochlin says, a fantasy may serve the same purpose and so may a psychotic hallucination, but the significant difference lies not in their aim but in their relation to reality. Many acts result after fantasies of restitutions for the loss evolve, but creativity is a highly sublimated act and one that is not destructive.

The common denominator artists share with children and everyone else is that "through the creative process something is being restored or realized," Rochlin maintains. In childhood play, as throughout life during sleep, fantasies, dreams, reveries—some unconscious, others "silently stated," some acted on—reveal a creative effort to find restitution for losses, he concludes. The rich fantasy life of the child, coupled with his emerging elaboration of dreams, indicates the creative process to be "intimately linked with loss and restitution, constant fear and dread of loss is not acceptable to man and forces restitution, the route to which is creativity."

Edmund Wilson, the literary critic, in *Axel's Castle* wrote of Marcel Proust that "following his beloved mother's death, he was obliged to find something to take her place and for the first time set himself seriously to work." The result of Proust's loss was *Remembrance of Things Past* which brought him great fame.

Franz Kafka used his tormenting fantasies as a child possibly more dramatically than any other writer. Speaking of his native city, Prague, he once declared, "This little mother has claws"—one of his fantasies about his mother, who was always busy, worked in the family business, a haberdashery store in his youth, and later an asbestos factory his father owned. His mother was also busy giving birth to children. Franz had two younger brothers who died in infancy and three younger sisters, later murdered in the Holocaust. As the oldest child and the only son to survive infancy, he received little warmth and love from either his mother or father, according to Richard H. Lawson in his moving biographical-critical study, *Franz Kafka*.

Kafka endured a "precarious emotional existence," in Lawson's words. For one thing, he always lived in the fantasied shadow of death, for with two brothers dead, he would fear the same fate. That shadow of death would also haunt his mother and father, and their fear would be mirrored in him, the survivor. He did not live long, died at forty-one of tuberculosis of the larynx at Kierling Sanatorium near Klosterneuburg, Austria.

His father, Hermann Kafka, whom Lawson describes as looming "larger than life" in the writings of his son, served three years in the Imperial and Royal Army when he was nineteen. He became a platoon leader and, when his hitch was completed, took up the career of an itinerant trader, ultimately settling in Prague. He married Julie Löwy, daughter of a prosperous and stable family of merchants, members of the German-Jewish establishment, and set up a haberdashery business at which he was very successful.

Lawson writes, "From very early there seems to have been an absence of sympathy—to put it mildly—between the father, all too harsh, and all too concerned about his business, and Franz, all too sensitive to the absent paternal love (or perhaps only badly misdirected). This estrangement Julie Kafka was unable to mediate in any very helpful way. Franz, feeling himself badgered, threatened, and silenced, followed his probably natural bent to turn inward."

The family cook walked him to the German school when he was six; his father was too busy and so was his mother. The cook was one of an ever-changing cast of family servants who entered and left Franz's life. His only stability seems to have been his governess, Marie Werner, who stayed several years.

He earned the early reputation of being a loner. He became interested as a young man in the German theater in Prague, wrote scenarios to be acted out by his sisters at home, also composed fragments of a novel. Lawson says that "probably theater and writing, as well as general academic excellence provided him with a kind of counterweight against what he felt to be paternal persecution." It is also probable the neglect by his mother in his very early years caused a number of the horrifying fantasies—

perhaps the most horrifying ever placed in such eloquent literary form on paper—described in his novels.

Writing was one of the many bones of contention between father and son. His father wanted him to enter the family business but Kafka became a lawyer at twenty-four, at least a field of which his father eventually approved, critical of his son's first choice of philosophy as a profession.

The fantasies in Kafka's books show his buried violence and fear, guilt beyond belief, and horror at life's harshness and unfairness without apparent cause or sense. Psychoanalysts would say his fantasies were defense against going mad (since madness was so much a part of his writings), his creative way of working out terrorizing feelings he did not understand, feelings that in a powerful, symbiotic way expressed how he felt about himself.

That he could sublimate his feelings thus was the mark not only of his genius but of some inner strength that allowed him to convert intense fear and terror into a literary, spell-binding drama of horror that has had no equal. Writing, to him, was the way he escaped a life he likened to the underworld of hell. The acclaim given Kafka shows that to some degree his terrified feelings stir in all of us.

He had difficulty separating in a physical sense, as well as emotional, from his parents, living in the crowded flat that was the parental home until he was thirty-one. Then he met Felice Bauer, to whom he became engaged in 1912. That year he completed *The Metamorphosis,* started work on *The Trial.* These two books emerged at a time he moved away from his mother and father, able at least in fantasy to write about his tormented feelings.

Kafka never married but had three fiancées. Felicia was his fiancée twice, and her friend, Grete Bloch, later asserted that Kafka was the father of her son. He had a fear of marriage and its effect on his writing, unconsciously feared sexuality and his repressed violence.

Lawson speaks of Kafka's "spare and perfectionist style." His lifelong friend and literary executor, Max Brod, encouraged him to publish, realizing the importance of his work. Kafka's novels lived up to Brod's expectations.

The Metamorphosis depicts Kafka's fantasy of a man turning into a cockroach, what he felt like as a child and adult. Never sent, or, as Lawson says, more likely never handed to his father, was a letter of over a hundred pages Kafka gave his mother. It was as "rich in self-accusation as in accusation of the 'dearest father' to whom it was addressed."

In this letter Kafka accused himself of being oversensitively fearful in the face of his father's unreflective, instinctive self-aggrandizement. It is not a fair, chivalrous fight between them, not a fight between honorable opponents, Lawson writes, but one in which the writer is confronted by a "bloodsucking vermin." Kafka draws two distinct character types: "the son, more a Löwy than a Kafka, odd, shy, quiet; the father, a Kafka through and through, forceful, strong, noisy, knowledgeable, unreflective—all those attributes that are necessary, as the son sees it, for a tolerable bourgeois marriage—and that he so significantly lacks."

Kafka asserts he was essentially raised by his domineering father, as a result of which he lost his natural self-confidence, replaced by a sense of guilt. Whatever he wanted to do, or did, was opposed or ridiculed by his father. Even when Kafka became interested in his Jewish roots, that too attracted the father's hostility—his own Judaism consisted only of "formalized, meaningless fragments."

Lawson says, "It is not entirely dialectic to suggest that there was an element of love, of admiration as well as disdain in their relationship, which, as far as personal contact went, deteriorated into a virtual non-relationship after Kafka finally left the paternal roof." At one point he fell in love with a married woman but she would not leave her husband. Kafka spent time in and out of sanitariums during bouts with tuberculosis.

His fantasy of his relationship with his father can be clearly seen in a passage from *The Metamorphosis*. Gregor Samsa, a traveling salesman who, through exhausting labor, has been supporting his parents and sister, awakes one rainy morning after troubled dreams to find himself transformed into a monstrous insect, a beetle or cockroach. Unable to go to work, he is virtually held prisoner by his family, while his formerly idle father, with new vigor, resumes work. The loathsome bug imprisoned in his room is violently persecuted by his father. His mother ineffectually pleads for Gregor, his sister tries to feed her metamorphosed brother. But he fails to find satisfaction or nourishment in the fresh food she places before him. Alternately ignored and persecuted, he gradually starves to death, "to the resurgent joy of his family," says Lawson.

More of Kafka's fantasies appear in *The Trial*, which he wrote within weeks of breaking his first engagement to Felicia Bauer. It is no difficult task, as Lawson comments, to relate the hero of this book, Josef K., to the situation of the author at the time he wrote it. The novel's events cover one year and Josef K.'s assassination takes place on the night before his thirty-first birthday, the age of Kafka when he left his parents' home. Lawson says the relationship between Josef K. and Franz Kafka "is perhaps the key to most other insights."

The Trial is the story of a man who is arrested, never informed for what crime and, after a year of interrogations, hearings, petitions and inaccessability to anyone he knows, is executed. In fantasy Kafka saw this as his life, the execution no doubt the threat of the tuberculosis that slowly killed him at forty-one. He is saying to the world that he faces death but does not know what crime he has committed; in fantasy the cruel executioner is his father.

The famous sculptor, the late Alberto Giacometti, did not try to hide his depression, known to his friends as a man who possessed an attitude of "earnest despair." His biographer James Lord asked if he ever thought of suicide.

"Every day," he said.

Edgar Allan Poe was another whose life was full of fantasies of despair, murder and horror. He lost through death several women important to him, starting with his mother who died when he was a child. His excessive drinking was also a sign he was trying to escape childhood fantasies of mourning, rage and hopelessness.

In contemporary murder mysteries one popular type is called the "whydunit." Dostoyevski was a pioneer in this area when he wrote *The Brothers Karamazov* in 1879, as Theodor Reik pointed out in *Curiosities of the Self*. He declared the character Dostoyevski conceived in Fyodor Mikhailovich had many "ardent murderous wishes." Reik said of Dostoyevski, "He must have wished his brother Michael dead," (he died in 1864) and also his brother's family, which he felt obliged to support. Dostoyevski also, Reik added, "must have wished for the death of his first wife, Marie Isaewa, with whom he was not happy, especially since he had a passionate sexual affair with Paulina Suslova before his wife died."

Reik concludes that Dostoyevski had "the imagination of a mass murderer and *The Brothers Karamazov* reveals only a small part of his fantasies."

To write about murder gives the author an outlet for his own murderous fantasies so that he does not have to act on them; he retains a partial outlet that lessens temporarily his guilt at such wishes, ones his conscience disapproves of. Writing about murder is what Freud called "sublimation" of murderous impulses. The reader also engages in such sublimation as he thrills to the murder, the chase and the final capture of the villain.

Alongside the capacity for conflict we all possess stands the human capacity for creativity, Margaret Brenman-Gibson, Ph.D., pointed out at the annual winter convention of the American Psychoanalytic Association at the Waldorf Astoria in New York on December 18, 1987. The meeting featured a psychoanalytic study by Brett Kahr, a psychologist, of London, England, about the tragic life of the dancer Nijinsky, who spent the last thirty years of his life as a schizophrenic patient in mental hospitals. Kahr showed slides that held clues to the fantasies in Nijinsky's famous but emotionally tortured life, fantasies that drove him to insanity. Kahr related these fantasies to Nijinsky's childhood with unstable parents and an older brother who lost his mind after falling through an open window.

Another kind of creativity is called the "Munchausen Syndrome," named after Baron Munchausen, a man who indulged in telling "tall tales," serving as inspiration for a series of stories, largely fictional, written by Rudolf Erich Raspe in the late eighteenth century. Sufferers of the Munchausen Syndrome live out the fantasy of being sick when there are no physical signs of illness. They feign symptoms, do it so well that doctors take them seriously. These very disturbed persons are often highly intelligent and well-informed about medical conditions. The creativity in this condition is a destructive one, however, that gives only temporary relief.

Their sophistication makes it hard for the medical profession to immediately detect that they are faking their symptoms. They play on the sympathy of friends, dramatize their life situation and feelings to manipulate others to assist them in any way possible. To make their story believable they may even inflict serious injuries on themselves. They have a chameleon characteristic in that they invent new symptoms to assure themselves of continued medical attention.

Severe neglect and rejection may often be found in the background of those who use fantasy in a destructive way and prey upon the sympathy of others. As children, they seem never to have felt loved and accepted. These conditions made it difficult for them to see reality, to show love and caring.

They simulate a variety of illnesses for the sole purpose of receiving medical attention. For instance, one man, seriously abused as a child physically, as well as emotionally, indulged in fantasies about illnesses that caused pain and suffering, such as cancer. For him, cancer constituted a powerful metaphor, an image of his low self-image—the dirty, rejected, diseased one—as well as the image of his abusive parents who, in his imagination, were still present, now within him: his tormentors, the cancer, that ripped him apart, threatened his life. (This man possessed, like most such patients, a need for masochistic pleasure.)

He was so proficient at faking his symptoms of the so-called side effects of cancer treatment that he was actually able to obtain additional treatment from several renowned hospitals for what seemed to be the consequences of chemotherapy and radiation. Finally, a physician at one hospital, through minute investigation and questioning, discovered flaws in his story that revealed the situation in all its tragedy.

Apart from the personal tragedy of the Munchausen Syndrome exists the practical consequences of the fact that valuable medical assistance is spent in vain when others, who are really sick, have to wait their turn for necessary medical care.

The Swedish film producer, Ingmar Bergman, in his autobiography *Laterna Magica* (The Magic Lantern) describes how in early childhood he resorted to lies and fantasies in the interest of survival. His father was a very strict disciplinarian and Ingmar, in contrast to his truthful brother, learned to use lies to save his skin. He created an inner person who had little to do with his real self. This resulted in his difficulty as a child in keeping apart his imagined self (fantasized self) and his real self, and he suffered the consequences far into his adult life, though using his suffering in part in his creativity.

Sometimes such a person comforts himself by knowing that though he lives in lies, he loves the truth, and this gives him a sense of reality. Bergman recalled his first lie when his family lived in a yellow house close to the hospital where his father served as a minister. Ingmar had been out with his brother and his friends in the park, throwing snowballs at the greenhouse, shattering panes of glass. The gardener suspected the boys and reported it to Ingmar's father.

All the boys except Ingmar confessed and were severely punished. Ingmar made the decision not to confess but to make up a story. He told his father he had fashioned loosely packed snowballs, then decided to throw them at his brother but, because his feet became cold, instead walked home. He later admitted that he said to himself, "This is the way one does it when one lies" (one creates a story).

Soon after this, he was invited to the circus where at first he became frightened by the scary, raging clowns, then fell asleep from all the excitement. He woke at the sound of delightful music and the sight of a young woman dressed in white, riding a black horse. He at once fell in love with her, in his imagination named her Esmeralda. He told a classmate, sworn to secrecy, his parents had sold him to the circus where he would be trained as an acrobat, appearing with Esmeralda.

But his friend betrayed him and the next day everyone knew about his "secret." His concerned teacher wrote a letter to Ingmar's parents, who confronted him, punished him severely for his "lies," made him feel forlorn, devastated and humiliated.

As revenge he chased the classmate who had betrayed his secret through the schoolyard with a knife, almost killed the teacher who tried to intervene, was suspended from school and beaten by his father. But in spite of all this maltreatment because of a fantasy, Ingmar continued to fantasize about his passionate adventures with Esmeralda.

Luckily he possessed a beloved grandmother and confided to her his inner thoughts—his first audience (as a child, we might say, his dream of getting a projector for his fantasies was thus gratified). The first film he saw, *Black Beauty,* about a horse (Esmeralda's black horse), left him deeply touched. From then on he was gripped by a fever that never left but drove him to become the Bergman the world knows as the creator of magnificent, original films that reflect the thoughts and fantasies not only of his tormented mind but the minds of all of us.

Grotjahn in *Beyond Laughter* talks of "fantasy and art as islands of freedom." He speaks of the "great clown," Emmett Kelly, as a creative artist, saying that there are moments of true artistic creation in the circus performance "when a step is taken from the funny to the beautiful and finally to the sublime." The clown then no longer represents something comic about which we laugh, but humor which makes us smile and understand, even at times brings tears.

The average person binds his energy to repress his fantasies but the artist is able to free enough energy to create. The artist may feel anxiety but somehow he is not as afraid of it as the uncreative person. In Grotjahn's words, "The neurotic does not dare to lift repressions and face his fantasies but treats them like the unopened box of Pandora."

All creativity is based on free access to the unconscious, Grotjahn states. He makes the analogy that while the psychoanalyst tries to interpret objectively the subjective world of fantasies to the patient, the artist interprets the fantasies subjectively: "He works with the Dionysian unconscious and gives it Apolline form. Where the artist is esthetic, the scientist is conceptual."

Fantasy is inherent in the artist though it can determine not only his work but, if destructive, how unhappy his life will be. Claude Monet used his fantasies not only for his glorious paintings, initiating the age of impressionism, but to live wisely to an old age, content with work and family. But Vincent Van Gogh was so tormented by fantasies he used them not only for painting but also to destroy himself when he was thirty-seven.

He feared he would never be successful as an artist, would have to depend on his brother to support him all his life. It is highest irony that his "Irises," painted in 1889 during his first week at the asylum at Saint-Rémy, was sold at Sotheby's in New York the night of November 11, 1987, for $53,000,000—the highest price ever paid for an art work at auction. The fierce bidding for this masterpiece was witnessed by an international gathering of 2,200 collectors, dealers, museum curators and officials.

Sometimes we hear the argument that if an artist or writer goes into analysis and faces his fantasies he will no longer be able to create, that his imaginative work comes out of his conflicts. This is false reasoning, since artists and writers and other creative persons have received psychoanalytic help to become far more productive.

One woman writer of fiction told a friend, "After I was psychoanalyzed I could write three times more material than before analysis. I felt far freer to delve into the lives of my characters."

Once the creative person faces his fantasies and conflicts, he discovers he possesses greater energy. He also finds his creative work more fulfilling, he enjoys it rather than thinks of it as a burden or a desperate struggle. His personal life is apt to be far happier too. He does not make unreal demands on those to whom he is close, nor allow them to make such demands on him.

Creativity is also found as part of the psychoanalytic situation in both patient and analyst, according to Dr. Hans Loewald. He calls the psychoanalytic treatment a "creation" involving a patient and his analyst—a fantasy creation in which both patient and analyst, in different ways, take part. During the treatment the patient develops what is called a "transference neurosis," meaning he displaces onto his analyst patterns of feelings and behavior that have their origin in the relationship with his parents, siblings and other important people from childhood. This unconscious process expresses itself in a repetition on an unconscious level of attitudes, fantasies and emotions.

The psychoanalytic situation thus is an emotional recapitulation of the patient's inner life history. Seen in this light it can be compared with the creation of a dream, like the Greek tragedy Aristotle described as "the imitation of action in the form of action." The fantasy character of the transference neurosis has been referred to as the fantasy aspect of the psychoanalytic situation.

In the eloquent words of Loewald, in his article, "Psychoanalysis as an Art and the Fantasy Character of the Psychoanalytic Situation," the "fantasy character of the transference neurosis has been referred to as the make-believe aspect of the psychoanalytic situation. In the promotion and development of the transference neurosis, analyst and patient conspire in the creation of an illusion, a play. The patient takes the lead in furnishing the material and the action of this fantasy creation, while the analyst takes the lead in coalescing, articulating and explicating the action and in revealing and highlighting it as an illusion. The patient experiences and acts without knowing at first that he is creating a play."

The analyst through his interventions reflects back to the patient what he does and says and also by transference interpretations that reveal the relations between the play and the original action the play imitates, Loewald explains. As director of the play the analyst must relive, recreate the action of the play and to direct the actors, "not by telling them what to do or how to act, but by bringing out in them what they often manage to express only fleetingly, defensively, in inhibited or distorted fashion."

A rare kind of creativity, which appears in books, plays, movies and television presentations, is humor—much needed and much appreciated by all societies through the ages. We all welcome a laugh in what Lucy Larcom, in her poem "Three Old Saws," called this "vale of tears" into which we are born. Humor is essential to our sanity, we feel at times. A laugh a day drives depression away, to paraphrase the old adage about an apple.

The person who possesses a sense of humor we find appealing, the one who does not, we avoid. There are all kinds of humorists: the ones who repeat jokes, the ones who make up jokes, the punster, the practical joker and the sarcastic or hostile humorist such as Joan Rivers on television.

Television is replete with programs that focus on laughter. It was evident in the presentation of the thirty-ninth annual Emmy Awards on September 20, 1987, how large a part humor plays—half the awards went to comedy, half to drama. When Bruce Willis, the star of *Moonlighting,* who plays the role of detective much of the time as sheer comedy, received the award for the best male dramatic appearance of the year, a Los Angeles television critic complained to the worldwide audience that this was not fair. Comedy even impinged on the dramatic category.

Comedy, which brings forth our laughter, is essential in helping us release fantasies and feelings we have repressed. Not only through television but in the movie theater, on the stage, in books and at parties where jokes abound, we release fantasies of aggression and sexual desire. Life would be far grimmer without a laugh.

To examine the close tie between fantasy and humor Freud wrote a 170-page book, *Wit and Its Relation to the Unconscious.* In his introduction he said, "our philosophical inquiries have not awarded to wit the important role that it plays in our mental life."

Known for his telling of numerous jokes to his colleagues, Freud maintained there was "an intimate connection between all psychic occurrences" and that wit in our society offered "a peculiar, overwhelmingly fascinating charm." He said a new joke operated almost as an event of universal interest, passed on from one person to another just like the news of the latest conquest.

One of his favorite jokes was that of the condemned prisoner who was led to his execution on a Monday. He remarked to his jailer, "Yes, this week is beginning well." This is called gallows humor. The one who hears this joke feels pity for the condemned man (tied to fantasies of self-pity) but the prisoner's indifference and stoicism saves the expenditure in the listener of the emotional energy involved in pity. Instead he can laugh, feel relief. The condemned man has proved that even an execution cannot break his strong spirit and the one who laughs identifies with this optimistic frame of mind.

Under "nonsense" jokes Freud gave the example of a guest who was served fish at the table and after putting both hands twice into the mayonnaise, ran his fingers through his hair. His neighbor looked at him with astonishment, at which he excused himself, saying, "Pardon me, I thought it was spinach." We laugh at nonsense jokes as the child laughs at the fantasy in them that ridicules oft-painful reality.

Most humor brings pleasure because it allows us, in disguised form, to release some of our hidden fantasies of sex and violence. In no other social area can we express vicariously these forbidden fantasies with such ease, receive such a temporary feeling of freedom—as though we put one over on our punitive parents.

In other words, the repressed returns and we laugh at it for the moment instead of suffering pain at the thought of it. We free some of the energy we have used to keep forbidden fantasies and desires under repression.

Fantasies in humor, in sexual desire, in hatred, in love, in marriage, in depression, in addiction, in perversion, in psychosomatic illnesses, in creativity, in our dreams—all these have been discussed in this book.

How can we feel more at ease with our fantasies so we may achieve happier lives? How can we help not only ourselves but our fellow human beings throughout the nation and the world live more peaceably so we do not threaten each other with extinction?

13
The Rewards of Knowing Your Fantasies

"Row, row, row your boat / Gently down the stream / Merrily, merrily, merrily, merrily / Life is but a dream," goes an old song, sung in schools throughout the nation, the words of which carry a fervent childhood wish.

But life is far from a dream; life is often difficult, harsh, hurtful. And some of our fantasies may destroy the dreamlike quality of our existence.

Fantasies operate from the cradle to the grave, determine in large part how we feel, think, act. The rewards of feeling more at ease with our fantasies, as stated earlier, are many. We may use fantasy either to enhance our life or to emotionally cripple us. The difference depends on our ability to become aware of a fantasy that is destructive, rather than allowing it to continue to rule us.

Fantasy is one of our first defenses against frustrations and losses of all kinds. We are entitled to fantasize whatever we wish, though not to act on fantasies that will harm us or others.

We will profit in many ways if we take the time and trouble to understand fantasies that have remained hidden and exert undue power, to understand too how and why they started and the reason they remain. In childhood, fantasies served a valuable function, met a vital emotional need. But they may harm if they persist too intensely into adulthood, cause us to feel angry and bewildered, unable to be true to what we think of as the real self.

The denial of a troublesome fantasy only fuels our strict conscience, makes us superjudgmental, causes us to feel guilty, not knowing why. Guilt may become an enemy that keeps us from putting our energy into love and work.

Facing buried fantasies helps us deal with the conflicts that underlie them, reveals the unreal demands we make on ourselves and others. It is the *unknown* fantasies controlling us that keep us from being aware of what we really think and feel—or "unreally" think and feel, as one psychoanalyst put it. Fantasies may block our ability to live at ease with those we love and to achieve our full capabilities in what we call "reality."

To understand the power of a fantasy we have to understand what "acting out" a fantasy means. In discussing this concept Freud said that the person who acts out "does not remember anything of what he has forgotten or repressed. . . . He reproduces it without, of course, knowing he is repeating it. . . . He cannot escape from this compulsion to repeat; and in the end we understand that this is his way of remembering." He added that the greater the resistance of the person to remembering a painful experience, "the more extensively will acting out (repetition) replace remembering."

The awareness of our deeper fantasies, which comes through remembering, is the heart of emotional healing. The moment we become aware of a painful fantasy, we then accept it as fantasy, not as the reality we have deluded ourself it is. We can fight what is conscious—we cannot fight what remains unknown. The unconscious is the burial ground of all our past fears, in addition to being the wellspring of most of our tormenting fantasies and all our primitive desires. It is only by exhuming the fantasies that cause pain that we halt their destructive power.

Many believe if only they had enough money all their problems would be solved. Money eases life's economic hazards but money does not solve the inner conflicts that cause harmful fantasies. To understand those conflicts we need to become aware of fantasies we have believed would destroy us if we admitted them to ourselves, let alone anyone else.

We all possess the same underlying fantasies. Each one of us hides wishes that stem from feelings of sexual desire, violence, greed. This is part of being human. There is no escape from such fantasies, they are as natural as the fact that the night (or nightmares at times) follows the day.

We all want total love, perfect love. We want to destroy anyone who interferes with our receiving love, or those more successful, who earn more money or achieve greater fame. We have to make peace with the inevitable frustrations and disappointments in life, for the greatest fantasy of all is that we will get everything we want.

We have to give up the demand for perfection in ourselves and others. There is nothing perfect in this world except perhaps the "perfect game" in baseball. This occurred only once in a World Series, on October 8, 1956, when Don Larsen of the New York Yankees pitched against the Brooklyn Dodgers, not allowing one hit.

Even when we give up unrealistic fantasies part of us still mourns for the lost pleasures of infancy, both the real ones and the imagined ones. But if we become realistic about what life offers we will find appropriate pleasures.

Not all fantasy is defensive or needs to be examined in terms of childhood conflicts. We may take heart in our creative and productive uses of fantasy. Fantasies of which we are unaware may often be used constructively in the mental process psychoanalysts call "sublimation." This leads to promotions in work, a sense of stronger identity, the ability to respect and trust ourselves and others, rather than to tear down or denigrate.

To acknowledge our hatreds and hostilities does not mean we act on them but that we are less likely to act on such unpleasurable feelings if we become aware of them. We are then more at peace with ourself and others. Those who feel deeply troubled by their lives may want to examine their fantasies more in depth through therapy to free themselves from unreal fears.

Our terror lessens as we realize that most of our rage and wish for vengeance belongs not to the present but flows from the past. All our thoughts are connected in chains of associated memories, interwoven with one another. They form networks—a personal inner network—that sometimes holds terror. A child's mind is not yet equipped to fight injustices, which leave psychic scars. But as we become aware of repressed fantasies and wishes of the past, realize they stem from terrifying moments of childhood, accumulated hours of seething, planning vengeance and acknowledge they were natural at the time, our terror evaporates.

It is important that parents encourage a child to talk about his fantasies, not make the child feel guilty for his natural fantasy of wishing to get even for a real or imagined cruelty that deserves punishment. He should be helped to explore his thoughts, accept his right to feel angry at either the real or imagined cruelty or neglect of a parent. Parents will learn much about themselves as a child if they listen to a child's fantasies. They will better understand not only their child but themselves.

One mother, advised to be more understanding with her five-year-old son, listened to his outbursts of rage when she denied him what he thought a pleasure but she thought harmful—in one case, a second dish of chocolate ice cream.

"Why *can't* I have a second dish?" he stormed.

"It isn't good for you," she explained.

"Who says so?" he demanded.

"All the health people say too many sweets destroy the teeth and body."

"They're wrong," he said. "I need more sweets."

"Why?" she asked.

"To make me feel sweet," he said.

She could not help laughing, for she knew the feeling well. As a child she had waged the same battles with her mother. She wanted to please her son yet not harm his health, so she asked, "Is there something else I can give that would substitute for a second portion of ice cream?"

He thought a moment, said, "A Hershey bar."

She laughed again. Then suggested gently, "How about a dish of sweet strawberries? Or a juicy plum?"

He hesitated, then said, willing to make a compromise, "Strawberries." Added, "With cream and sugar."

She compromised too. "Okay."

They each won the battle without becoming angry. She recaptured her fantasies and feelings as a child when her mother refused to compromise and was able not to repeat the same destructive scene but show her son everyone had to make compromises at times for his own good.

Our acts often reveal our fantasies. A secretary was sent by her employer to pick up a package on the east side of Manhattan, a city she knew well. Yet she found herself stepping off the bus on the west side, berated herself for being "stupid," wasting time. As she rode the bus to the east side she wondered why she had made the mistake. She thought of the pleasant evenings she had once spent with a man she loved, who lived near the Hudson River, she had often wished to see him again. She realized that she had unconsciously taken a bus to his home rather than one to carry out her chore.

In a sense she also punished herself for this, to her, forbidden fantasy, for she knew the relationship with this man would never have worked out.

She realized too the extra time it would now take to deliver the package to her employer would bring a rebuke, perhaps jeopardize her job. She felt like a "bad" girl who had "messed up" an important errand.

Fantasy affects not only individuals but nations. A growing group of men and women concerned for the welfare of the universe in this age of nuclear warfare that could destroy the world believe it is "uncivilized" to wage war; they feel it shows we have not come far from our primitive ancestors living in caves.

War is described as "a group fantasy" that gives people the opportunity to act out their infantile fantasies of murder and sex, according to Lloyd DeMause, psychohistorian, founder of the International Psychohistorical Society.

He explains: "For instance, as an essentially male homosexual ritual, war allows men to avoid the conflicts of heterosexuality by leaving behind their wives and girl friends and going to the front to penetrate other men with projectiles. War is dominated by homosexual imagery, such as President Lyndon Johnson's claim during Vietnam that 'I didn't just screw Ho Chi Minh: I cut his pecker off.' Then there is President Ronald Reagan's recent 'disinformation' campaign saying that Colonel Khadafy is a homosexual."

He adds that group fantasies during wars "resemble very closely the phallic display fantasies found in male homosexual pornographic literature, and, invariably the most bellicose section of the nation is composed of those men who had the most punitive upbringing and the most problems with repressed homosexuality."

During war nations "act out massive orgasmic violence against men, women and children, completely without guilt," he maintains. "A recent magazine cover proclaimed war is a sexual turn-on . . . the secret love of a man's life . . . the closest thing to what childbirth is for women." This appeared in *Esquire*, 1984.

DeMause notes, "The psychological benefits of the war group-fantasy can be seen by noting the jump in Gross National Product during wars, far exceeding just the increase in war goods. During wars, nations pull together in a unified, enthusiastic effort to produce far more than they ever had in the past, because with the manic defense well in place they can sidestep the usual limitations due to guilt which normally drag down productivity during peaceful periods."

Just as individuals feel guilty about their unacceptable fantasies, wishes and acts, and provoke punishment for the guilt, so do nations. When the populace and the leaders they choose feel an intolerable guilt for their fantasies of greed, envy and wish to conquer other nations, they unconsciously arrange, as children do, to be punished, DeMause says. They seek wars with other nations, sacrifice innocent lives and often are defeated, as this country was, in a sense, in Vietnam. The defeat for the moment eases their guilt. It is no accident that wars seem to occur every few decades with terrifying regularity.

Political scientists and psychohistorians, who study history from a psychological perspective rather than dates of battles, discover that the wars of nations are not very different from marital and child battles, says DeMause, also director of the Institute for Psychohistory.

He has explored extensively the relationship between the fantasies of voters and the leaders they elect in his books *Foundations of Psychohistory* and *Reagan's America*. He suggests voters unconsciously elect guilt-ridden leaders so that the populace will be punished for their violent fantasies and the guilt they feel over *their* murderous and greedy wishes. The elected leaders carry the nation to war "as a sacrificial ritual when we feel we are 'bad' and guilty and deserve punishment," DeMause says. We no longer, like our primitive ancestors, offer our children in sacrifice to the gods; instead we wage war on other nations, kill their children and their mothers.

The reasons we unconsciously wish to wage war, like the reasons individuals choose to engage in murderous acts, involve many childhood fantasies. Motives behind the need to go to war have been the subject of study for two decades by research associates at the Institute for Psychohistory. There has been a focus on the fantasies expressed "in the words and images used by national leaders and the media *prior* to wars," DeMause explains.

He reports: "We have been surprised to find consistent patterns of group fantasies which nations share and use as trial actions in the process of finding an enemy and beginning a war." These fantasies, circulated in the public dialogue during the early buildup of tensions include "growing guilt over sinfulness, despair about ever achieving happiness, increasing rage and fears of ego collapse, and, finally, powerful wishes to sacrifice youth as representatives of forbidden sexuality and rebelliousness."

He adds that the conclusions reached by research "form a coherent theory of war which is truly *psychogenic*, as opposed to the purely economic theories of war most common today." Among the conclusions: "war is a wish, not a response or a 'mistake' and involves a period of regression similar to the regressions experienced by individuals during psychotic episodes. This group regression is signaled by violent group fantasies that reflect growing rage and fears of national collapse, desires for national rebirth through violence and fantasies of the cleansing of sinfulness."

Another conclusion holds that "war involves grandiose sexualization of inner conflict, accompanied by group fantasies of rape and orgasmic violence, projected into an appropriate 'enemy' who has agreed to participate in a period of mutual sacrifice." And still another: "War is a sacrificial ritual in which the blood of soldiers is drained away to cleanse the nation and remove its sinfulness and make it 'good' again, so the guilt of the individuals and the nation will be eased."

DeMause proposes the establishing on an international basis of a Nuclear Tensions Monitoring Center whose purpose would be to describe, measure and publicize increases in violent group fantasies in each of the nuclear nations. It would also provide psychological help in decreasing nuclear tensions. This help is already being given on a small scale by psychotherapists in a number of communities in this country as they aid children in school and their parents to combat the fear of the nuclear bomb and devastation.

Declaring that "the most effective help the mental health profession can provide for a world preparing for a suicidal nuclear war, is to *make the unconscious conscious,* just as the profession has been trained to do in the case of individuals," DeMause explains. "Since an unconscious wish derives its power to be acted on through its state of repression, the group-fantasy of having a cleansing nuclear war can only be prevented from being acted out by continuous interpretation of both the wish and its myriad defense systems."

He has proposed that psychotherapists, psychiatrists, psychohistorians, political psychologists and other specialists trained in the analysis of unconscious mental life establish the Nuclear Tensions Monitoring Center. Anyone concerned with the avoidance of nuclear war is asked to take part. Ideally, the center would have a branch in each of the nuclear nations, though it could begin to function with only one center—in this country, where the mental health profession is largest.

We may draw the conclusion that the reason the world wages so many wars is that the people and their leaders are unable as yet to act with maturity and thoughtfulness either for their own good or that of other nations. They act instead on the level of the fantasies possessed by the infant—wish for power, greed, envy, fear, guilt. We may compare the psychic state of the world to that of the primitive, savage thinking of the infant. We have not as yet reached the level of emotional development and mature thought where we elect leaders able to consider another nation's needs, to feed the starving throughout the world, to honestly strive to avert the destruction of the planet.

We might think of the history of "civilization" as an attempt to conquer the power of personal fantasies so that they do not destroy us. But we still cannot claim to be very "civilized," for we project on "enemy" countries the fantasies within that torment us as a way of getting temporary relief from our own inner terror. Charity toward our inner fears should begin at home so we do not hurl them at distant "enemies," for then our weapons will prove a boomerang.

We can find peace within only as we become aware of fantasies of hate against those who have hurt us or who we imagine have hurt us. And fantasies that stem from strong sexual desires that seek endless outlet (in order to assure continuance of the human race, which on the one hand we try to destroy, on the other, preserve).

If we can courageously tackle some of the deeper fantasies buried over the years, know they will no longer hurt us if we air them to reason, we gain that sense of self-esteem, of inner integrity that holds many rewards, not only for ourselves but for those we cherish.

The more we understand and face the infant that sometimes dominates us, the stronger becomes the trust in ourselves. This trust brings the desired sense of identity, the awareness we are, after all, human, imperfect and possessed by fantasies that can either hurt or help us, depending on how aware we are of them.

This is true "power"—a power that keeps us from harming ourselves and others who are near and dear, the power of love over hate.

To "know thyself" means "know thy fantasies." Know what you truly (or untruly) feel, think, wish. Know that underneath your civilized self lies a strong primitive self that often fights the humane rules of society. The civilized self has to accept the primitive self, know it is natural, in order to make peace with it.

We cannot have everything, we cannot be perfect but that does not prevent us from loving, from caring, from protecting those we love from pain, as well as protecting the self.

To quote Freud, echoing Socrates, the life that goes "unexamined" is not worth living. To face your fantasies, to separate the unreal ones from the ones that may become realities and enhance your existence, constitutes examination of the self. It leads to a happier, more peaceful way of life.

Bibliography

Arlow, Jacob. "Unconscious Fantasy." *Journal of the American Psychoanalytic Association,* vol. 31, no. 3, 1985.

Bergler, Edmund. *The Psychology of Gambling.* New York: Hill and Wang, 1957.

Bergman, Ingmar. *Laterna Magica.* Stockholm: Norstedts Forlagy, 1987.

Bettelheim, Bruno. *The Uses of Enchantment: The Meaning and Importance of Fairy Tales.* New York: Alfred A. Knopf, 1976.

Cannon, Walter B. *Bodily Changes in Pain, Hunger, Fear, and Rage.* London: D. Appleton-Century Company, 1929.

Chessick, R. D. "The Pharmacogenic Orgasm in the Drug Addict." *Archives of General Psychiatry,* vol. 3, 1960.

DeMause, Lloyd. *Foundations of Psychohistory.* New York: The Psychohistory Press, 1975.

Deutsch, Helene. *Psychology of Women.* New York: Grune & Stratton, 1944.

Eisenstein, Victor W., ed. *Neurotic Interaction in Marriage.* New York: Basic Books, 1956.

Fine, Reuben. *The Healing of the Mind.* New York: David McKay, 1971.

———. *The Development of Freud's Thought.* New York: Jason Aronson, 1973.

Fraiberg, Selma H. *The Magic Years.* New York: Charles Scribner's Sons, 1959.

Freud, Sigmund. *Leonardo da Vinci: A Study in Psychosexuality.* New York: Random House, 1947.

———. *The Interpretation of Dreams.* New York: Basic Books, 1970.

———. *Studies on Hysteria.* New York: Basic Books, 1957.

———. *The Basic Writings of Sigmund Freud.* New York: Random House. 1938.

Greenacre, Phyllis. "The Family Romance of the Artist." *The Psychoanalytic Study of the Child.* Vol. XIII. New York: International Universities Press, 1958.

Groddeck, George. *The Meaning of Illness.* New York: International Universities Press, 1977.

Grossman, William I. "The Self As Fantasy: Fantasy as Theory." *Journal of the American Psychoanalytic Association,* vol. 30, no. 4, 1982.

Grotjahn, Martin. *Beyond Laughter.* New York: McGraw-Hill, 1957.

———. *The Voice of the Symbol.* Los Angeles: Mara Books, 1971.

Havens, Leston. "A Theoretical Basis for the Concepts of Self and Authentic Self." *Journal of the American Psychoanalytic Association,* vol. 34, no. 2, 1986.

Hendrick, Ives. *Facts and Theories of Psychoanalysis*. New York: Alfred A. Knopf, 1950.

Horney, Karen. *Neurosis and Human Growth*. London: Routledge and Kegan Paul, 1951.

Jacobson, Edith. *Contribution to the Metapsychology of Cyclothymic Depression in Affective Disorders, Psychoanalytic Contribution to Their Study*. Phyllis Greenacre, ed. New York: International Universities Press, 1953.

Kohut, Heinz. *Analysis of the Self*. New York: International Universities Press, 1971.

Kernberg, Otto. *Borderline Conditions and Pathological Narcissim*. New York: Jason Aronson, 1975.

Kestenberg, S. Judith. *Children and Parents*. New York: Jason Aronson, 1975.

Lawson, Richard H. *Franz Kafka*. New York: Ungar, 1987.

LeShan, Lawrence. *You Can Fight For Your Life*. New York: Evans and Company, 1977.

Loewald, Hans W. "The Waning of the Oedipus Complex." *Journal of the American Psychoanalytic Association*, vol. 27, no. 4, 1979.

Mahler, Margaret S. *The Selected Papers of Margaret S. Mahler*, Vol. 2, *Separation-Individuation*. New York: Jason Aronson, 1971.

———. *The Psychological Birth of the Human Infant*, with Fred Pine and Anni Bergman. New York: Basic Books, 1975.

———. *Children and Parents, Psychoanalytic Study in Development*. New York: Jason Aronson, 1975.

Meissner, W. W. "Can Psychoanalysis Find Its Self?" *Journal of the American Psychoanalytic Association*, vol. 34, no. 2, 1986.

Miller, Alice. *Prisoners of Childhood*. New York: Basic Books, 1981.

Niederland, William G. *The Schreber Case. Psychoanalytic Profile of a Paranoid Personality*. New York: Quadrangle/The New York Times Book Co., 1974.

Pollock, George H. "Mourning and Adaptation." *International Journal of Psycho-Analysis*, parts 4–5, 42, 1961.

———. "Temporal Anniversary Manifestations: Hour, Day, Holiday." *Psychoanalytic Quarterly*, 9, 1971.

Proffer, C. R., Editor, *Letters of Nicolai Gogol*. Ann Arbor: University of Michigan Press, 1967.

Reik, Theodor. *Curiosities of the Self: Illusions We Have About Ourselves*. New York: Farrar, Straus & Giroux, 1965.

Rochlin, Gregory. *Griefs and Discontents: The Forces of Change*. Boston: Little, Brown and Company, 1965.

———. *The Masculine Dilemma: A Psychology of Masculinity*. Boston: Little, Brown and Company, 1980.

Rothstein, Arnold. "Fear of Humiliation." *Journal of the American Psychoanalytic Association*, vol. 32, no. 1, 1984.

Sachs, Wulf. *Black Hamlet*. Boston: Little, Brown and Company, 1947.

Schafer, Roy. "The Pursuit of Failure and the Idealization of Unhappiness." *American Psychologist*, April 1984.

Sechehaye, M. A. *Symbolic Realization.* New York: International Universities Press, 1951.

Segal, Julius and Yahraes, Herbert. *A Child's Journey.* New York: McGraw-Hill Book Company, 1978.

Sharpe, Ella. *Dream Analysis.* London: The Hogarth Press, Ltd., 1949.

Socarides, Charles W. *Beyond Sexual Freedom.* New York: Quadrangle, The New York Times Book Company, 1975.

Spitz, René A. *The First Year of Life.* New York: International Universities Press, 1965.

Spotnitz, Hyman. *Psychotherapy of Preoedipal Conditions.* New York: Jason Aronson, 1976.

————. *Treatment of the Narcissistic Neuroses,* with Meadow, Phyllis W., Ph.D. New York: The Manhattan Center for Advanced Psychoanalytic Studies, 1976.

Stoller, Robert J. *The Transsexual Experiment.* New York: Jason Aronson, 1968.

Strean, Herbert S. *The Extramarital Affair.* New York: The Free Press, 1980.

Tec, Leon. *The Fear of Success.* New York: New American Library, 1976.

Wertham, Fredric. *Dark Legend.* New York: Doubleday & Company, 1950.

Winnicott, D. W. *Through Paediatrics to Psycho-Analysis.* New York: Basic Books, 1975.